Student Migration from Eastern to Western Europe

This book explores European student migration from the perspectives of Eastern European students moving to Western Europe for study.

Whilst most research on student migration in Europe focuses on the experiences of Western European students, this book uniquely casts a light on Eastern European student migrants moving to the 'West.' Mette Ginnerskov-Dahlberg deploys a novel approach to the subject by drawing on insights gleaned from a longitudinal study of master's students pursuing an education abroad and their multifaceted journeys after graduation. Thereby, she brings their narratives to life and highlights the changes and continuities they experienced over a period of seven years, fostering an understanding of student mobility as an activity enmeshed with adult commitments and long-term aspirations. Using Denmark as a case study of a host country, Ginnerskov-Dahlberg analyses the trajectories of these students and situates their experiences within the wider socio-historical context of Eastern European post-socialism and the contemporary dynamics between EU and non-EU citizens in the welfare state of Denmark – reflecting issues playing out on the global stage today.

This book will be a valuable resource for students and scholars of migration and mobility studies, as well as human geography, sociology, higher education, area studies, and anthropology.

Mette Ginnerskov-Dahlberg is a senior lecturer and a researcher associated to the research unit Sociology of Education and Culture (SEC) at Uppsala University, Sweden.

'Based on a detailed ethnography of students from Eastern Europe in Denmark, this book makes a major contribution to the growing literature on student migration. It challenges the myth that international students are a privileged elite and unveils their complex and precarious journeys as students, workers and graduates, as well as their transition from youth to adulthood.'

Russell King, *School of Global Studies, University of Sussex, UK*

'Based on engaging ethnographic accounts, this book offers a very timely contribution to the field of international student mobility, scholarly and politically. Through its nuanced and historically anchored analysis of new regional flows of student migrants, it compels us to rethink dominant ideas of contemporary student migration and more broadly fundamental dynamics between mobility and immobility.'

Karen Valentin, *Associate Professor, the Danish School of Education, Aarhus University, Denmark*

'This book makes an extremely valuable and timely intervention into increasingly vibrant debates around the internationalisation of higher education and international student mobility. Drawing on longitudinal ethnographic fieldwork over a number of years to construct the experiences and narratives of students, the book proffers a compelling and original argument around their mobility from Eastern to Western Europe. It is a must-read for all scholars working in this area.'

Johanna L. Waters, *Professor of Human Geography, University College London, UK*

Routledge Studies in Development, Mobilities and Migration

This series is dedicated to the growing and important area of mobilities and migration, particularly through the lens of international development. It promotes innovative and interdisciplinary research targeted at a global readership. The series welcomes submissions from established and junior authors on cutting-edge and high-level research on key topics that feature in global news and public debate.

These include the so called European migration crisis; famine in the Horn of Africa; riots; environmental migration; development-induced displacement and resettlement; livelihood transformations; people-trafficking; health and infectious diseases; employment; South-South migration; population growth; children's wellbeing; marriage and family; food security; the global financial crisis; drugs wars; and other contemporary crisis.

Contemporary European Emigration
Situating Integration in New Destinations
Brigitte Suter and Lisa Åkesson

Europe and the Refugee Response
A Crisis of Values?
Edited by Elzbieta M. Gozdziak, Izabella Main and Brigitte Suter

Nigerian and Ghanaian Women Working in the Brussels Red-Light District
Sarah Adeyinka, Sophie Samyn, Sami Zemni and Ilse Derluyn

Family Practices in Migration
Everyday Lives and Relationships
*Edited by Martha Montero-Sieburth, Rosa Mas Giralt,
Noemi Garcia-Arjona and Joaquín Eguren*

Student Migration from Eastern to Western Europe
Mette Ginnerskov-Dahlberg

For more information about this series, please visit: www.routledge.com/
Routledge-Studies-in-Development-Mobilities-and-Migration/book-series/
RSDM

Student Migration from Eastern to Western Europe

Mette Ginnerskov-Dahlberg

Routledge
Taylor & Francis Group

LONDON AND NEW YORK

First published 2022
by Routledge
2 Park Square, Milton Park, Abingdon, Oxon OX14 4RN

and by Routledge
605 Third Avenue, New York, NY 10158

Routledge is an imprint of the Taylor & Francis Group, an informa business

© 2022 Mette Ginnerskov-Dahlberg

British Library Cataloguing-in-Publication Data
A catalogue record for this book is available from the British Library

Library of Congress Cataloging-in-Publication Data
Names: Ginnerskov-Dahlberg, Mette, author.
Title: Student migration from Eastern to Western
Europe / Mette Ginnerskov-Dahlberg.
Description: 1st Edition. | New York : Routledge, 2022. |
Series: Routledge Studies in Development, Mobilities and Migration |
Includes bibliographical references and index.
Identifiers: LCCN 2021006661 (print) | LCCN 2021006662 (ebook)
Subjects: LCSH: Student mobility–Europe. | Graduate student mobility. |
Students, Foreign–Education (Higher)–Denmark. |
Emigration and immigration–Political aspects–Europe, Eastern. |
Emigration and immigration–Economic aspects–Europe, Eastern. |
Emigration and immigration–Social aspects–Europe, Eastern. |
Education and state. | Ethnology–Denmark.
Classification: LCC LB3064.4.E85 G56 2022 (print) |
LCC LB3064.4.E85 (ebook) | DDC 378.1/982691–dc23
LC record available at https://lccn.loc.gov/2021006661
LC ebook record available at https://lccn.loc.gov/2021006662

ISBN: 978-0-367-52073-1 (hbk)
ISBN: 978-0-367-52075-5 (pbk)
ISBN: 978-1-003-05628-7 (ebk)

Typeset in Sabon
by Newgen Publishing UK

Contents

Acknowledgements   viii

1   Introduction   1

2   Methodology and analytical tools   27

3   'Go West!' Eastern European students' motivations for
    pursuing an education in Denmark   52

4   'Thrivers' and 'dead guys': The lives of Eastern European
    students in the West   88

5   Should I stay or should I go? The social and
    geographical trajectories of Eastern European graduates   138

6   Conclusion   180

    Index   193

Acknowledgements

I want to begin by thanking all the wonderful student migrants who were willing to share their experiences and thoughts with me throughout the years. Without your narratives, there would be no book to begin with.

Even if a book is primarily driven by intellectual curiosity, it also requires financial assistance. I therefore graciously acknowledge the financial support from the Independent Research Fund Denmark, Aarhus University, and the Department of Education at Uppsala University.

I want to thank Lisanne Wilken and Stig Thøgersen for valuable insights on the initial drafts as well as the group members of the project, 'Internationalisation and Social Practice within the field of Danish Higher Education' at Aarhus University. Thank you Russell King, Martin Bak Jørgensen, and especially Karen Valentin for giving me the confidence that I should turn my doctoral dissertation into a book. Thank you Lars Christiansen for sharpening my written English and providing me with shelter in Aarhus.

I am grateful for my dear colleagues from the research group Sociology of Education and Culture (SEC) at Uppsala University. I especially want to acknowledge the continuous support and encouragement from Mikael Börjesson, which have been invaluable in my post-graduation journey.

Finally, I want to send my warmest regards to the main pillars in my life without whom this book never would have seen the light of day. To my best friend, Janne, whose warmth and empathy I never want to be without. To my dear parents, Bente and Jesper, for ALWAYS being there and believing in me. Your eyes and affection for the exposed and marginalised in society serve as an incredible source of inspiration – even for this study. To my incredible husband, Josef, whose strength, love, and intellect blow me away on a daily basis. A shout out to both you and Janne for patiently reading and commenting on all the drafts that preceded this book. Finally, to my beloved son, Aske, who serves as a daily reminder that, after all, there are more important matters in life beyond the peculiar world of academia. You and pappa are the brightest stars in my sky.

1 Introduction

It was 1:00 am, my alarm clock went off. There was nothing I wanted more than to stay under my warm covers, and yet I forced my heavy body to get up. It was a Saturday night and I had arranged with Bogdan, a master's student from Romania, to assist him in delivering newspapers. I jumped on my bike and went out into the dark night. Parallel to his university studies in Denmark, Bogdan had been a newspaper deliverer for almost two years now. Together we arrived at a large, grey building where the newspapers were to be handed out. The vast majority of Bogdan's colleagues originated from Eastern European countries and they communicated in languages that I could not understand. Some smoked cigarettes and others drank a cup of coffee while mentally preparing for the night. Bogdan and I equipped ourselves with neon-coloured vests to become visible in the dark. We loaded the bike trailer with newspapers and rode our bikes towards the city centre where our route was located. Bogdan needed to navigate an enormous bunch of keys to get through, what in my eyes looked like an urban labyrinth of gates and stairways. I was fascinated by the dexterous manner in which he moved between keys and mailboxes with striking ease and elegance. So many stairs. So many newspapers. Surrounded by drunk youngsters in the streets, seemingly belonging to a different world than us, we carried on for several hours. Finally, around 5:00 am, the newspaper wagon was empty and I could happily return to my bed knowing that I would get a good night's sleep for the foreseeable future. For Bogdan, however, this work routine would repeat itself for six out of seven nights a week.

The vignette is based on field notes from the very beginning of my study of Eastern European master's students in Denmark (2013–2020). It provides a good indication of a life condition foreign to most international students, yet one that characterised many of my interlocutors' studies abroad. This group of individuals often had to balance the highly diverse roles of university students and low-skilled workers. For Bogdan,[1] newspapers represented his financial lifeline in Denmark and, indeed, a necessity for even attending classes at the university; yet, they also hindered him from prioritising his studies. His part-time job thus had an ambiguous connotation: 'It fucked up my life and saved my life!' When Bogdan initially decided to study in

Denmark, he never imagined that newspapers would occupy such a central position in his life. In Romania, his days mostly revolved around reading and writing and he had just published his first novel. As my fieldwork progressed, I realised that Bogdan was far from the only student working night shifts at the newspaper centre. Many students from post-socialist countries – especially those originating from the European Union (EU) – shared a similar fate abroad. Thus, I was taken aback by the precarious conditions, which seemingly characterised the lives of some international students where hard, physical jobs were a precondition for studying in Denmark. Certainly, this discovery challenged my preconceptions of what an international student *is*.

International student migration/mobility has often been depicted as an activity involving privileged individuals in search of social and cultural capital accumulation, entailing the inherent assumption that a degree abroad is linked to a longer term strategy to return to the country of origin after graduation (Barnick, 2010; Börjesson, 2005; Brooks and Waters, 2011; Cairns, 2014; Kenway and Fahey, 2007; Munk, 2009). Other scholars have suggested that studying abroad may function as a 'time out' from adult commitments (Amit, 2010a, p. 67), driven by a desire to 'experience something new, exciting and fun' (Trower and Lehmann, 2017, p. 285). The internationalisation of education, Johanna Waters (2012, p. 124) claims, has led to the internationalisation of 'choice,' entailing that privileged individuals can 'opt-out' of competitive domestic education systems in favour of alternatives abroad. Elizabeth Murphy-Lejeune (2002, p. 75) calls student travellers in Europe 'an elite' because 'they show the way towards the future. Even though their number is small, they are the "yeast" which will facilitate European mobility.' In a similar vein, Jane Kenway and Johannah Fahey (2007, p. 168) argue that the 'cosmopolitan Euro student' roaming the European educational landscape is no ordinary traveller but an individual with a background characterised by 'certain educational and class privileges' and indeed 'spatial emancipation.'

This conceptualisation of educational mobility as a 'light' and privileged variant of migration relates to a more general perception of youth in affluent Western countries, where youth travelling has been identified with the supposed extension of youth and delayed transition into adulthood (Amit, 2011). According to Vered Amit (2010b, p. 13), there persists a dominant 'notion that study abroad is a good, in and of itself, tends to be accepted as a common-sensical truth, largely impervious to countervailing or unavailable evidence.' The belief in the power of 'international experience' is not a novel phenomenon but can be traced to the seventeenth century and the grand tours undertaken by young European elites seeking self-development and cultural refinement (Amit, 2010b; Cresswell, 2006; Winberg, 2018).

An increasing number of studies, however, advocate for a broader and more multifaceted conceptualisation of student migration/mobility. According to Russell King and Parvati Raghuram (2013, p. 135), we should abandon 'the simplistic image of the international student as a privileged individual from a relatively well-heeled background' and acknowledge them as 'complex subjects who are much more than just students whose only function is life in higher education.' Methodologically, this has at least two important implications: Firstly, that global student flows should be examined within broader practices of migration (Findlay et al., 2012; Fong, 2011; Luthra and Platt, 2016; Olwig and Valentin, 2015; Valentin, 2015; Wanki and Lietaert, 2018). Studies increasingly show how education outside the national borders is entangled with aspirations of more permanent settlement rather than a wish to return directly to their home countries after graduation (Baas, 2010; Brooks and Waters, 2011; Findlay et al., 2017, 2012; Mosneaga, 2014; Robertson, 2013; Robertson and Runganaikaloo, 2014; Soong, 2014). Lesleyanne Hawthorne (2010) even argues that long-term migration represents a strong and longstanding motivation for international study. Moreover, in a time where opportunities to enter the EU are becoming increasingly restricted, the student category stands out as one of the few legitimate options for migration (Luthra and Platt, 2016).

Secondly, greater attention should be paid to the multiple roles (e.g. as family members, actual or potential workers, refugees, and asylum-seekers) that international students inhabit next to their studies (King and Raghuram, 2013). As exemplified in the vignette from my fieldwork, many student migrants are simultaneously low-skilled workers (see also Maury, 2017; Valentin, 2015) – something which also confronts the notion that students must be in possession of sufficient financial means to cover the costs of living in a foreign country before going abroad. Moreover, acquisition of skills and knowledge, generally associated with student migration, has become important in the selection, admission, and integration of other migrant categories – making skills a fundamental element of all migrants' lives (Raghuram, 2013).

As international students appear to have become a more varied group in terms of socio-geographical origins and motives for going abroad, they also evoke contradicting connotations in public debates (Genova, 2016; Valentin, 2012; Wilken and Dahlberg, 2017). On the one hand, they are solicited as desirable migrants because of the skills they bring and develop in the receiving destinations (King and Raghuram, 2013; Mosneaga, 2015). Since the beginning of the 21st century, international students have increasingly been viewed as prospective highly skilled workers and means for boosting knowledge-intense labour markets and countering ageing populations (Alho, 2020; Hawthorne, 2009; Mosneaga and Winther, 2013). On the other hand, international students are not unconditionally 'welcome' (Luthra and Platt, 2016). In an intra-EU context, the 'freedom of movement of persons' has been problematized due to the potential threat some argue that they pose to national welfare goods (Barbulescu and Favell, 2020). In addition, immigration laws restrict the future opportunities for residence and work of non-EU graduates (Luthra and Platt, 2016).

In their co-written article, King and Raghuram (2013, p. 134) highlight the pressing need for 'detailed ethnographic research with other types of student-migrants, for instance those who move from the global South to Europe, North America, Australia, and elsewhere, to document their complex lives in the academic, social, cultural, and economic realms.' In particular, researchers have highlighted how there remains a shortage of studies focusing explicitly on student flows from Eastern European countries (Chankseliani, 2016; Favell and Recchi, 2011; Genova, 2016; Marcu, 2015). With this book, founded upon a longitudinal and ethnographically informed study, I seek to address this research lacuna by offering a window into the multifaceted experiences and narratives of a group of students from different Eastern European countries attending higher education in a (non-Anglophone) Western European country and their lives as they unfold following their graduation in various localities.

Scope of the book

The disintegration of the block of socialist countries in combination with the enlargement of the EU in May 2004 and January 2007 provided new members from Eastern and Central European countries with an unprecedented 'space of opportunity' to move freely within the EU territory (King, 2018, p. 1). They were granted a privilege, which for years had only been enjoyed by their Western European counterparts. The EU's Eastern enlargement has been referred to as the most significant event affecting intra-European migration since the end of the Second World War (Baláž and Karasová, 2017; Favell, 2008; King and Karamoschou, 2019). Between 2000 and 2011, the numbers of EU citizens from Central and Eastern European countries residing in other member states grew more than five-fold to 5.1 million, with the two largest national groups on the move being Romanians (2.3 million) and Poles (1.6 million) (King and Williams, 2018, p. 2). With the newfound opportunities to cross borders, young people from post-socialist countries are increasingly looking towards Western Europe – not least via the channel of higher education (Genova, 2016; Lulle and Buzinska, 2017; Marcu, 2015). In Denmark, a small country of around 6 million inhabitants located in Northern Europe, the new flow of mobile individuals have also made their entrance into the educational landscape. Within the last decades, the number of students coming to study in Denmark from the EU's 'newer' member states has increased at a rapid pace from 600 in 2004 to approximately 10,000 in 2015. In comparison, the number of international students from the 'old' EU/EEA countries grew from 1,000 to around 6,000 (UFM, 2018).

One feature which makes Denmark particularly attractive for EU-citizens is the fact that tertiary education is tax-funded and therefore free of charge for Danish citizens and – because of the EU principle of non-discrimination on grounds of nationality – other citizens of the EU as well (Wilken and Dahlberg, 2017). In sharp contrast, since 2006 students from outside the EU or the European Economic Area have been obliged to pay tuition fees. A controversial ruling by the Court of Justice of the EU in early 2013 made EU citizens eligible to receive the Danish study grant 'Statens Uddannelsesstøtte,' colloquially known as 'SU.' With approximately 800 euros per month, the Danish study stipend is the most generous in the EU. However, in contrast to Danish citizens, incoming students must qualify as mobile workers in order to receive the desirable study stipend, which in practice means that they are required to have a stable job of minimum 10–12 hours per week. Following the EU verdict, the number of non-Danish EU citizens that received the SU increased at an incredible speed: From 400 individuals in 2011–2012 to almost 9,700 in 2016 (Scheuer, 2017). The majority of these students originated from the EU's newer member states. However, it is important to emphasise that the overall number of international students coming to the country has not been noticeably affected by the EU verdict (UFM, 2018).

As indicated, the large inflow of international students has increasingly been problematized in European countries. Due to the conditions discussed above, incoming students from the EU's newer member states have sparked particular controversy in Denmark. Some Danish politicians have raised concerns that these student groups enrol in Danish universities to take advantage of the fee-free tertiary education and the possibility of obtaining study grants – only to leave the country shortly following their graduation. During the election to the European Parliament in May 2019, the 'populist' 'Danish People's Party' singled out Eastern European students as an endangerment to the established order. In one election poster, they portrayed the EU as a dictatorship, forcing the Danish state to finance the education of foreign citizens where Eastern European students were portrayed as a group particularly focused on exploiting the Danish welfare system.

Despite endangering forecasts and warnings of an 'invasion' (Justesen and Bang, 2014) of students from Eastern European countries in Denmark and the 'explosion' of study grant payments to EU students (Adelsteen, 2014) surprisingly little research has been conducted on their motives and experiences as well as their social and geographical trajectories after graduation. At-times one-sided, the portrayal of Eastern European students – as calculating, profit-seeking individuals – provides an important incentive for unravelling their lives and stories in depth. This book thus aspires to bring a 'human face' (Smith and Favell, 2006) to these individuals by shedding light on the micro, ethnographic level of the mobility experience of full-degree students from different Eastern European countries. Assisted by theoretical tools found in the literature on narrativity and dramaturgy, the book engages with the experiences and narratives of the mobile individuals but also the ways that structural conditions and inequalities, such as economy and immigration regulation, affect their mobility experience and possibilities for long-term migration. This book builds on a longitudinal ethnographic fieldwork (2013–2020) among full-degree students enrolled in English medium, master's programmes at a larger university in Denmark, and interviews following their graduation. It strives to capture the continuities and changes that these individuals undergo in Denmark, but also their shifting geographical locations, visa matters, career interruptions, fluid personal relations and obligations, re-imagined futures, settlements, and re-settlements upon graduation. As such, the book offers valuable insights into the scarce literature on international students' study-to-work transition (Alho, 2020; Bryła, 2018; Geddie, 2010; Mosneaga and Winther, 2013).

Eastern European students on the move

In the following sections, I provide a more detailed description of the point of departure for my interlocutors' educational journey, namely the socio-geographical context where they have come of age. I begin by discussing the roots of dominant conceptualisations of Eastern Europe today.

The narrative construction of Eastern Europe

The collapse of the Iron Curtain in 1989 paved the way for reunification of Europe's estranged eastern and western parts. Despite the fact that more than three decades have passed since the 1989 revolutions and that some Eastern European countries have become official members of the EU, scholars have highlighted how Europe still suffers from a mental dividing line across the continent which has proven highly difficult to eradicate (Galasińska and Galasiński, 2010). According to Attila Melegh (2006), the societal developments post-1989 were characterised by a strong paradox: The breakdown of communism gave birth to aspirations of 'normalcy' among Eastern European nations, which basically means 'Western conditions' and a sacred cocktail of diversity, freedom, democracy, and market economy. The entrance into a non-communist era also renewed hopes that the distinct Eastern category in Europe would dissolve 'or at least the rapid evaporation of its unpleasant connotations and a gradual "reintegration" of Europe' (Melegh, 2006, p. 1). Instead, people found dreams of normalcy replaced with what many experienced as a state of abnormality due to the rise of nationalism and disintegrative tendencies around the shifting borders of Europe – leaving the East–West divide intact.

According to Larry Wolff (1994, p. 3), mental maps are often hardy and highly resistant to time. Moreover, they do not necessarily follow suit with altering political realities. Thus, the shadows of the Iron Curtain persist with remarkable tenacity because the *idea of Eastern Europe* lives on, even in the absence of any physical barrier. As indicated, the 'return' to Europe has proven to be vastly more difficult than initially expected (Galasińska and Galasiński, 2010). One of the reasons for this, Wolff claims, is that the symbolic East–West division of the European continent did not arise with communism but predates the Cold War. In his book, *Inventing Eastern Europe: The Map of Civilization on the Mind of the Enlightenment*, Wolff (1994) accentuates how the stubborn separation between Eastern and Western Europe has its roots in the period of Enlightenment where thoughts about Western superiority gained ground. His take-home message is clear: The East–West distinction is anything but natural despite its resilient nature; rather, Eastern Europe is a 'product' of Western Europe. Indeed, the identity of a place is very much bound up with the narratives that are told of them and the narratives that rise to dominance (Massey, 1995). The founders of these narratives were, according to Wolff, prominent Western thinkers and travellers during the Enlightenment. As such, they are responsible for Eastern Europe's ambivalent position in Europe today – 'a paradox of simultaneous inclusion and exclusion, Europe but not Europe' (Wolff, 1994, p. 7). In the Western travellers' writings, the region came to be identified with backwardness – an image which bolstered the perception of Western Europe as the cradle of civilisation (Wolff, 1994).

A central issue in dominant East–West conceptualisations remains the aspect of modernity – a notion that has been and continues to be theorised as distinctive and Western in its origin (Mayblin et al., 2016, p. 4). According to Maria Todorova (2009, p. 12), 'the element of time with its developmental aspect has been an important, and nowadays the most important, characteristic of contemporary perceptions of East and West.' There has been an outspoken assumption that Eastern Europe needs to 'catch up' with the modern West – a perception that has gained momentum following the end of communism (Melegh, 2006). Moreover, these narratives have also manifested themselves at an individual level. Nataša Kovačević (2008, pp. 5–6) claims that the internalisation of the stigma of inferiority is accompanied by an outspoken tendency among Eastern Europeans to have to prove themselves as 'civilized, developed, tolerant, or multicultural enough' in order to be recognised and accepted as 'true' Europeans.

Out of sight, out of mind? Coming of age in post-socialist Europe

Communist 'trademarks,' such as state ownership of virtually all economic assets, central economic planning, and government by communist parties to which no organised opposition was permitted, dissolved almost overnight in 1989 in East-Central Europe and in 1991 in South-Eastern Europe when the Soviet Union took its last breath (Roberts, 2009). Since then, Eastern European countries have taken different paths:

> The change to Eastern European societies has been not only fundamental, but has also taken different directions in different states: most of the post-socialist countries have joined the European Union, while some have had to cope with civil wars and separatist movements, including the former Yugoslavian countries as well as Moldova, Georgia and Ukraine, whereas Belorussia and Russia have chosen a more authoritarian way.
>
> (Schwartz and Winkel, 2016, p. 3)

Today young people have lived most of their lives without material reminders of the Iron Curtain and hence their knowledge of communism comes 'only from schoolbooks, movies or the memories of older friends and family members' (Schwartz and Winkel, 2016, p. 3). While communism may be out of sight, Ken Roberts (2009, p. 4) claims that its legacy remains deeply ingrained in the minds of the people and continues to structure how the present is experienced. Matthias Schwartz and Heike Winkel (2016, p. 3) make a similar observation: 'The common social and cultural heritage of the socialist era is still more or less present, as are the consequences of its downfall, such as rapid privatisation, the economisation of public goods and contested political systems.' Indeed, Eastern European nations have faced enormous challenges when having to reimagine, adjust, and reorganise the societal setup in their aspirations of moving politically and socially more westward:

> The social, political and economic alterations in Europe have been accompanied by radical changes in the public and private discourses in [post-socialist] countries. A new 'more European' style of political discourse had to be invented; new history; new textbooks; new laws; new constitutions had to be written to both reflect and construct the new realities.
>
> (Galasińska and Galasiński, 2010, p. 2)

Attempts to implement a 'Western developmental model' led to a total reorganisation of public policy and social organisation attuned to the principles of free market, private property, and democratic and transparent governance. These alterations were driven with the hope of achieving the economic development, prosperity, and living standards equivalent to Western Europe (Manolova, 2017). However, such aspirations are not to be confused with the total replacement of all social phenomena with a completely new mode of life, and there is no clear-cut line between communism and post-communism but indeed strong threads of continuity (Humphrey, 2002). Charles Walker and Svetlana Stephenson (2010) underline that Eastern European countries remain in a state of transformation despite the 'end-of-history' rhetoric surrounding the transitions from state socialism to democracy and neo-liberal capitalism. The development of post-socialist countries results in many individuals feeling disadvantaged by the process of transition and feeling a certain powerlessness due to the lack of control of what is happening around them (Morokvasic, 2004; Rabikowska, 2013).

Essentially, the collapse of the socialist system and the demise of planned economy drove many citizens into poverty (Abbott et al., 2010). Scholars have shown how feelings of disappointment have given birth to a growing sense of nostalgia for life during communism (Ghodsee, 2011; Hann, 2002; Rekść, 2015) – even among younger generations who never experienced communism firsthand (Nikolayenko, 2008). A survey conducted in the poorest EU member state, Bulgaria, revealed that 62 per cent of the asked Bulgarians thought of themselves as economically worse off than during communism and that only 13 per cent felt they were better off in 2009 than under communism (Ghodsee, 2011). Overall, the survey showed how people to an increasing extent were willing to swap democratic freedoms for economic prosperity. Despite the fact that Professor of Russian and East European Studies, Kristen Ghodsee (2011, p. 178), regards Bulgaria as 'an extreme case,' she underscores how similar tendencies characterise a broad range of ex-socialist countries where people are becoming increasingly tired of the chaos that has accompanied democratic reforms (see also Abbott et al., 2010 for a similar analysis on Moldova). Thus, this longing for the past has seemingly grown out of the present's incapability to fulfil current desires (Ghodsee, 2011).

An unprecedented 'space of possibilities'

It is against this backdrop of sweeping societal transformation that young people from post-socialist Eastern Europe come of age (Burrell, 2011). Young people today grow up in a radically different environment than their parents. While previous generations were subjected to authoritarian paternalism, the post-socialist period has been characterised by opposite trends, including the incorporation into the global economic and cultural flows from which previous generations were protected (Abbott et al., 2010; Walker and Stephenson, 2010). Hence, youth today have no direct experience with the censorship, closed borders, and totalitarian propaganda characteristic of the living conditions during communism (Genova, 2016).

Post-socialist youth today belong to a generation who have grown up with increasingly open borders (Roberts, 2009; Schwartz and Winkel, 2016; Wilken and Dahlberg, 2017). Undoubtedly, these newfound possibilities for mobility stand in marked contrast to the lives of previous generations. Between 1945 and 1989, freedom of movement within communist countries was strictly regulated (Bianchi and Stephenson, 2014). Repressive measures put in place by communist state apparatuses meant that citizens were not allowed to travel freely across borders – the communist travel restrictions 'were almost universally despised' (Ghodsee, 2011, p. xv) – which kept international migration at very low levels (Massey, 2003). The 'draconian restrictions' (Bianchi and Stephenson, 2014, p. 4), however, did not rule out all tourist activities. Travels were primarily organised by state enterprises, trade unions, and youth organisations with the overall aspiration to cultivate the ideal socialist citizen and foster solidarity among socialist nations (Bianchi and Stephenson, 2014; Sliwa and Taylor, 2011). Thus, prior to 1989 and 1991, foreign travel was primarily restricted to other socialist countries.[2]

As emphasised, the range of choices available for young people in Eastern Europe has increased when it comes to cross-border mobility, especially for

EU citizens who can now make use of the same mobility rights as young people in Western European countries (Favell, 2008). The new generations thus enjoy an unprecedented 'space of possibilities,' which previous generations were denied (Morokvasic, 2004, p. 9). The end of the bipolar world and the collapse of the communist regimes led to unprecedented cross-border movement and heralded a new phase in European migrations, described as one of the most extensive migration flows in contemporary European history (Marcu, 2017). Massive migration outflows have affected some countries more than others. Romania, for example, witnessed an out-flow of approximately almost 2 million citizens to other European countries (mostly Spain and Italy) between 2005 and 2013 – a number which corresponds to 9.3 per cent of the country's total population (Baláž and Karasová, 2017, p. 17). Moreover, mobile Eastern Europeans are often younger than the overall population in both sending and receiving countries (Marcu, 2017).

The generations who grew up in the light of marked socio-political change and increased transnational possibilities of mobility may be thought of as 'European searchers' (Szewczyk, 2015, p. 155). As noted earlier, the large waves of young people leaving Eastern European countries today are to a great extent the result of open border policies that emerged due to the disintegration of the block of socialist countries and the enlargement of the EU (Lulle and Buzinska, 2017). The considerable differences in living standards between Eastern and Western European countries partly explain why migration has become an attractive option for many young people born and raised in post-communist countries (Roberts, 2009; Sandu et al., 2018). Yet, researchers have also been cautious to underline that the urge to migrate cannot be reduced to an economic logic (Manolova, 2018; Sliwa and Taylor, 2011). Moreover, one should be careful to assume that economic success in the host countries can explain migrants' propensity to stay abroad. For instance, the study by Erik Snel et al. (2015) on Central and Eastern European migrants in the Netherlands accentuates how factors such as migrants' level of transnational activities and socio-cultural integration in the host countries play an important role in shaping their return intentions.

As indicated, we cannot automatically assume that studies on youth mobility in Western European countries are directly transferable to youth mobility in Eastern European countries (Roberts, 2009; Schwartz and Winkel, 2016). A study conducted by Dumitru Sandu et al. (2018) on youth mobility in Europe presents relevant insights into the differences between the mobility patterns of young individuals from Eastern European and Western European countries. Whereas the migration motivations of young people from Eastern European countries were structured around jobs and welfare, young people from Western European countries emphasised life-style factors. One explanation is found in the high rates of youth unemployment in Southern and Eastern Europe, which have forced young people to 'think internationally' when sketching their grand plans for the future

(Abbott et al., 2010, p. 582). Anne White (2010, p. 578) argues that the high migration levels from Poland since 1989 entail that young people have been 'socialised into migration.' Thus, the expectation that young people eventually will have to work abroad is installed in their minds from a very early age. Since youth from the new EU member states tend to look for more favourable work conditions in the more western parts of the Union, concerns have been raised about the so-called brain drain that might have a negative impact on the development of Eastern European countries (Guth and Gill, 2008). Looking outside the EU, a similar picture is found in a study by Pamela Abbott et al. (2010) on young people in Moldova – a post-Soviet country covering one of Europe's poorest regions and one of the regions with the highest rates of emigration. Despite the fact that the country is not an EU member, young people feel increasingly compelled to look for opportunities outside the Moldovian boundaries. The majority of these individuals aim for countries inside the borders of the EU and more generally destinations in the West.

In the period between 1997 and 2013, approximately three-quarters of all intra-European migrants were concentrated in six countries (the UK, France, Germany, Switzerland, Italy, and Spain), all of which are situated in Western Europe (Baláž and Karasová, 2017, p. 23). The uneven distribution of individuals travelling within the EU and the scale of migration from East to West have prompted a pronounced fear in Western European countries that low-cost workers from the new member states will flood their labour markets (Sliwa and Taylor, 2011; van Riemsdijk, 2010). Thus, Eastern European workers have often been constructed as 'undesirable others' who pose an overriding threat to the established social order and welfare provisions enjoyed by locals (Manolova, 2018). In addition, studies underline how Eastern Europeans are subjected to different types of discrimination practices at the labour market in Western European countries, such as receiving lower wages than natives and lower returns on their educational qualifications vis-à-vis other migrant groups (Fox et al., 2015).

Previous studies on student migration/mobility in Europe

The European Commission has been highly focused on emphasising the benefits of youth mobility in Europe and more generally the principle of free mobility between EU member states (Cairns, 2014). The Erasmus programme of higher education and student mobility, established in 1987, is by many scholars considered a cornerstone in creating a new generation of mobile young Europeans – what has been termed 'the Erasmus generation' (Cairns, 2014, p. 16). Approximately 30 years after its launch, more than 3 million students have crossed borders as part of the Erasmus scheme (King, 2018, p. 2). For that reason, EU programmes promoting student mobility have often been proclaimed as maybe the most successful component of EU policy to date (Brooks and Waters, 2011), and students on the move viewed as frontrunners of European integration. According to Emmanuel Sigalas (2010, p. 261), one of the original goals of the Erasmus programme was to promote personal interaction between young Europeans and, in turn, a European identity. In this light students are instrumental for creating a sense of 'Europeanness' and a Europe that is closely knit, since they, due to their young age, may be more prone to learn from each other (King and Raghuram, 2013).

It has been suggested that these political ideals put forward by the EU may have created a bias in research addressing mobile students in Europe, making academics especially interested in whether the experience of a European student exchange paves the way for a European identity (Papatsiba, 2005). A number of studies addressing young Europeans' motivation for studying abroad focus on students participating in officially mediated student mobility programmes such as the Erasmus programme (Baláž and Williams, 2004; Bryła, 2018; King and Ruiz-Gelices, 2003; Lesjak et al., 2015; Munk, 2009; Sigalas, 2010; Van Mol and Timmerman, 2014). The majority of studies on student migration/mobility in Europe, however, engage with individuals coming from Western, Anglophone countries, while less is known about the characteristics and experiences of students coming from post-socialist countries (Marcu, 2015). In the following, I will discuss the empirical findings of this sparse literature, which focus explicitly on the perspectives of Eastern European full-degree students studying abroad.

A key focus of these studies is *why* students from post-socialist countries pursue an education abroad. In her study of young undergraduates from Bulgaria and Romania studying in Spain and the UK, Silvia Marcu (2015) debunks the notion that all mobile students belong to an elite trying to secure privileged positions upon their return to their home country. In fact, Marcu shows how her interlocutors mainly belonged to the lower-middle classes and accentuates that their decision to study abroad was based on very different 'life-strategy expectations' (2015, p. 71). These include permanent settlement and family reunification, uncertain mobility as a tool for future competition, and mobility for return. Several of the students perceived a Western European degree to be a future weapon against poverty in their home countries and particularly instrumental for upholding their families financially. Hence, the students' motivations for pursuing an education abroad were strongly connected to the well-being of their loved ones. Further nuances as to what drives Eastern European students to pursue an education abroad can be found in Lulle and Buzinska's (2017) study on Latvian students abroad. The authors highlight how patterns of inequality in Latvia, including a lack of access to higher education, have created a climate that turns education elsewhere in Europe into an attractive option. Since state-funded scholarships in Latvia are difficult to access, do not cover basic needs and living costs, and are accompanied by loans with interest payments of up to 5 per cent per year, young people are increasingly prevented from attending higher education at home (Lulle and Buzinska,

2017, p. 1368). For Latvian students, countries with free education (such as the Scandinavian countries) therefore constitute a way to bypass local circumstances. Lulle and Buzinska (2017, p. 1375) argue that 'study abroad, at least for some, is not a privileged choice but rather a viable alternative if securing a state-funded place in Latvia fails.' Some students were driven by aspirations of labour migration and/or romantic attachment to a foreign partner. Like Marcu's study, their findings nuance the notion of privilege and accentuate how various factors not directly connected to their university studies may have a pivotal impact on the students' decision to go abroad.

While Jessica Guth and Bryony Gill's (2008) study focuses on the perspectives of Polish and Bulgarian doctoral candidates (i.e. not under-graduate students) who have 'gone West' (to the UK and Germany), it presents some relevant and interesting insights into the participants' motiv-ation for going abroad and their subsequent reflections on returning. The study accentuates the link between education abroad and the students' plans for longer-term settlement. Guth and Gill suggest that the socio-economic factors and the characteristics of labour markets in sending coun-tries, vis-à-vis host countries, possess a bearing influence on the students' mobility. Besides traditional economic concerns (such as the prospect of a higher salary), their findings also underscore that the doctoral candidates' mobilities were driven by reasons such as universities' science expenditure. The study, thereby, underlines the importance of paying attention to the subtler nuances when it comes to the role of economy in transnational movement. In terms of return, the interviewees were focused on destinations that could offer 'the best opportunity available to them' (Guth and Gill, 2008, p. 837). While some of the students were dissatisfied with their social life abroad, they were, at the same time, discouraged by the thought of returning to their home countries due to the job market awaiting them. As such, the latter observation illustrates how students on the move some-times experience a conflictual relationship between different desires such as wanting to stay close to one's social network at home and the possibility for relevant employment after graduation.

Some studies focus specifically on students from post-Soviet countries – a group that, according to Maia Chankseliani (2016), make up 8 per cent of the global body of internationally mobile students. Chankseliani argues that students from these countries seek to escape conditions such as low tertiary capacity and high youth unemployment and therefore seek out destinations which are expected to offer good-quality higher education and where living conditions are culturally and economically appealing (see also Cairns and Sargsyan, 2019). She further raises the issue of educational mobility poten-tially leading to 'brain drain,' yet at the same time, she argues that 'the desire to permanently migrate show that such motivation cannot be linked with student outbound mobility' (Chankseliani, 2016, p. 312). In Sarah Holloway et al.'s (2012) study of Kazakhstani students pursuing higher education in the UK, the 'key driver of their mobility was a desire to obtain a qualification that would make them stand out from other graduates in their chosen labour market, and thus (re)produce themselves as economically successful citizens' (Holloway et al., 2012, p. 2285). While the mobile individuals were predominantly oriented towards the domestic labour market, such return aspirations should be viewed in the light that the scholarships, which gave the students access to overseas education, had a 'return to Kazakhstan' as a precondition.

Finally, I wish to draw attention to Elena Genova's (2016) ethnographic study of Bulgarian students in the UK, which specifically sheds light on their experiences of residing abroad and the multiple identities they take on in the host country. Genova (2016, p. 397) underlines the interplay between four main student identifications the students face in the increasingly foreign-hostile context: 'Bulgarians,' 'students,' 'European citizens,' and 'migrants.' Her analysis accentuates the fluidity of identity and how certain events abroad affect processes of identity construction. The Bulgarian students' experiences abroad – and not least the hostility that they encountered – triggered a strong sense of patriotism, which resulted in the precedence of national identity over the others. Genova thereby stresses how occurrences of 'othering' of Eastern Europeans not only occur among labour migrants, as have been reported elsewhere (Favell, 2008; van Riemsdijk, 2010), but also at the student level. In general, the Bulgarian students did not feel recognised as 'fellow European citizens' abroad, which made them 'cling on' to their student identity to counter negative stereotypes.

Internationalisation in Denmark

While there is a long tradition for cooperation within the Nordic countries and for assisting students from the Global South with educational opportunities, it was not until the mid-2000s that Danish universities adopted a more systematic approach to internationalisation (Wilken and Dahlberg, 2017). Like in many other European countries, the new focus on internationalisation can be understood in light of the Bologna process, which paved the way for the use of standard templates in educational provision (Börjesson, 2017; Brooks and Waters, 2011; Findlay et al., 2012). Following the European standardisation of 1999 and onwards, Danish universities adopted a three-tier structure (BA–MA–PhD), introduced ECTS-points, and launched a broader range of English-medium courses and degree programmes (Wilken and Dahlberg, 2017).

Like most OECD countries, Denmark has, since the mid-2000s, witnessed a steady increase in the inflow of international students and welcomes around 22,000 international full-degree students annually – almost half of which study at the master's level (UFM, 2018). The Danish government has, in its efforts to make Denmark competitive in the global economy, focused on attracting foreign talent through marketisation and national profiling of Denmark as a destination for mobile students

(Valentin, 2012). Aija Lulle and Laura Buzinska (2017), for instance, argue that Denmark has figured as the most visible country in the Baltic higher education market, when compared to other Nordic countries, and has broadly advertised its highly ranked universities and innovative English-medium degree programmes. When taking a closer look at the distribution of nationalities in Danish universities, the neighbouring country Norway sends most students (2,839 students) followed by Germany, Romania, Sweden, Lithuania, Bulgaria, Poland, and Hungary (UFM, 2015a). Hence, the majority of international students in Denmark come from neighbouring countries and the EU's newer member states. More than 80 per cent of international students in Denmark travel from countries inside Europe and, on a global level, Denmark hosts approximately 3 per cent of the world's international students (OECD, 2017). The above distribution of nationalities reflects, among other things, the dual system where non-EU citizens are recruited according to a market logic while EU citizens are not (Börjesson, 2017).

The Danish government has increasingly been preoccupied with retaining international students in Denmark following their graduation. International students stand as one of the key target groups under Denmark's talent attraction agenda oriented at accommodating national labour market shortages (Mosneaga, 2015). In 2015, the Ministry of Higher Education and Science (UFM), the Danish ministry in charge of research and education above high school/upper secondary school, published a report that sought to shed light on critical factors for making graduates stay in the country (UFM, 2015b). The report suggested that merely 55 per cent of the study's participants resided in Denmark in the immediate years following their graduation and that Scandinavian students were the most prone to leave the country. A report conducted by the Danish think tank Kraka in 2016 underlined that Eastern European students attending higher education in Denmark are more likely to stay than, for instance, Scandinavian students. The report singled out the income differences between their home countries and Denmark as the main reason why Eastern European students are seemingly more prone to staying in Denmark following their graduation (Vasiljeva, 2016). Despite ambitions of retaining international students in the country, the Danish government presented the high number of graduates leaving shortly after having obtained a degree as the main reason for reducing the number of English-language degree programmes in Denmark (UFM, 2018). The initiative, they claimed, sought to restore the balance between the inflow and outflow of international students.

According to Dana Minbaeva et al. (2018), Denmark suffers from a 'Danish talent paradox.' While the country excels in its ability to enable and grow talent internally, it is much less successful in attracting and retaining international graduates. In addition to a general lack of openness towards foreign culture and people, the constant changes in immigration regulations appear to be a barrier for non-EU citizens to settle down on a more permanent basis (Minbaeva et al., 2018). Moreover, international student retention is filtered through immigration policies and delicate policy environments that often make a poor fit with the ongoing globalisation of higher education (Mosneaga and Agergaard, 2012). Immigration regulations that apply to the status of international students after graduation vary widely depending on whether one has a passport from an EU/EEA country or not (Mosneaga and Winther, 2013). In Chapter 5, which deals with the students' social and geographical trajectories following their graduation, I go more in-depth with the most important policies facilitating international students' transition into the Danish labour market.

Eastern European students in Denmark

To my knowledge, no scientific research has been conducted specifically on Eastern European students in Denmark besides the present study (see also Wilken and Dahlberg, 2017) or in any other Scandinavian country for that matter. Nevertheless, there is valuable knowledge to be gained from the public reports available on Eastern European students in Denmark. In this section, a background constituted by these reports is presented in order to contextualise the case of this student group in Denmark.

Eastern European students have become increasingly visible in the Danish educational landscape. Students from the EU's 'newer' member states make up approximately 41 per cent of all international students in higher education (UFM, 2018). Half of these students come from three countries: Romania, Lithuania, and Poland. A factor that appears to distinguish students from the EU's Eastern European member states and students from other EU member states is their financial model abroad. In an article co-written with Lisanne Wilken, I emphasised how Eastern European students usually receive minimal financial support from their parents and therefore have to work to support themselves in Denmark (Wilken and Dahlberg, 2017). In contrast, Nordic students tend to bring study grants from their home countries, and Western and Southern EU students often receive financial support from their parents.[3] The high number of SU receivers from Eastern European countries also suggests a pronounced dependency on establishing a financial base abroad among this group in particular. In 2018, the country with the most SU receivers was Romania (1,327) followed by Slovakia (1,067), Germany (1,039), Poland (974), Hungary (854), and Lithuania (804) (UFM, 2019).

A report,[4] conducted by Professor Steen Scheuer for The Danish Confederation of Trade Unions (LO), suggests that Eastern European students' dependence on a paid job positions them in a vulnerable position in Denmark (Scheuer, 2017). According to Scheuer, more than one-third of the Eastern European students who participated in the LO's investigation had been subjected to social dumping in Denmark and had been paid far less than the official minimum wage. Scheuer presents two potential scenarios of how Danish employers may take advantage of incoming EU students.

First, employers can pay the students less than the minimum salary, thereby exploiting the fact that the students – despite their low salary – can get by in Denmark financially because they also get SU. Alternatively, employers may pay students for 10 hours of work per week, but in reality they are expected to work considerably more. In both cases, the employers use students' possibility to get SU as an excuse to pay the students less (in some cases much less) than the minimum wage or to make them work more hours.[5] The report further emphasises that the majority of students were unaware of the minimum wage in Denmark and may have been uninformed that they, to use Scheuer's (2017, p. 20) words, were subjected to 'gross exploitation.'

It is furthermore relevant to note the *types of jobs* that Eastern European students usually hold while studying in Denmark. Scheuer (2017) underlines that only 15 per cent of the students had part-time jobs requiring higher education qualifications, while more than 50 per cent worked within the cleaning, hotel, and restaurant industries. This entails that the majority of Eastern European students had low-skilled jobs unrelated to their educational path. Similar results were presented in a survey-based report by the Danish government (DAMVAD, 2013).[6] The survey examined the career plans of international students attending higher education in Denmark and showed that 74 per cent of the study population had part-time jobs to cover their living expenses abroad. Only 32 per cent of the students coming from EU's member states (where the majority came from Eastern European countries) worked in fields related to their studies, which stood in sharp contrast to, for instance, the Nordic students, where 74 per cent had jobs related to their fields of interests. Since the report emphasised the importance of a part-time job during one's studies for employment following graduation, it is also striking to note that only 17 per cent of all international students in the survey had done an internship (DAMVAD, 2013, p. 25). While some might argue that there is nothing remarkable about university students working in low-skilled jobs next to their studies, there appears to be a marked difference between the situation of Danish and Eastern European students. Since the first group consists of native speakers who receive SU without work obligations, they hypothetically have a broader palette of jobs to choose from (Wilken and Dahlberg, 2017). They can also work fewer hours a week if they wish to do so and take up unpaid internships – a potential way to further their career after graduation.

As underlined, this book does not focus solely on the experience of Eastern European students originating from EU countries, the so-called *EU-movers*, but also students travelling from countries outside the EU (popularly referred to as post-Soviet countries and the Balkans). Essentially, all non-EU students came to Denmark accompanied by rather generous scholarships, and hence did not pay tuition fees. In addition, they also received a monthly amount to cover their living expenses (approximately the equivalent of the Danish SU, i.e. approximately 800 euros per month). Therefore, students receiving scholarships are usually not dependent on a job next to their university studies. Non-EU students, in general, are furthermore restricted from working more than 20 hours per week and full time in June, July, and August. In this book, I use the students' different life conditions to not only investigate the ways that structural factors affect their subjective experience of living and studying in Denmark but also to explore how legal statuses – in this case EU citizens and non-EU citizens – enable differentiated mobility possibilities after graduation.

Structure of the book

Chapter 2, *Methodology and analytical tools*, outlines the book's methodological and theoretical framework. I begin by discussing the two 'main waves' of data collection, which make up the heart of this ethnographic, longitudinal study, followed by a characterisation of my interlocutors and a reflection on my role(s) in the field. I then turn to a discussion of the book's narrative approach for bringing my interlocutors' personal experiences to the forefront and contextualise the stories they narrate in relation to grander historical and cultural narratives. To accentuate 'the micro politics of interpersonal interaction' (Phibbs, 2007, p. 2) and how my interlocutors' narrations are shaped by their practices, a complementary analytical toolset is found in theories of dramaturgy.

Chapter 3, '*Go West!' Eastern European students' motivations for pursuing an education in Denmark*, marks the beginning of the book's empirical part. It highlights some of the multifaceted factors that initially made the Eastern European students pursue a master's degree in Denmark. The students' narrations indicate that the meanings they attach to their home countries' 'material environment' – i.e. the socio-economic, historical, and political context – are imperative when seeking to understand why they eventually pursue a master's degree in Denmark. I discuss how my interlocutors experienced a state of existential immobility while residing in their home countries due to an alarming gap between their desires and possibilities to act on these, and how they narrated their mobility as a search for 'normality.' Such difficulties of aligning their lives with the desired life trajectory turns an education in Denmark – symbolically located in the global West – into an attractive option. The chapter ends with a discussion of how we should understand the students' specific choice of Denmark as a study destination and the role that economic considerations (i.e. free tuition and scholarships) play in their educational mobility.

Chapter 4, '*Thrivers' and 'dead guys': The lives of Eastern European students in the West*, explores the students' experiences of life in Denmark and their narratives of selfhood in relation to the material and symbolic boundaries that they encounter in Denmark. I discuss how students' (from EU countries) dependence on low-skilled jobs affects their sense of self and how few seem prepared for the unparalleled level of precariousness that in many cases awaits the EU movers in Denmark. The chapter also engages with the narratives of the Eastern European students who do not have this financial pressure, that is, the non-EU students sponsored by a scholarship. I discuss how these students are surrounded by a different level of freedom that allows them to engage in activities that they value. The comparison between narratives of Eastern European students funded by scholarships and the self-financing EU students serves to illustrate the ways that structural factors – such as the financial means at one's disposal – affect the students' experiences of studying abroad. Finally, the chapter discusses how my interlocutors find their 'Eastern Europeanness' discredited as well as their strategies for managing this 'Eastern European stigma.' The book thus accentuates how being a student is not a singular identity but often one of many.

Chapter 5, *Should I stay or should I go? The social and geographical trajectories of Eastern European graduates*, highlights the multifaceted paths of my interlocutors following their graduation. I am particularly interested in the ways they narrate their present lives (the future that they hoped for) with respect to the goals they had set for themselves when they initially arrived in Denmark, how a Danish degree (from interdisciplinary study programmes) positions them upon graduation, and the ways they imagine the future from their current positions. The analysis is divided into three overall parts: One part focuses on the narratives and strategies of the graduates keen on staying in Denmark; the second part unravels the narratives of 'the homecomers' and how homecoming is experienced highly differently, and finally, the third part examines the paths of the graduates engaging in onward journeys.

In addition to synthesising the study's analytical findings, Chapter 6, *Conclusion*, discusses the main themes that emerged in the chapters in relation to current literature on student migration. I also address the book's methodological contributions to the literature – stressing, in particular, how a longitudinal study of international students' lived realities can count for how attitudes and narratives change over time, particularly depending on where and how life unfolds.

Notes

1 The names of all individuals participating in this study are fictious to ensure their anonymity.
2 Raoul Bianchi and Marcus Stephenson (2014), underscore that there persisted significant variations of how much individuals could travel depending on the nationality of their passport. Hungary and the former Yugoslavia were examples of countries with relatively lenient travel restrictions. The latter country stood out with free movement to the West (Samaluk, 2016). While the red passport, in theory, provided Yugoslavian citizens with the possibility to travel to almost all of Europe and beyond, Steff Jansen (2009) argues that many Yugoslavs (like most of the world's population) did not take advantage of this opportunity.

3 In her study of Eastern European undergraduates in UK and Spain, Silvia Marcu (2015) also found that it was imperative for the students to get a paid job quickly following their arrival if they wanted to study in Spain.
4 The report builds on the experience of 2,353 individuals from different Eastern European countries.
5 Kvist (2014) highlights a similar risk.
6 DAMVAD conducted the report on behalf of the Danish government. The analysis builds on the experience of 4,949 international students pursuing an education in Denmark. The majority of these (70 per cent) are full-degree students, 21 per cent are exchange students, and 9 per cent are PhD students. The analysis, however, focuses on the responses of the full-degree students.

References

Abbott, P., Wallace, C., Mascauteanu, M., Sapsford, R., 2010. Concepts of citizenship, social and system integration among young people in post-Soviet Moldova. J. Youth Stud. 13, 581–596. https://doi.org/10.1080/13676261.2010.489605
Adelsteen, P. 2014. Velfærdsturister: Nødvendigt at sikre Danmark. *Politiken*. 28 January 2014.
Alho, R., 2020. 'You need to know someone who knows someone': International students' job search experiences. Nord. J. Work. Life Stud. https://doi.org/10.18291/njwls.v10i2.120817
Amit, V., 2011. 'Before I settle down': Youth travel and enduring life course paradigms. Anthropologica 53, 79–88.
Amit, V., 2010a. The limits of liminality: Capacities for change and transition among student travellers, in: Rapport, N. (ed.), Human Nature as Capacity. Berghahn Books, New York.
Amit, V., 2010b. Student mobility and internationalisation: Rationales, rhetoric and 'institutional isomorphism.' Anthropol. Action 17, 6–18.
Baas, M., 2010. Imagined Mobility: Migration and Transnationalism Among Indian Students in Australia. Anthem Press, London.
Baláž, V., Karasová, K., 2017. Geographical patterns in the intra-European migration before and after Eastern enlargement: The connectivity approach. Econ. Cas. 65, 3–30.
Baláž, V., Williams, A.M., 2004. 'Been there, done that': International student migration and human capital transfers from the UK to Slovakia. Popul. Space Place 10, 217–237. https://doi.org/10.1002/psp.316
Barbulescu, R., Favell, A., 2020. Commentary: A citizenship without social rights? EU freedom of movement and changing access to welfare rights. Int. Migr. 58, 151–165. https://doi.org/10.1111/imig.12607
Barnick, H., 2010. Managing time and making space: Canadian students' motivations for study in Australia. Anthropol. Action 17. https://doi.org/10.3167/aia.2010.170103
Bianchi, R.V., Stephenson, M.L., 2014. Tourism and Citizenship: Rights, Freedoms and Responsibilities in the Global Order. Routledge, New York.
Börjesson, M., 2017. The global space of international students in 2010. J. Ethn. Migr. Stud. 43, 1256–1275. https://doi.org/10.1080/1369183X.2017.1300228

Börjesson, M., 2005. Transnationella utbildningsstrategier vid svenska lärosäten och bland svenska studenter i Paris och New York. Uppsala Universitet, Uppsala.

Brooks, R., Waters, J., 2011. Student Mobilities, Migration and the Internationalization of Higher Education. Palgrave Macmillan, New York.

Bryła, P., 2018. International student mobility and subsequent migration: The case of Poland. Stud. High. Educ. 1–14. https://doi.org/10.1080/03075079. 2018.1440383

Burrell, K., 2011. Opportunity and uncertainty: Young people's narratives of 'double transition' in post-socialist Poland. R. Geogr. Soc. 43, 413–419.

Cairns, D., 2014. Youth Transitions, International Student Mobility and Spatial Reflexivity: Being Mobile. Palgrave Macmillan, UK.

Cairns, D., Sargsyan, M., 2019. Student and Graduate Mobility in Armenia. Springer.

Chankseliani, M., 2016. Escaping homelands with limited employment and tertiary education opportunities: Outbound student mobility from post-Soviet countries. Popul. Space Place 22, 301–316. https://doi.org/10.1002/psp.1932

Cresswell, T., 2006. On the Move: Mobility in the Modern Western World. Routledge, London.

DAMVAD, 2013. Internationale studerende i Danmark (Research report). Styrelsen for Universiteter og Internationa- lisering, Styrelsen for Fastholdelse og Rekruttering, Aarhus Universitet and VIA University College.

Favell, A., 2008. The new face of east – west migration in Europe. J. Ethn. Migr. Stud. 34, 701–716. https://doi.org/10.1080/13691830802105947

Favell, A., Recchi, E., 2011. Social mobility and spatial mobility. Sociol. Eur. Union 50–75.

Findlay, A., Prazeres, L., McCollum, D., Packwood, H., 2017. 'It was always the plan': International study as 'learning to migrate.' Area 49, 192–199. https://doi. org/10.1111/area.12315

Findlay, A.M., King, R., Smith, F.M., Geddes, A., Skeldon, R., 2012. World class? An investigation of globalisation, difference and international student mobility. Trans. Inst. Br. Geogr. 37, 118–131.

Fong, V.L., 2011. Paradise Redefined. Stanford University Press, Stanford.

Fox, J.E., Moroşanu, L., Szilassy, E., 2015. Denying discrimination: Status, 'race,' and the whitening of Britain's new Europeans. J. Ethn. Migr. Stud. 41, 21. https:// doi.org/10.1080/1369183X.2014.962491

Galasińska, A., Galasiński, D., 2010. The Post-communist Condition: Public and Private Discourses of Transformation. John Benjamins, Amsterdam.

Geddie, K.P., 2010. Transnational Landscapes of Opportunity? Postgraduation Settlement and Employment Strategies of International Students in Toronto, Canada and London, UK. University of Toronto, Toronto.

Genova, E., 2016. To have both roots and wings: Nested identities in the case of Bulgarian students in the UK. Identities 23, 392–406. https://doi.org/10.1080/ 1070289X.2015.1024125

Ghodsee, K.R., 2011. Lost in Transition: Ethnographies of Everyday Life after Communism. Duke University Press, Durham, NC.

Guth, J., Gill, B., 2008. Motivations in east – west doctoral mobility: Revisiting the question of brain drain. J. Ethn. Migr. Stud. 34, 825–841. https://doi.org/10.1080/ 13691830802106119

Hann, C., 2002. Postsocialism: Ideals, Ideologies, and Practices in Eurasia. Routledge, New York.

Hawthorne, L., 2010. The growing global demand for students as skilled migrants, in: Findlay, C., Tierney, W.G. (Eds.), Globalisation and Tertiary Education in the Asia-Pacific: The Changing Nature of a Dynamic Market. World Scientific Publishing Co Pte Ltd, London.

Hawthorne, L., 2009. The growing global demand for international students as skilled migrants, in: The Migration Policy Institute Talent (Ed.), Competitiveness and Migration: The Transatlantic Council on Migration. Verlag Bertelsmann Stiftung, Brussels.

Holloway, S.L., O'Hara, S.L., Pimlott-Wilson, H., 2012. Educational mobility and the gendered geography of cultural capital: The case of international student flows between Central Asia and the UK. Environ. Plan. Econ. Space 44, 2278–2294. https://doi.org/10.1068/a44655

Humphrey, C., 2002. Does the category 'postsocialist' still make sense?, in: Hann, C. (Ed.), Postsocialism: Ideals, Ideologies, and Practices in Eurasia. Routledge, New York.

Jansen, S., 2009. After the red passport: Towards an anthropology of the everyday geopolitics of entrapment in the EU's 'immediate outside.' J. R. Anthropol. Inst. 15, 815–832. https://doi.org/10.1111/j.1467-9655.2009.01586.x

Justesen, A., Bang, M., 2014. Tidobling af Øststuderende i Danmark. Accessed May, 2021. www.altinget.dk/eu/artikel/tredobling-af-udenlandske-studerende-i-danmark

Kenway, J., Fahey, J., 2007. Policy incitements to mobility: Some speculations and provocations, in: Epstein, D., Boden, D., Deem, R., Rizvi, F., Wright, S. (Eds.), World Year Book of Education 2008: Geographies of Knowledge, Geometries of Power – Framing the Future of Higher Education. Routledge, New York.

King, R., 2018. Theorising new European youth mobilities. Popul. Space Place 24. https://doi.org/10.1002/psp.2117

King, R., Karamoschou, C., 2019. Fragmented and fluid mobilities: The role of onward migration in the new map of Europe and the Balkans. Migr. Etn. Teme 35, 141–169.

King, R., Raghuram, P., 2013. International student migration: Mapping the field and new research agendas: Mapping the field and new research agenda in ISM. Popul. Space Place 19, 127–137. https://doi.org/10.1002/psp.1746

King, R., Ruiz-Gelices, E., 2003. International student migration and the European 'Year Abroad': Effects on European identity and subsequent migration behaviour. Int. J. Popul. Geogr. 9, 229–252. https://doi.org/10.1002/ijpg.280

King, R., Williams, A.M., 2018. Editorial introduction: New European youth mobilities. Popul. Space Place 24, e2121. https://doi.org/10.1002/psp.2121

Kovačević, N., 2008. Narrating Post/communism: Colonial Discourse and Europe's Borderline Civilization, BASEES/Routledge Series on Russian and East European Studies; 47. Routledge, London.

Kvist, J., 2014. Velfærdsturisme og afkobling af ret og pligt, in: Christiansen, N.F., Kvist, J., Kærgård, N., Petersen, K. (Eds.), På Kryds Og Tværs i Velfærdsstatens Univers: Festskrift Til Jørn Henrik Petersern. Syddansk Universitetsforlag, Odense.

Lesjak, M., Juvan, E., Ineson, E.M., Yap, M.H.T., Axelsson, E.P., 2015. Erasmus student motivation: Why and where to go? High. Educ. 70, 845–865. https://doi.org/10.1007/s10734-015-9871-0

Lulle, A., Buzinska, L., 2017. Between a 'student abroad' and 'being from Latvia': Inequalities of access, prestige, and foreign-earned cultural capital. J. Ethn. Migr. Stud. 43, 1362–1378. https://doi.org/10.1080/1369183X.2017.1300336

Luthra, R., Platt, L., 2016. Elite or middling? International students and migrant diversification. Ethnicities 16, 316–344. https://doi.org/10.1177/1468796815616155

Manolova, P., 2018. 'Going to the West is my last chance to get a normal life': Bulgarian would-be migrants' imaginings of life in the UK. Cent. East. Eur. Migr. Rev. 1–23. https://doi.org/10.17467/ceemr.2018.01

Manolova, P., 2017. On the Way to the Imaginary West: Bulgarian Migrations, Imaginations, and Disillusionments. (Unpublished thesis). Birmingham University, Birmingham: Department of Political Science and International Studies.

Marcu, S., 2017. Tears of time: A Lefebvrian rhythm analysis approach to explore the mobility experiences of young Eastern Europeans in Spain. Trans. Inst. Br. Geogr. 42, 405–416. https://doi.org/10.1111/tran.12174

Marcu, S., 2015. Uneven mobility experiences: Life-strategy expectations among Eastern European undergraduate students in the UK and Spain. Geoforum 58, 68–75. https://doi.org/10.1016/j.geoforum.2014.10.017

Massey, D., 2003. Patterns and Processes of International Migration in the 21st Century. Presented at the Conference on African Migration in Comparative Perspective, Johannesburg, South Africa.

Massey, D., 1995. Places and their pasts. Hist. Workshop J. 39, 182–192.

Maury, O., 2017. Student-migrant-workers. Nord. J. Migr. Res. 7, 224–232. https://doi.org/10.1515/njmr-2017-0023

Mayblin, L., Piekut, A., Valentine, G., 2016. 'Other' posts in 'other' places: Poland through a postcolonial lens? Sociology 50, 60–76. https://doi:10.1177/0038038514556796.

Melegh, A., 2006. On the East-West Slope: Globalization, Nationalism, Racism and Discourses on Central and Eastern Europe. Central European University Press, New York.

Minbaeva, D., Andersen, T., Lubanski, N., Navrbjerg, S.E., Torfing, R.M., 2018. Macro talent management in Denmark, in: Vaiman, V., Sparrow, P., Schuler, R., Collings, D.G. (Eds.), Macro Talent Management: A Global Perspective on Managing Talent in Developed Markets. Routledge, London.

Morokvasic, M., 2004. 'Settled in mobility': Engendering post-wall migration in Europe. Fem. Rev. 77, 7–25. https://doi.org/10.1057/palgrave.fr.9400154

Mosneaga, A., 2015. Managing international student migration: The practices of institutional actors in Denmark. Int. Migr. 53, 14–28. https://doi.org/10.1111/imig.12071

Mosneaga, A., 2014. Student migration at the global trijuncture of higher education, competition for talent and migration management, in: Tejada, G., Bhattacharya, U., Khadria, B., Kuptsch, C. (Eds.), Indian Skilled Migration and Development: To Europe and Back. Springer India, New Delhi.

Mosneaga, A., Agergaard, J., 2012. Agents of internationalisation? Danish universities' practices for attracting international students. Glob. Soc. Educ. 10, 519–538.

Mosneaga, A., Winther, L., 2013. Emerging talents? International students before and after their career start in Denmark: International students in Denmark. Popul. Space Place 19, 181–195. https://doi.org/10.1002/psp.1750

Munk, M.D., 2009. Transnational investments in informational capital: A comparative study of Denmark, France and Sweden. Acta Sociol. 52, 5–23.

Murphy-Lejeune, E., 2002. Student Mobility and Narrative in Europe: The New Strangers, Routledge Studies in Anthropology. Routledge, London.

Nikolayenko, O., 2008. Contextual effects on historical memory: Soviet nostalgia among post-Soviet adolescents. Communist Post-Communist Stud. 41, 243–259. https://doi.org/10.1016/j.postcomstud.2008.03.001

OECD (2017), Education at a Glance 2017: OECD Indicators. OECD Publishing, Paris, https://doi.org/10.1787/eag-2017-en.

Olwig, K.F., Valentin, K., 2015. Mobility, education and life trajectories: New and old migratory pathways. Identities 22, 247–257. https://doi.org/10.1080/1070289X.2014.939191

Papatsiba, V., 2005. Political and individual rationales of student mobility: A case-study of ERASMUS and a French regional scheme for studies abroad. Eur. J. Educ. 40, 173–188.

Phibbs, S., 2007. Four dimensions of narrativity: Towards a narrative analysis of gender identity that is simultaneously personal, local and global. N. Z. Sociol. 23, 47–60.

Rabikowska, M., 2013. Everyday of memory – between communism and post-communism. Peter Lang Ag, Internationaler Verlag der Wissenschaften, Berlin.

Raghuram, P., 2013. Theorising the spaces of student migration. Popul. Space Place 19, 138–154. https://doi.org/10.1002/psp.1747

Rekść, M., 2015. Nostalgia for communism in the collective imaginations. Procedia Soc. Behav. Sci. 183, 105–114. https://doi.org/10.1016/j.sbspro.2015.04.852

Roberts, K., 2009. Youth in Transition: Eastern Europe and the West. Palgrave Macmillan, Basingstoke.

Robertson, S., 2013. Transnational Student-Migrants and the State: The Education-Migration Nexus. Palgrave Macmillan, Basingstoke.

Robertson, S., Runganaikaloo, A., 2014. Lives in limbo: Migration experiences in Australia's education – migration nexus. Ethnicities 14, 208–226. https://doi.org/10.1177/1468796813504552

Samaluk, B., 2016. Migration, consumption and work: A postcolonial perspective on post-socialist migration to the UK. Ephemera 16, 95.

Sandu, D., Toth, G., Tudor, E., 2018. The nexus of motivation-experience in the migration process of young Romanians. Popul. Space Place 24, e2114. https://doi.org/10.1002/psp.2114

Scheuer, S., 2017. Misbrug af østeuropæiske studerende på det danske arbjedsmarked. LO – Landsorganisationen i Danmark. https://lo.dk/wp-content/uploads/2017/11/2221- ny-su-rapport-oesteuro-stud-2017.pdf

Schwartz, M., Winkel, H., 2016. Eastern European Youth Cultures in a Global Context. Palgrave Macmillan, UK.

Sigalas, E., 2010. Cross-border mobility and European identity: The effectiveness of intergroup contact during the ERASMUS year abroad. Eur. Union Polit. 11, 241–265. https://doi.org/10.1177/1465116510363656

Sliwa, M., Taylor, B., 2011. 'Everything comes down to money'?: Migration and working life trajectories in a (post-)socialist context. Manag. Organ. Hist. 6, 347–366. https://doi.org/10.1177/1744935911406103

Smith, M.P., Favell, A., 2006. The Human Face of Global Mobility: International Highly Skilled Migration in Europe, North America and the Asia-Pacific. Transaction Publishers, New Brunswick, NJ.

Snel, E., Faber, M., Engbersen, G., 2015. To stay or return? Explaining return intentions of Central and Eastern European labour migrants. Cent. East. Eur. Migr. Rev. 4, 5–24.

Soong, H., 2014. Transnational Students and Mobility: Lived Experiences of Migration. Routledge, London.

Szewczyk, A., 2015. 'European generation of migration': Change and agency in the post-2004 Polish graduates' migratory experience. Geoforum 60, 153–162. https://doi.org/10.1016/j.geoforum.2015.02.001

Todorova, M., 2009. Imagining the Balkans. Oxford University Press, New York.

Trower, H., Lehmann, W., 2017. Strategic escapes: Negotiating motivations of personal growth and instrumental benefits in the decision to study abroad. Br. Educ. Res. J. 43, 275–289. https://doi.org/10.1002/berj.3258

UFM, 2019. Status for udviklingen iantallet af EU/EØS-arbejdstagere sommodtager SU. Uddannelses- og Forskningsministeriet. Accessed January 2021. www.ft.dk/samling/20201/almdel/UFU/bilag/3/2256895/index.htm

UFM, 2018. Offentlige indtægter og udgifter ved internationale studerende. Uddannelses- og Forskningsministeriet. Accessed January 2021. https://ufm.dk/publikationer/2018/filer/offentlige-indtaegter-og-udgifter-ved-internationale-studerende.pdf

UFM, 2015a. Internationale studerende i Danmark. Uddannelses- og Forskningsministeriet. Accessed January 2021. https://ufm.dk/publikationer/2015/filer/internationale-studerende_mlogo.pdf

UFM, 2015b. Internationale studerende i Danmark. Hvad har betydning for om internationale studerende bliver i Danmark efter endt studie? Uddannelses- og Forskningsministeriet. Accessed January 2021. https://ufm.dk/publikationer/2015/filer/internationale-studerende_mlogo.pdf

Valentin, K., 2015. Transnational education and the remaking of social identity: Nepalese student migration to Denmark. Identities 22, 318–332. https://doi.org/10.1080/1070289X.2014.939186

Valentin, K., 2012. Caught between internationalisation and immigration: The case of Nepalese students in Denmark. Learn. Teach. 5. https://doi.org/10.3167/latiss.2012.050304

Van Mol, C., Timmerman, C., 2014. Should I stay or should I go? An analysis of the determinants of intra-European student mobility. Popul. Space Place 20, 465–479. https://doi.org/10.1002/psp.1833

van Riemsdijk, M., 2010. Variegated privileges of whiteness: Lived experiences of Polish nurses in Norway. Soc. Cult. Geogr. 11, 117–137. https://doi.org/10.1080/14649360903514376

Vasiljeva, K., 2016. Hvordan fastholder vi udenlandske stu- derende i Danmark? Kraka, Copenhagen.

Walker, C., Stephenson, S., 2010. Youth and social change in Eastern Europe and the former Soviet Union. J. Youth Stud. 13, 521–532. https://doi.org/10.1080/13676261.2010.487522

Wanki, P., Lietaert, I., 2018. 'Bushfalling': The ambiguities of role identities experienced by self-sponsored Cameroonian students in Flanders (Belgium). Identities 1–19. https://doi.org/10.1080/1070289X.2018.1475975

Waters, J.L., 2012. Geographies of international education: Mobilities and the reproduction of social (dis)advantage. Geogr. Compass 6, 123–136. https://doi.org/10.1111/j.1749-8198.2011.00473.x

White, A., 2010. Young people and migration from contemporary Poland. J. Youth Stud. 13, 565–580. https://doi.org/10.1080/13676261.2010.487520

Wilken, L., Dahlberg, M.G., 2017. Between international student mobility and work migration: Experiences of students from EU's newer member states in Denmark. J. Ethn. Migr. Stud. 43, 1347–1361. https://doi.org/10.1080/1369183X.2017.1300330

Winberg, O., 2018. Den statskloka resan: Adelns peregrinationer 1610–1680. Uppsala University, Uppsala.

Wolff, L., 1994. Inventing Eastern Europe: The Map of Civilization on the Mind of the Enlightenment. Stanford University Press, Stanford, CA.

2 Methodology and analytical tools

The chapter consists of two overall parts where I lay out the methodological approach and theoretical foundation of the book. I begin the first part by outlining the two 'main waves' of data collection that make up the heart of this ethnographic, longitudinal study, which is followed by a characterisation of the interlocutors, such as their nationality, class identification, and how I 'recruited' them. I then turn to a reflexive account of my role(s) in the field, touching on various research problematiques such as the 'blurred lines' between being a researcher and a friend as well as my role as a Western European subject examining the experiences of Eastern European subjects. Finally, I wrap up the methodological reflections by discussing my strategy for analysing the large corpus of empirical material collected over a period of seven years.

The second part of the book presents the theoretical framework, which is grounded in the literature on narrativity and, in particular, Margaret Somers' (1994, 1992) conceptualisation of 'narrative identity.' With its focus on ontological, public, meta, and conceptual narratives, Somers' conceptual toolbox seems particularly well rounded for grasping how the Eastern European students' experiences and sense of self emerge through a complex relationship between different types of narratives that are entangled on both the micro and the macro levels. To accentuate 'the micro politics of interpersonal interaction' (Phibbs, 2007, p. 2), a complementary analytical toolset is drawn from the field of dramaturgy, specifically Erving Goffman's (1963, 1956) work on the presentation of self and stigma. To illuminate further the process of exchanging one status position for another – a potential consequence of international mobility – Douglas Ezzy's (1993) concept of divestment passage will be added to the conceptual framework of dramaturgy. Given the explorative approach of the present study, I will, throughout this book, continuously discuss the empirical findings in relation to insights and complementary analytical concepts found in studies dealing with similar phenomena and the literature on international student mobility/migration.

Two waves of data collection

The study builds on an ethnographic approach to data gathering and analysis, with the combination of in-depth interviews and participant observation as its primary methods. The data on which this book is based were collected over a period of seven years, 2013–2020, in different locations with varying intensity, mainly within Danish borders but also on field expeditions to a handful of Eastern European countries. The first wave of data collection played out in the timespan of 2013–2015. During this period, I mostly focused on the environment surrounding the university where the students studied. From September 2013 and the subsequent four months, I followed several courses at two interdisciplinary master's programmes located at faculties within social science and humanities. Besides the possibility to obtain a first-hand impression of the dynamics in an international classroom, my presence constituted an excellent opportunity to meet the same group of students on a regular basis and to establish meaningful relations with them. By becoming a natural part of the study environment and regularly engaging with the students, I received invitations to various social events at the departments as well as more intimate gatherings in their private homes. Becoming familiar with the events, feelings, rules, and norms in the field (O'Reilly, 2005) allowed me to go beyond some of the restraints inherent in a classic interview situation. I focused on initiating occasions for interaction and hanging out with students in cafés, restaurants, their homes, and their workplaces, and I even accompanied some of my interlocutors to worship in their local church. Often, I met up with students for a coffee and a chat after they had attended classes at the university, which was highly valuable for understanding the rhythm of their everyday lives.

In 2015, I went on a trip with a student (in this book referred to as Bogdan) to his home country, Romania, which lasted approximately one month. The trip offered a unique opportunity to explore the environment of a European Union (EU) member state where an increasing number of young individuals use their right of free mobility and pursue education abroad. In Romania, I also interviewed and hung out with two students still enrolled at master's programmes in Denmark but who, due to lack of money, had returned home to live with their parents in order to finish their master's thesis. In addition to this trip, I also made shorter travels in 2018 and 2019 to Hungary and Poland, where I met a few students who were then currently residing in their country of origin, following their graduation in Denmark. These expeditions gave me a first-hand view of the lives of 'the returnees' by conversing with them in their then-current living environments. This offered me a chance to take part in their narratives of what they experienced back home and how they imagined their lives to unfold, which I could contrast with their narratives of the present and the future presented to me in Denmark years earlier. Besides these trips abroad, I have also met some of the students who managed to stay in Denmark after the completion of their studies all within Copenhagen.

In addition to numerous informal conversations with interlocutors, I planned, conducted, and recorded narrative interviews with 62 master's students (involving 32 different nationalities and 4 different continents).[1] As emphasised, this book predominantly focuses on the perspectives and narratives of 27 students from 14 Eastern European countries. It is, nevertheless, important to underline that the insights from the remaining interviews were instrumental in carving out this 'Eastern European focus' when accentuating the different life conditions co-existing within the broader student body and motivations for going abroad. A researcher's understanding of a given field is always informed through other settings and worlds (Atkinson, 2014). Conducting interviews with students from all over the world highlighted how many students from post-socialist EU countries lived under precarious conditions while studying in Denmark. It also made me aware that their decision to study abroad was often entangled with aspirations of long-term migration; whereas, many students originating from Western countries went abroad with a wish to return to their home countries following their graduation – initially at least.

In the timespan of 2013–2015, I interviewed the students repeatedly to obtain a more systematic understanding of how their experiences and perceptions would transform while in Denmark. On average, I conducted two scheduled, semi-structured, in-depth interviews with the 27 Eastern European master's students in Denmark. I tried to schedule the first round of interviews when the students had just arrived and the following when they had settled in. Shanti Robertson (2018) emphasises the importance of interviewing international students more than once during their time abroad. In her study on international students in Australia, she shows how friendship networks change over time and are crucial for the transformation of self that students undergo in their new country of residence. This insight would most likely not have been as clear had she interviewed the students at one point in time only. In line with Robertson's observation, one of my interlocutors characterised his first year in Denmark as a 'pink period,' which stood in sharp contrast to his second year abroad where he ran into unforeseen financial problems and had to return to his home country. Had I only interviewed him once during the beginning of his stay in Denmark, I would have described his experiences as predominantly joyful and, thus, missed significant nuances of his stay abroad.

The period following the students' graduation, 2015–2020, marks the second and indeed more scattered wave of the data collection. For obvious reasons – such as most graduates (including myself) moving to other countries or to different cities *within* the borders of Denmark – data collection could not be conducted in the same systematic manner as between 2013 and 2015. Despite the challenges involved in longitudinal research, various social media platforms (such as LinkedIn, Facebook, and Instagram) have to varying extent allowed me to stay in contact with the majority of my interlocutors. In addition to numerous conversations, emails, and short messages, I have repeatedly conducted digital video interviews with 22 of my interlocutors on Skype. As mentioned, I have also visited several graduates in their new destinations on different trips not only to cities within Denmark but also to Hungary and Poland.

The interlocutors

This book predominantly builds on the experiences and narratives of 27 Eastern European full-degree, master's students. While the selection of interlocutors is vital for the researcher, it is important to recognise that factors such as their accessibility and inclination to share their experiences shape the outcome of the study. As pointed out by Charlotte Davies (2008, p. 89), ethnographers are, in many cases, selected by interlocutors and not the other way around. Although I aimed for an equal gender balance and diverse ethnonational backgrounds among the students, I could not afford to turn down any potential interlocutors fitting the social category 'Eastern European master's student' studying at the specific university of my investigation. Here, it is important to stress that the students were not chosen with the ambition of investigating the role of factors such as gender and class per se but above all the intention to study 'Eastern European students' and, thus, to include as broad a range of their experiences as possible. Moreover, I specifically focus on master's students for several reasons. Firstly, the majority of English-speaking programmes in Denmark are found at the master's level, making it the most internationalised level (UFM, 2018). Secondly, pursuing a full international master's degree involves a different educational investment than, for instance, credit mobility, where students in the end will graduate from their own university in their home country.

My initial student sample consisted of 13 women and 14 men who were all between 22 and 30 years of age as of 2013. Included in this sample are the perspectives of individuals from the following countries: Romania, Hungary, Poland, Estonia, Bulgaria, the Czech Republic, Serbia, Bosnia and Herzegovina, North Macedonia, Montenegro, Moldova, Ukraine, Georgia, and Belarus. While these countries may be grouped under the broad referent 'post-socialist countries,' it is evident that they are also characterised by heterogeneous political and cultural environments as well as distinct historical developments (Schwartz and Winkel, 2016). Particularly important for this study is that some of the countries are EU members and others are not. The varying EU statuses of the countries entail that my interlocutors do not have the same juridical opportunities for international mobility and that they, therefore, study and graduate on different terms in Denmark. However, as discussed earlier, there are also important commonalities between these countries, which create a common frame for analysing the students' narratives in relation to each other (Roberts, 2009). These 'children of transition' (Genova, 2017) have all come of age in a time heralded by great social and economic upheaval and they have coped with the social, political, and economic challenges of similar nature (Burrell, 2011). As emphasised, I did not set out to study 'Eastern European students'; rather, I chose to focus on this group because of the marked similarities in their narratives and experiences. For example, Marcu (2015, p. 74) also noted that she 'detected no differences in behaviour in terms of experiences and expectations among students from Bulgaria and Romania' studying in Spain and the UK. In other words, the justification of my empirical focus on 'Eastern European students' is based on the interplay between inductive reasoning, emerging from my fieldwork, and deductive reasoning, particularities of the group presented in the literature. I will discuss how differences among the students' experiences, rather than a question of their nationality per se, seemed to be mostly structured around issues of money (i.e. the money at their disposal abroad and if they had to work to support themselves) and their legal status after graduation (EU vs. non-EU citizen).

When asked about their socio-economic backgrounds, most of my interlocutors estimated that they had grown up in 'middle-class' families. According to Ingo Schröder (2008, p. 13), scholars have paid less attention to the emergence of the new middle classes of post-socialist Eastern Europe. The new middle classes, Schröder claims, are quite heterogeneous in terms of economic backgrounds. They, furthermore, share a particular lifestyle and a certain openness towards cultural influences from the West. In this book, I am not preoccupied with verifying my interlocutors' class descriptions. While I do discuss how some students are confronted with markedly different socio-economic realities abroad, I do this on the basis of their own narrations. I will furthermore discuss the ways that their legal status as either EU or non-EU citizens affects their experiences of coming to Denmark, residing abroad, and, indeed, their post-graduation journeys, because their narrations suggest that this distinction matters. In contrast, I found no significant differences between the experiences and narratives presented by men vis-à-vis women in my sample and will thus make no noteworthy gender cases.

Blurred lines

When doing fieldwork, researchers are bound to occupy specific social role(s) in the local context, which in many ways is a determining factor for what kind of information they can access. Roles are not static and researchers may choose to downplay or emphasise certain roles (Hasse, 1995). While conducting this study, I never tried to mask my researcher identity and always made myself available for discussing my interlocutors' potential concerns as well as the extent of their involvement in the study. At the same time, I was conscious of 'toning down' my position as a researcher during everyday interactions:

We want them to forget, for a time at least, that we are outsiders. We want to develop sufficient rapport and to have them so comfortable as community participants that they will share insights and information that only insiders would know. We regard this as the strength of our method.

(Dewalt et al., 1998, p. 273)

Moreover, too much focus on the researcher role might affect people's behaviour in ways that may invalidate the research (Hammersley and Atkinson, 1995, p. 265). The progression of my fieldwork involved a trans-formation into different and more informal roles where I went from Mette 'the researcher' to Mette 'the friend' whom the students would confide in. Thus, I became highly involved in their lives and one of my interlocutors, for instance, wrote me the following in an e-mail:

You know, in psychological therapies, questions are not just requests for information, many times questions are also what are called 'interventions,' i.e. things therapists do to show something to the patient, or to produce some new meaning, etc. You are not my therapist, but a friend (a new one, but a friend indeed), and you ask me things that make me think in new ways.

Another student wrote on his online blog that I had become the most important individual for support and encouragement during his initial months in Denmark. He wrote that he was taken aback by this develop-ment, since he was not initially interested in being interviewed by me. In line with the student's reflections, I found that some interlocutors regarded me as a safe haven with whom they could discuss issues related to hardship while digesting what some students experienced as a turbulent period. The fact that some students found themselves in a vulnerable situation in Denmark, especially when residing far away from family and friends, might have made them more prone to disclose intimate details about their lives. However, in contrast to an interview situation, which typically denotes a power hier-archy rather than a reciprocal relationship (Oakley, 2016), personal infor-mation did not just flow in one direction. Hence, the student migrants were not only 'feeding' my study with information about their lives but they also learned much more about me than the name of my academic title and my research interests. According to Ann Oakley (1981, p. 41), the best way to find out about people's lives when interviewing 'is best achieved when the relationship of the interviewer and interviewee is non-hierarchical and when the interviewer is prepared to invest his or her personal identity in the relationship.' Albeit, blurred lines in the field, Kathleen Dewalt et al. (1998) claim, may also give rise to ethical dilemmas:

The fieldworker is traveling alongside community members, par-ticipating in events, work leisure activities, hanging out. Community

companions will probably not be aware that the fieldworker will faith-
fully record an account of these events as soon as possible, and that this
will form a data core for analysis. Even if fieldworkers make it clear that
they will 'write a book' or report in their experiences, informants may
not realize that what they share as 'gossip' during informal conversations
will form part of this report.

(Dewalt et al., 1998, p. 273)

Especially when an ethnographer is doing long-term participant observation, interlocutors may forget that they are research objects (Hammersley
and Atkinson, 1995; O'Reilly, 2005). On several occasions, students actually touched on my dual role as a researcher and a friend. While drinking
a beer together at a café in the city centre, one of my interlocutors asked
me if I was taking mental notes of our conversation. Another time a student smilingly asked me if my anthropological interest in him made me
curious about his whereabouts. Incidents like these suggested that they
thought about my intentions and whether I had a genuine interest in
them as actual persons or if they mainly constituted valuable data for
my study.

While I, in line with Dewalt et al.'s argument above, consider these blurred
lines and the close relationships with the interlocutors a strength of this study,
I also believe that the intimate bond requires continuous reflections on the
information that your role in the field gives you access to. Closeness to one's
interlocutors necessitates a constant focus on the responsibility to handle
personal and intimate information with care and discretion (Dewalt et al.,
1998, p. 273). While ethics is always a matter of context, it is important to
stress that I, for instance, refrain from publishing or passing on information
that potentially could embarrass or distress my interlocutors (Hammersley
and Atkinson, 1995, p. 280). Besides avoiding using my interlocutors' actual
names as well as the name of their study programmes, their dorms, the university they attend, and even the city in Denmark where they live and study,
I do not employ confidential information that I received from conversations
with the students in my analysis. Indeed, I concur with Karen O'Reilly's
(2005, p. 63) argument that ethics, in the end, is about causing as little harm
in the field as possible and keeping aware of one's own effects on the study's
participants and data.

Reflexive observations

According to Charlotte Davies (2008), anthropologists have been highly
focused on their level of participation in the field – taking this as an indicator of the quality of their work – and paid less attention to the degree to
which they as ethnographers influence their empirical material. Thus, Davies
underlines the importance of 'reflexive observation,' meaning that the ethnographer should be 'sensitive to the nature of, and conditions governing,

their own participation as a part of their developing understanding of the people they study' (Davies, 2008, p. 73). Researchers enter the field as persons with specific cultural and social backgrounds and certain ways of communicating (Dewalt et al., 1998) – personal features, which undoubtedly shape the data they can access.

In the following, I discuss an important personal feature in relation to my interlocutors, namely my role as a Western European researcher who examines the experiences of Eastern European research subjects, and the influence of power relations in the field for conducting qualitative research. As emphasised, the categories 'Eastern Europe' and 'Western Europe' do not merely describe geographical areas but similarly denote unbalanced symbolic geographies. The Slovenian author Leon Marc (2009), for instance, objects to the term 'Eastern European,' which he associates with being 'lesser European.' The negative stereotypes associated with the Eastern Europe referent meant that I initially felt uncomfortable using the expression during interviews and conversations with students. I was uncertain if they (in line with the experience of Marc) would find such distinctions offensive or hurtful, especially when coming from a 'Western European' researcher. Therefore, I always made sure to use the terms 'Eastern European' and 'Eastern Europe' with great care and consideration.

According to Andrew Sayer (2005), 'class' is by many experienced as an embarrassing and unsettling subject. Thus, in many social situations it 'would be considered insensitive to refer to class, particularly to the class of someone to whom we are talking or who is within earshot' (Sayer, 2005, p. 1). In her study of emic class-distinctions among Danish women, Stine Faber (2008, p. 87) presents a similar observation. Many of her interlocutors appeared uncomfortable when talking about class, making it a somewhat tricky topic to investigate. In line with my own experience, Faber felt slightly uncomfortable when posing questions to the women related to social class differences. As indicated, I too found that questions concerning 'global class' were shrouded with a certain sensitivity as well as an underlying fear of stepping on my interlocutors' toes when addressing such topics. Moreover, I gradually realised that the student migrants were more prone to talk about feelings related to the potential stigmatising effect of coming from Eastern Europe during informal conversations than in the more formal interview situations conducted at the university.

Doing fieldwork in Romania also made me aware of the influence of the unbalanced power hierarchy between East and West in more subtle ways. Before the trip, Bogdan 'warned' me that people would look up to me simply due to my Danish nationality, and indeed, in line with his prediction, I noticed that my 'Danishness' attracted a great deal of attention at various places during our travel. As emphasised, I spent much time with Bogdan's family in their house, and when people phoned his mother, she would proudly state that 'the Dane' was visiting. Incidences like these underlined that I was not a neutral individual but simultaneously incorporated into narratives beyond my mere existence and imaginaries of societal progression. During social gatherings, locals frequently asked me various questions about the Danish welfare model and if I reckoned it was possible to obtain a similar societal structure in Romania. It was evident that they had very detailed assumptions about my persona, even before I had spoken a word. While travelling with Bogdan in Romania, my Danish nationality thus seemed to symbolise a value in itself – it was not only a marker of my place of birth but became to some extent also a marker for my value as a human being. Hence, I clearly sensed that my nationality also affected the way that people would interact with me and, consequently, come to shape my data. Because, in the end, anthropologists do their analyses on the basis of empirical material generated through ethnographic fieldwork – such as fieldnotes and interview transcripts – that is founded upon the interaction between the ethnographer and his or her interlocutors.

Identifying analytical patterns

While this study from the very onset focused on the experiences of international students attending English-medium master's programmes in Denmark, I did not enter the field armed with a rigid hypothesis or a strictly predetermined research design. Rather, this study is highly explorative in nature (Atkinson, 2014). The fieldwork was guided by what O'Reilly (2005, p. 63) calls an 'iterative–inductive approach' entailing a process whereby the researcher 'enters into an ongoing simultaneous process of deduction and induction, of theory building, testing and rebuilding.' This approach acknowledges that it is almost impossible to start out without any preconceived ideas or any theories while holding that the researcher should strive to keep an open mind and allow the data to speak for itself to the extent that it is possible. As emphasised, the explicit focus on Eastern European students emerged *during* the fieldwork when it became apparent that students from post-socialist countries shared highly similar motivations for pursuing an education in Denmark as well as a number of common challenges and experiences abroad that set them apart, in particular, from students from Western European countries.

Alongside my fieldwork, I fleshed out the field notes and transcribed the interviews on my own as an integrated part of the analytical process (Elliott, 2005). To confront the task of schematising the information produced through the numerous conversations and observations, I sorted my data into different themes. The thematisation already began as the data collection period progressed. As I gradually became aware of consistent narrative patterns, I focused on exploring these themes more in depth during the interviews and conversations with my interlocutors. For instance, the cost of living in Denmark and the money available to the students were topics that gradually took up more space in my research design. Following my explorative approach, the theoretical concepts presented in the next section were not determined from the beginning but emerged and developed throughout the research process – from the initial data gathering to the final analysis. Having accounted for the research strategy and methods, the next section moves into the theoretical framework of the book.

Theoretical tools

This book draws on a narrative and dramaturgical approach for bringing a contextualised interpretation of the student migrants' experiences to the forefront. Marita Eastmond (2007, p. 250) holds that narratives can enlighten us on 'how social actors, from a particular social position and cultural vantage point, make sense of their world.' Therefore, a narrative approach brings the experiences of people to the centre and constitutes a window into how they make sense of their everyday lives. Through its insistence on getting a deeper understanding of the human experience, a narrative approach often entails an inborn wish to give voice to people or groups unheard due to their marginalised positions in society (Cederberg, 2014; Johnson, 2016). For unravelling the multiple layers that constitute the stories my interlocutors tell, I especially draw on the theory of narrative presented by Margaret Somers (1994, 1992). Somers' analytical focus on reinterpreting historical data, however, entails that the dynamic aspects of inter-personal social encounters are not the main fix point of her analysis (Phibbs, 2007). To unravel the ways that individuals orientate themselves in relation to their experience of interactions and practices, I suggest that a performative perspective, in particular Goffman's (1963, 1956) work, constitutes a valuable supplement.

The intricate route from lived experience to text

In the early 1980s, the human and social sciences witnessed a renewed interest in life stories and personal narratives. Following the repudiation of the realist tradition of representing lives and cultures, researchers turned to explore the subjective dimension of social life through an interpretive narrative approach of 'the human experience' (Josselson and Lieblich, 1995, p. ix). According to Catherine Riessman, the meaning of the term 'narrative' can be derived by relating it to a similar expression located in the more common term 'story':

> Narratives (stories) in the human sciences should be defined provisionally as discourses with a clear sequential order that connect events in a meaningful way for a definite audience and thus offer insights about the world and/or people's experiences of it. The notion of story should thus be understood in a broad manner. It is through narratives that people communicate and assign meaning to their experiences through the stories they tell.
>
> (Riessman, 2008, p. 3)

In the narrative approach, storytelling is regarded as a fundamental part of the life and it is, essentially, through narratives that we make sense of our experiences. In other words, when we are involved in something, we construct a story based on our interpretation of what just took place. A story is, therefore, not an objective account but an 'arbitrary imposition on the flow of memory, where the narrator highlights certain aspects while downplaying others' (Bruner, 1986, p. 7).

In his study of 'job loss narratives,' Ezzy (2000) examines how people draw on different narratives when explaining a similar phenomenon. More specifically, he shows that unemployed people, in their autobiographical stories, narrate a job loss in competing ways. In simplified terms, narratives of job loss can be divided into two overarching strands: 'heroic job loss narratives' and 'tragic job loss narratives' (Ezzy, 2000, p. 123). Heroic job loss narratives involve a positive telling whereby a job loss typically is presented as something empowering. The narrator, thereby, downplays the role of social forces and relationships as explanations for behaviour and draws on the narrative form of a heroic journey emphasising autonomy and agency. Tragic job loss narratives, on the other hand, tend to suppress the individual's responsibility or agency as the cause of job loss. Instead, it draws on a so-called victim narrative that blames other people or impersonal social forces. Ezzy's study illustrates how narratives always entail interpretation and how experiences of a similar phenomenon vary depending on the interaction between the lived event and the lifeworld of the narrator. A person's interpretations of a set of events and the form its corresponding narrative will take are therefore not only determined by the lived experience but also, indeed, constituted by a 'complex interweaving of events, narrative strategies, the influences of other people, and biographical history' (Ezzy, 2000, p. 130).

Ezzy's empirical findings suggest that a narrator enjoys a good portion of freedom when interpreting her own experiences and arranging past events into a fitting story. Hence, the organisation of experiences into a coherent narrative should not be viewed as an 'innocent act' but infers a privileged position (Brænder et al., 2014, p. 143). The reduction of experience, however, is not necessarily a deliberate and rational act. According to Eastmond (2007, p. 250), we automatically reduce our experiences as it 'in its vitality and richness, always far exceeds the expression which a person can give it.' The purpose of narrative analysis, then, is not to come as close to 'the real life' as possible. Narratives are not to be treated as exact copies of lived experience – they should, instead, be viewed as 'creative constructions' of the past in a particular context of the present (Eastmond, 2007, p. 250). This does not entail that narratives are 'free fiction' or even solely the reflection of an individual psyche, rather they are shaped by structures that exist *beyond* a person's inner world (Atkinson, 2014). Narratives are products of interactions between the broader cultural discourses and the material circumstances and experiences of the individual (Elliott, 2005). Thus, individual narratives are always entangled in wider cultural and social narratives that people draw on when they tell their stories of what they go through and experience (Cederberg, 2014; Miller, 2005; Schmidt, 2010). Even the most intimate and seemingly subjective experiences are given meaning through these shared narrative formats (Plummer, 1995). Following this line of thought, narrative researchers have problematized the common assumption that memory is 'a private issue,' as pointed out by Atkinson (2014):

> Memory is a cultural phenomenon, and is to an extent a collective one. What is memorable is a function of the cultural categories that shape what is thinkable and what is not, what is counted as appropriate, what is valued, what is noteworthy and so on.

> (p. 97)

In other words, individuals can creatively construct narratives but the way they perceive their experiences are always limited and framed by the cultural categories at their disposal as well as their position within different social contexts. Arthur Frank (2013) exemplifies this point in his autobiographical work on critical illness; he writes:

> People tell their own stories about illness, but what seems worth telling, how to format the story, and how others make sense of the story all depend on shared ways of narrating illness.

> (p. xiv)

For the present study of Eastern European students in Denmark, narratives may be understood as *devices* through which my interlocutors 'weave' their lives into 'discursive structures which are the materialization and reproduction of power arrangements' (Melegh, 2006, p. 127). As the students tell their life stories, they simultaneously reproduce a specific way of looking upon the world. Their narratives thereby function as 'critical intermediaries in the materialization and reproduction of the power arrangements concerned' (Melegh, 2006, p. 6). As indicated, people do not have unlimited creative freedom in the fabrication of narratives but are constrained by the given 'stock of narrative patterns' (Melegh, 2006, p. 127). The students' narratives are shaped by the social context of, for instance, a Danish university or more broadly the Danish society. Still, they are not exact imprints of pre-established narratives or discourses. People can combine elements of different narratives in the narration of their life story and, thereby, individualise the shape of the narrative (Melegh, 2006).

Narrative identity

Out of the extensive literature on narrative theory, I especially draw on Margaret Somers' (1994, 1992) work on *narrative identity*.[2] By encapsulating knowledge from various academic disciplines – such as anthropology, economy, sociology, law, and history – Somers' theoretical framework is useful for unravelling the multi-layered narratives that people employ when navigating and making sense of their lives. Somers' work on narrativity provides an active, processual view on how identities transform over time and are anchored in different socio-economical and geopolitical contexts (see also Elliott, 2005). With its attentiveness to both ideological and material aspects, Somers' approach seems highly fitting for dealing with questions of transnational mobility where individuals are confronted with changing life worlds. In this present book, I draw on Somers' work to illuminate the multiple layers that constitute the stories that Eastern European students present when they try to make sense of themselves and their experiences in Denmark. Fundamentally, Somers (1994) advocates for a reconfiguration of identity through the concept of narrative. With the notion of 'ontological narrativity,' she addresses a turn in social science whereby narratives not only are viewed as a method or a question of representation but indeed as an ontological condition of social life (see also Ferber, 2000). Narratives, then, are the medium through which people come to know, understand, and make sense of the world and it is importantly through narratives that we craft our social identities:

> [This new strand of research] is showing us that stories guide action; that people construct identities (however multiple and changing) by locating themselves or being located within a repertoire of emplotted stories; that 'experience' is constituted through narratives; that people make sense of what has happened and is happening to them by attempting to assemble or in some way to integrate these happenings within one or more narratives; and that people are guided to act in certain ways, and not others, on the basis of the projections, expectations, and memories derived from a multiplicity but ultimately limited repertoire of available social, public, and cultural narratives.
>
> (Somers, 1994, p. 606)

As the quote illustrates, the conceptualisation of narrative identity involves the fundamental assumption that narrativity is a principal condition of social existence, social action, and structures. Therefore, it is neither possible to speak of experiences independent from narrative contexts nor narratives external to social life (see also Ferber, 2000). The human existence is itself 'told' (Somers, 1994, p. 621).

According to Atkinson (2014), ethnographers and other qualitative researchers often assume that they deal with social actors whose lives and identities are relatively stable. With the notion of narrative identity, Somers accentuates the fluidity of identity when highlighting how narratives are processual and relational – a theoretical perspective, which complements the book's longitudinal approach where the focus remains on change. The merging of narrative with identity entails an analytical focus on the aspect of *time*, *space*, and *relationality*. Thus, social categories such as gender or race should never be treated as fixed entities in the singular (Somers, 1994). Rather, people's experiences of a social category vary considerably and are ultimately a question of space and place as well as the larger matrix of relations they currently are entangled in, such as their family patterns and the social events they assign meaning to in their individual life stories. As such, social actors are restrained in the fabrication of narratives, which are limited in scope, and, as indicated earlier, ultimately a question of the distribution of power (Somers, 1994). Because of the limited options, when it comes to the construction of individual or public narratives, individuals may experience despair and powerlessness due to the inability to accommodate certain happenings within a range of available cultural, public, and institutional narratives (Somers, 1994). Nick Crossley (2001) gives a good description of how we never 'have' ourselves completely:

> As embodied beings we are perceptible to others. We fall within their perceptual field and, in this sense, they 'have' us too. Our embodiment is thus necessarily alienated. We are never in complete possession of ourselves. More to the point, our perceptible being is captured in schemas of collective representation. From the moment of birth, and even before, our anatomical state and embodied visibility are made to signify social meanings and we, accordingly, are positioned in social space. Indeed, we only come to have ourselves by first enjoining this intersubjective order and learning to see ourselves from the outside, as 'other.'
>
> (p. 141)

Crossley's point is clear: We are never in total control of our bodies and the narratives attached to us. By birth, we are parachuted into a symbolic system of meaning over which we have little or no control. Thus, others' views on a person are constitutive of his or her 'self,' regardless of whether it conflicts with or supports the 'narrative of self' that person tries to convey. For example, the meanings attached to the colour of one's skin may vary considerably depending on the social context. Similar arguments can be made about social class, and Somers (1994) criticises researchers who automatically assume a correlation between class attributes and action as if there exists an inherent link between the two. We cannot build our analysis on the assumption that people act in the same way because one of their primary identities seemingly fits neatly into a single social category. Rather, the position of individuals in their current relational setting is a more appropriate indicator of their actions.

Narratives are not set in stone but constitute objects of struggle and dominant narratives can be challenged by counter-narratives. Somers (1994) emphasises how gender studies and critical race studies have advocated for the importance of constructing new public narratives and symbolic representations that defy traditions of exclusion. This also means that struggles over narration ultimately are 'struggles over identity' (Somers, 1994, p. 631). Researchers should accordingly try to avoid a priori assumptions. Instead, social categories are to be explored a posteriori by empirical evidence and historical reasoning (Somers, 1994, p. 612). In order to capture the narrativity of social life, a totalising mode of imagining 'society' must be swapped for a relational one. Here, Somers proposes to substitute the metaphor of a *relational setting* for society (Somers, 1994, p. 626). On a broader level, Somers objects to what she refers to as an artificial divide between social sciences and narrative research. She ascribes this division to an outdated perception among social scientists when it comes to the conceptualisation of narratives. According to Somers (1994, p. 614), narratives are often mistaken for a representational form and method for presenting social and historical knowledge. She points to how the neglect of narratives in social science is a part of a broader exclusion of issues dealing with expressions of social being and identity in favour of norms and value-centred research dealing with agents and agency. One theoretical ambition is to bridge this dichotomy:

> I argue in this article that the association of identity and ontology with philosophy or theoretical psychology on the one side, and action with interests, norms, or behaviour on the other, is a limited model and deprives social scientists of the deeper analysis that it is possible to achieve by linking the concepts of action and identity. To get these benefits, however, we must reject the decoupling of action from ontology, and instead accept that some notion of social being and social identity is, willy-nilly, incorporated into each and every knowledge statement about action, agency, and behaviour. Just as sociologists are not likely to make sense of action without focusing attention on structure and order, it is unlikely we can interpret social action if we fail to also emphasize ontology, social being, and identity. We thus enlarge our analytical focus when we study social action through a lens that also allows a focus on social ontology and the social constitution of identity.
>
> (Somers, 1994, pp. 615–616)

As the quote accentuates, we can only understand patterns of behaviour if we recognise the different levels of narratives in which actors are entangled – from the most individual narratives, bound only to a single person, to the broadest and most global narratives, spanning across different societies. The next section outlines the four interrelated dimensions of narrativity, which constitute the cornerstone of Somers' conceptual framework.

Four narrative levels

In Somers' writings, we encounter a distinction between four narrative levels (Somers, 1994, 1992; Somers and Gibson, 1994). The first narrative level, 'ontological narratives,' discusses the stories that we craft to make sense of our own lives:

> We use ontological narratives to define who we are, not just to know what to do. Locating ourselves in narratives endows us with identities – however multiple, ambiguous, ephemeral or conflicting they may be (hence, the term narrative identity).
>
> (Somers, 1992, p. 603)

The quote accentuates how narrative identities are never complete but always in the process of being formed (Phibbs, 2007). Indeed, identities can be multiple, ambiguous, or contradictory exactly because narrative is neither a priori nor fixed. Social practice is embedded and emerges from this level and mutually constitutes what individuals are and how they act: 'People act, or do not act, in part according to how they understand their place in any number of given narratives – however fragmented, contradictory, or partial' (Somers, 1992, p. 603).

Ontological narratives are tightly interwoven with the second narrative layer, namely 'public narratives,' which refers to 'those narratives attached to cultural and institutional formations larger than the single individual, to intersubjective networks or institutions, however local or grand' (Somers, 1994, p. 619). They range from the intimate narratives told in the family and among groups of friends to those of the workplace, the church, the government, and the nation. As emphasised in the previous section, public narratives are not neutral but are shaped by actors, which are in turn formed by particular understandings of the world that tend to enforce one meaning over another and may be the object of contestation (Phibbs, 2007, p. 2).

Public narratives link to the third dimension of narrativity called 'metanarrativity,' also referred to as the 'master and metanarratives,' which implies narratives that we, as contemporary actors in history and social scientists, are entwined within (Somers, 1994, p. 619). The difference between public narratives and master narratives is ultimately a question of scale. According to Somers, metanarratives may be conceptualised as 'the epic dramas of our time: Capitalism vs. Communism, the Individual vs. Society, Barbarism/Nature vs. Civility' (Somers, 1994, p. 619). Suzanne Phibbs (2007, p. 3) describes master narratives as 'public narratives that are so pervasive that their temporal and spatial origins are obscured.' In this book, I specifically focus on dominant metanarratives of 'the East' and 'the West' within the context of Europe and how they influence the aspirations of students' mobility but also how their ontological narratives are weaved into 'the East-West civilizational slope' (Melegh, 2006, pp. 127–128).

The fourth and final level, which Somers refers to as 'conceptual narrativity,' has a different character since it refers to the explanations constructed by social researchers:

Because neither social action nor institution-building is solely produced through ontological and public narratives, our concepts and explanations must include the factors we call social forces, market patterns, institutional practices, organizational constraints.

(Somers, 1994, p. 620)

Somers calls for critical interrogation of the categories social scientists employ while conducting research. A central *problematique* concerns developing concepts that capture and reconstruct the narratives and relationships of individuals over time and space through which practice is guided, identities are constructed, and social interaction is mediated *without* abstracting them into new ahistorical and essentialist concepts. In other words, tools that enable us to analyse the conditions and interactions of the narratives that produce identity and practice – while always keeping their specific social contexts in mind. Having outlined the main narrative approach, which will guide the analysis, the next section delves into the literature of dramaturgy.

Performing narratives

While a narrative approach is helpful for shedding light on the stories people tell to make sense of their lives and actions, I suggest that a performative perspective constitutes a valuable supplement for drawing attention to how people's changing circumstances and practices constantly shape, challenge, and reorganise how they present their narratives to others. It is, however, important to stress that the extent to which the narratives and actions of the Eastern European students are aligned will not be evaluated. Quite the contrary, the proposed narrative epistemology holds that there is no objective reality 'behind' the narrative. Correspondingly, theories of performativity suggest that there is no essence or origin to be found outside the multiplicity of performances that make up our everyday lives (e.g. Schein, 1999). The complementary nature of the two theoretical strands has been noted by others. Mark Liechty (2003), for instance, combines both perspectives in his study of cultural practices among the new middle classes in Nepal. While Lietchy draws on the work of Judith Butler, the main theoretical source of inspiration in this study comes from Goffman's situational analysis of how the self is formed through everyday interactions.

In *The Presentation of Self*, Goffman (1956, pp. i, 93, 154) introduces a 'dramaturgical perspective' of human action and identity-making that is based on notions and expressions usually associated with the world of theatre. In the dramaturgical perspective, social life is played out on stages where performers act to steer their audiences' impressions and, ultimately, to define the meaning of the social situation at hand. As the individual performs – that is, taking on particular roles on the social stages that characterise a person's everyday life – s/he becomes a personality or, perhaps more accurately, is developing and alternating characters to play out in interactions with others. The dramaturgical concept of 'the self,' then, is unsettled and multi-layered in the sense of engaging in a never-ending inner dialogue between identities or roles.

Goffman's (1956) understanding of the human being is reflexive in the sense that people can direct how they present themselves and throughout a performance adjust the role in relation to how they aim for a particular audience to perceive them. At the same time, the role is intertwined with the stages where it is played out and, thus, cannot be detached from the frames that characterise these settings – the materials, routines, proper ways of speaking, moving, and so on (e.g. Goffman, 1956, pp. 21–22). There is, in other words, a moral dimension to performing – an obligation from the performer, other team members, and the audience to act in accordance to what each of them have learnt to be an appropriate behaviour for just that role on this particular stage (Goffman, 1956).

Just as a person's ontological narrative is entangled in public and master narratives beyond the individual's control, the performer's freedom to act is regulated by the audience's impressions and scripts associated with the social situation at hand. This limitation is simultaneously an opening to present oneself as the person the audience expects regardless of if the role being acted out harmonises with one's self-image. In other words, for Goffman (1956), social life is played out on stages where people are more or less willing to take on roles that are linked to certain expectations. To live up to these expectations, to avoid performance disruptions, and, ultimately, to protect one's self-image, people will actively try to master the arts of managing others' impressions of themselves within their performance by defining the social situation in their role within it. These impression managements are put in place by presenting a specific front of oneself (with the help of clothes, posture, way of speaking, etc.) that can define the interaction or scene that will take place for the particular set of actors and audience that constitute a stage (Goffman, 1956).

Since human beings are dynamic and multi-layered, they not only play a single role of the self but act in accordance with a diverse set of social roles. In the present case of Eastern European students, one can imagine a variety of roles they play out on an everyday basis: The role of a student within a certain discipline, as a son or a daughter, as a low-skilled worker, and so on. According to Goffman (1956, p. 22), members of a particular group or class are not equally invested in all social roles but 'tend to invest their egos primarily in certain routines, giving less stress to the other ones which they perform.' One can imagine that some students are more attached to certain social roles or routines than others, which they then want to keep at the forefront of daily interactions while hiding others. This also entails that the roles most central to one's self-image are surrounded by certain vulnerability. If the performance of an individual is discredited – which implies a mismatch between one's moral expectations of how the performance ought to be played out and the actual performance – the person might question his/her self-image (Goffman, 1956). When acting on the social stages of our everyday lives, we are therefore always on our guard to practice expressive control in order to keep the performance believable and manage the audience's impressions of oneself (Goffman, 1956, p. 33). Performers will present a particular front and conceal or downplay actions that are incompatible with their idealised version of themselves (Goffman, 1956, p. 26). As every actor is involved in impression management, there are parallel acts of fronting and mystification taking place in every interaction.

Following Goffman's theoretical toolbox, one could argue that students develop a sense of self through playing a set of roles on the stages that make up their everyday lives. The students will have developed distinctive fronts and hold different roles more dearly than others but the setting and the scenes they act on will be patterned. At every stage, they interact with other actors and audiences (local and international students, professors, shop owners, employers, etc.) that either reinforce or challenge their identities – or to use Somers' concepts, their ontological narrations. Seen in the light of narrativity, their ontological narratives will alter depending on the stage they perform on and the audiences in front of them – is it local students or international students, employers or employees, and do they originate from 'Western Europe' or 'Eastern Europe'? I suggest that this dramaturgical take on narrativity can bring about a dynamic and nuanced conceptualisation of the complex identity formation that student migrants engage in.

Divestment passages

In order to capture the complex transformation of narrative identity that takes place when the Eastern European students migrate from the social setting of their home countries to Denmark, more specific concepts are called for. Together with Howard Becker and Anselm Strauss, Goffman is said to have made up 'The second Chicago school,' which has been seen as an extension of the original symbolic interactionist programme (Becker, 1999). Strauss, in particular, has written extensively on symbolic interactionism and, together with Barney Glaser, he developed the popular notion of 'status passage.' Status passage has its roots in the work by Arnold van Gennep (e.g. 1960) on rites of passage – a term addressing the transition of an individual or a group from one social status to another. According to Glaser and Strauss (2010, p. 2), a status passage entails an individual's 'movement into a different part of a social structure, or a loss or gain of privilege, influence, or power, and a changed identity and sense of self, as well as changed behaviour.' Status passage theory, then, revolves around the relation between a person's social environment and their interpretation of this environment and their position within it (Ezzy, 1993, p. 48). Van Gennep initially suggested that rites of passage could be separated into three subcategories: rites of separation, transitional rites, and rites of integration. Ezzy expands this thread and proposes a clearer distinction between the two types of status passages – divestment passages and integrative passages – and the problems they might cause for managing one's daily performances:

> *Integrative passages* usually entail a transitional period followed by integration into a clearly delineated new status entered through a ceremonially specified process. Marriage ceremonies and membership recognition, for example both focuses on celebrating and establishing the passages in their new identities. On the other hand, *divestment passages* emphasise separation from a status and often contain extended transitional phases of uncertain duration. Divestment passages are, in one sense, negatively achieved. Divorce, becoming sick, unemployment and the death of a partner are all typically associated with the failure to successfully maintain or continue in a role.
>
> (Ezzy, 1993, p. 49)

Ezzy accentuates how divestment passages may have considerable consequences for a person's mental health – thereby nuancing the assumption that lowered mental health is a 'psychological manifestation of some mechanical response to an individual's environment' (Ezzy, 1993, p. 49). Experiences of lowered mental health, Ezzy claims, can be analysed with the help of sociological identity theory. He underlines that desired role performances, conducive for a positive self-understanding, are dependent on setting up certain life-plans that aims to sustain continual legitimation of one's identity. Thus, it may have enormous consequences for the individual if s/he fails to uphold the routines or interaction patterns necessary for doing so:

> Failure or success in the attempt to sustain a meaningful life has a very direct effect on the psychological integrity of the individual. If individuals are not successful in finding social involvements conducive to the performance of valued identities and therefore to the development of positive self-evaluations, this may result in anxiety, self-doubt and lowered self-esteem through the identity processes of social comparisons, reflected appraisals and self-perceptions.
>
> (Ezzy, 1993, p. 50)

While there is a temporal dimension to all statuses (Glaser and Strauss, 2010), transnational mobility often constitutes a situation whereby social status has to be renegotiated and redefined. For migrants, the relational dimension of identity can be particularly significant. For example, a person might choose to exchange a sense of community and reciprocity in a village setting for the economic opportunity yet relative anonymity of a major city (Conradson and Mckay, 2007). During this process, migrants' sense of selves will be shaped by a combination of the new relations in the destination setting and the distance from those in the sending context. International mobility, then, provides opportunities for new forms of subjectivity and emotion to emerge, whether positive or negative (Conradson and Mckay, 2007). Mobility involving a divestment passage may be conceptualised as a clash between a more or less established sense of self in a familiar setting with an involuntarily and forced identity in a new context. In symbolic inter-actionist terms, this clash generates a complex dialectics between 'the me' and 'the I' – that is, between 'the historical part of the self' (established in one place through narratives, occupation, roles played, etc.) and 'the active part of the self' (that is, to face the altered conditions for one's identity in the new environment) (Schubert, 2006).

It is obviously an empirical question as to whether Eastern European students undergo an integrative passage or a divestment passage abroad – that is, if their transition into the new destination constitutes a celebration or crisis of identity. There are, however, several studies indicating that Eastern European migrants are highly exposed to divestment passages while residing in the West (e.g. Fox et al., 2015; Manolova, 2018). According to Adrian Favell (2008, p. 711), many Eastern European migrants are subjected to 'sharp downward mobility' in Western European countries. This means that highly skilled migrants often have to settle for '3D jobs' – dirty, dull, and dangerous jobs – and face a situation where their educational level does not correspond with the jobs that await them abroad.

Stigma

In this book, I analyse the Eastern European students' lived realities abroad through the concepts developed in yet another of Goffman's famous works, *Stigma: Notes on the Management of Spoiled Identity* (1963). According to Goffman (1963, p. 14), 'stigma, then, is really a special kind of relationship between attribute and stereotype.' To unpack the meaning of this definition, Goffman situates stigma in relation to more general patterns of interaction. When two individuals interact, they tend to make characterisations of each other. These characterisations are grounded in each's assumptions of what the other person 'ought to be' rather than the attributes the person actually possess, that is, his/her 'virtual social identity' not his/her 'actual social iden-tity' (Goffman, 1963, p. 12). When the persons eventually learn about the other's actual attributes, they will correspondingly notice the discrepancy between their initial assumptions of the other (the virtual social identity) and what the other 'really is like' (actual social identity). Based on this new information, a reclassification of the person (from the social category ini-tially given to him/her to a more or less anticipated one) can take place. With the term stigma, Goffman (1963, p. 12) aspires to capture attributes so dominant that the other person becomes 'reduced in our minds from a whole and usual person to a tainted, discounted one.' A stigmatised indi-vidual thus holds 'deeply discrediting' attributes in interactions. In contrast, individuals who do not depart negatively from particular expectations he refers to as 'normals' (Goffman, 1963, p. 15). However, as Goffman (1963, p. 13) reminds us, 'it should be seen that a language of relationships, not attributes, is really needed.' A stigma, then, is something you can possess but the attribute's stigmatising effect depends on the interaction – it is not 'discreditable as a thing in itself' (Goffman, 1963, p. 13). This leads us to the notion that stigmatising attributes are associated with a virtual social identity, not automatically detectable by all (i.e. can be mistaken for something else), and are not necessarily discrediting in all interactions.

Goffman (1963, p. 14) operates with three categories of stigma: 'abominations of the body,' 'blemishes of individual character,' and 'the tribal stigma.' The last category indicates a discrediting 'of race, nation, and religion [...] that can be transmitted through lineages' and is the most fitting when discussing stereotypes associated with originating from Eastern Europe. Once again it is important to stress that a tribal stigma is not a component that all individuals from a particular region or a nation hold but a *relational* attribute that might or might not turn out to be discrediting in specific social interactions. If relating this line of thought to the present book, people may not regard the student as an individual in their own right because they are blinded by a stereotypical characterisation of what an Eastern European person 'ought to be like.' In this case, the student's virtual social identity overshadows his/her actual social identity.

Moreover, Goffman (1963, p. 69) holds that individuals are not fully governed by the discrediting attributes they possess but may engage in 'stigma management' aimed at concealing stigmatising attributes by overemphasising other personal features. Since people 'are likely to give no open recognition to what is discrediting,' discredited individuals will often find themselves in a situation where they feel uncertain of what 'to display or not to display; to tell or not to tell; to let on or not to let on; to lie or not to lie; and in each case, to whom, how, when, and where' (Goffman, 1963, p. 57). If individuals know for certain that the stigmatising attribute is their tribal affiliation (i.e. race, nation, religion, etc.), they can choose to align or detach themselves from the tribe or group:

> The stigmatized individual exhibits a tendency to stratify his 'own' according to the degree to which their stigma is apparent and obtrusive. He can then take up in regard to those who are more evidently stigmatized than himself the attitudes the normals take to him. Thus do the hard of hearing stoutly see themselves as anything but deaf persons, and those with defective vision, anything but blind. It is in his affiliation with, or separation from, his more evidently stigmatized fellows, that the individual's oscillation of identification is most sharply marked.
>
> (Goffman, 1963, pp. 129–130)

Following the quote, Goffman 'offers' people agency to challenge the structures of their everyday interactions – nonetheless by, so to speak, sacrificing one's own tribe. Here, one might draw a parallel to Somers' emphasis on how narratives may constitute objects of struggle and that people can challenge dominant narratives that they find limiting. Following Goffman's work, it is important to emphasise that 'Eastern European heritage' is not an attribute that automatically is stigmatising. Moreover, it is highly possible that people are unaware that some of their attributes, which they throughout their lives have experienced to be neutral or even positive, are discredited in some parts of the world. For that reason, they may find themselves in 'the sense of not knowing what the other people are "really" thinking about him' (Goffman, 1963, p. 25). To understand the ways that students make sense of themselves and how they reflect on their societal position in Denmark, we have to engage with the empirical material.

Notes

1 Associate Professor Lisanne Wilken participated in some of the initial interviews.
2 There are several other scholars who work with the concept of narrative identity. See, for instance, Ezzy (1998) and his discussion of the concept.

References

Atkinson, P., 2014. For Ethnography. Sage, London.
Becker, H.S., 1999. The Chicago School, so-called. Qual. Sociol. 22, 3–12.
Brænder, M., Kølvraa, C.L., Laustsen, C.B., 2014. Samfundsvidenskabelig tekstanalyse. Hans Reitzels Forlag, København.
Bruner, E.M., 1986. Introduction, in: Turner, V.W., Bruner, E.M. (Eds.), The Anthropology of Experience. University of Illinois Press, Urbana.
Burrell, K., 2011. Opportunity and uncertainty: Young people's narratives of 'double transition' in post-socialist Poland. R. Geogr. Soc. 43, 413–419.
Cederberg, M., 2014. Public discourses and migrant stories of integration and inequality: Language and power in biographical narratives. Sociology 48, 133–149.
Conradson, D., Mckay, D., 2007. Translocal subjectivities: Mobility, connection, emotion. Mobilities 2, 167–174. https://doi.org/10.1080/17450100701381524
Crossley, N., 2001. The Social Body: Habit, Identity and Desire. Sage, London and Thousand Oaks, CA.
Davies, C.A., 2008. Reflexive Ethnography: A Guide to Researching Selves and Others. Routledge, London.
Dewalt, K., Dewalt, B., Wayland, C., 1998. Participant observation, in: Bernard, H.R. (Ed.), Handbook of Methods in Cultural Anthropology. AltaMira, Walnut Creek, CA, pp. 259–299.
Eastmond, M., 2007. Stories as lived experience: Narratives in forced migration research. J. Refug. Stud. 20, 248–264.
Elliott, J., 2005. Using Narrative in Social Research: Qualitative and Quantitative Approaches. Sage, London.
Ezzy, D., 2000. Fate and agency in job loss narratives. Qual. Sociol. 23, 121–134.

Ezzy, D., 1998. Theorizing narrative identity. Sociol. Q. 39, 239–252.

Ezzy, D., 1993. Unemployment and mental health: A critical review. Soc. Sci. Med. 37, 41–52.

Faber, S., 2008. På jagt efter klasse. Aalborg Universitet: Institut for Sociologi, Socialt Arbejde og Organisation. Aalborg.

Favell, A., 2008. The new face of East–West migration in Europe. J. Ethn. Migr. Stud. 34, 701–716. https://doi.org/10.1080/13691830802105947

Ferber, A.L., 2000. A commentary on aguirre: Taking narrative seriously. Sociol. Perspect. 43, 341–349. https://doi.org/10.2307/1389800

Fox, J.E., Moroşanu, L., Szilassy, E., 2015. Denying discrimination: Status, 'race,' and the whitening of Britain's new Europeans. J. Ethn. Migr. Stud. 41, 21. https://doi.org/10.1080/1369183X.2014.962491

Frank, A., 2013. The Wounded Storyteller. The University of Chicago Press, Chicago.

Genova, E.S., 2017. Migration and the 'Children of the Transition': Unravelling the Experiences of Young, Highly Skilled Bulgarians in the UK. University of Nottingham, Nottingham.

Glaser, B.G., Strauss, A.L., 2010. Status Passage. AldineTransaction, New Brunswick, NJ.

Goffman, E., 1963. Stigma: Notes on the Management of Spoiled Identity. Prentice-Hall, Englewood Cliffs, NJ.

Goffman, E., 1956. The Presentation of Self in Everyday Life, University of Edinburgh Social Sciences Research Centre monographs; 2. University of Edinburgh Social Sciences Research Centre, Edinburgh.

Hammersley, M., Atkinson, P., 1995. Ethnography – Principles in Practise. Routledge, London and New York.

Hasse, C., 1995. Fra journalist til Big Mamma – Om sociale rollers betydning for antropologens datagenerering. Tidsskr. Antropol. 31, 53–65.

Johnson, H.L., 2016. Narrating entanglements: Rethinking the local/global divide in ethnographic migration research. Int. Polit. Sociol. 10, 383–397. https://doi.org/10.1093/ips/olw021

Josselson, R., Lieblich, A., 1995. The Narrative Study of Lives. Vol. 3, Interpreting Experience. Sage, Thousand Oaks, CA.

Liechty, M., 2003. Suitably Modern: Making Middle-class Culture in a New Consumer Society. Princeton University Press, Princeton, NJ.

Manolova, P., 2018. 'Going to the West is my last chance to get a normal life': Bulgarian would-be migrants' imaginings of life in the UK. Cent. East. Eur. Migr. Rev., 8, 1–23. https://doi.org/10.17467/ceemr.2018.01

Marc, L., 2009. What's So Eastern About Eastern Europe. Oldcastle Books, Harpenden.

Marcu, S., 2015. Uneven mobility experiences: Life-strategy expectations among Eastern European undergraduate students in the UK and Spain. Geoforum 58, 68–75. https://doi.org/10.1016/j.geoforum.2014.10.017

Melegh, A., 2006. On the East-West Slope: Globalization, Nationalism, Racism and Discourses on Central and Eastern Europe. Central European University Press, New York.

Miller, T., 2005. Making Sense of Motherhood: A Narrative Approach. Cambridge University Press, Cambridge.

Oakley, A., 2016. Interviewing women again: Power, time and the gift. Sociology 50, 195–213. https://doi.org/10.1177/0038038515580253

Oakley, A., 1981. Interviewing women: A contradiction in terms?, in: Roberts, H. (Ed.), Doing Feminist Research. Routledge & Kegan Paul, London.

O'Reilly, K., 2005. Ethnographic Methods. Routledge, London.

Phibbs, S., 2007. Four dimensions of narrativity: Towards a narrative analysis of gender identity that is simultaneously personal, local and global. N. Z. Sociol. 23, 47–60.

Plummer, K., 1995. Telling Sexual Stories: Power, Change and Social Worlds. Routledge, London.

Riessman, C.K., 2008. Narrative Methods for the Human Sciences. Sage, London.

Roberts, K., 2009. Youth in Transition: Eastern Europe and the West. Palgrave Macmillan, Basingstoke.

Robertson, S., 2018. Friendship networks and encounters in student-migrants' negotiations of translocal subjectivity. Urban Stud. 55, 538–553. https://doi.org/10.1177/0042098016659617

Sayer, A., 2005. The Moral Significance of Class. Cambridge University Press, Cambridge.

Schein, L., 1999. Performing modernity. Cult. Anthropol. 14, 361–395. https://doi.org/10.1525/can.1999.14.3.361

Schmidt, J., 2010. Migrating Genders: Westernisation, Migration, and Samoan fa'afafine. Ashgate, Farnham.

Schröder, I., 2008. The classes of '89: Anthropological approaches to capitalism and class in Eastern Europe, in: Schröder, I. and Vonderau, A. (Eds.), Changing Economies and Changing Identities in Postsocialist Eastern Europe, LIT Verlag Münster, Münster, pp. 3–25.

Schubert, H.-J., 2006. The foundation of pragmatic sociology: Charles Horton Cooley and George Herbert Mead. J. Class. Sociol. 6, 51–74. https://doi.org/10.1177/1468795X06061284

Schwartz, M., Winkel, H., 2016. Eastern European youth cultures in a global context. Palgrave Macmillan, UK.

Somers, M.R., 1994. The narrative constitution of identity: A relational and network approach. Theory Soc. 23, 605–649.

Somers, M.R., 1992. Narrativity, narrative identity, and social action: Rethinking English working-class formation. Soc. Sci. Hist. 16, 591. https://doi.org/10.2307/1171314

Somers, M.R., Gibson, G.D., 1994. Reclaiming the epistemological 'other': Narrative and the social constitution of identity, in: Calhoun, C (Ed.), Social Theory and the Politics of Identity. Blackwell, Oxford and Cambridge, pp. 37–99.

UFM, 2018. Offentlige indtægter og udgifter ved internationale studerende. Uddannelses- og Forskningsministeriet. Accessed April 2021. https://ufm.dk/publikationer/2018/filer/offentlige-indtaegter-og-udgifter-ved-internationale-studerende.pdf

van Gennep, A., 1960. The Rites of Passage. University of Chicago Press, Chicago.

3 'Go West!'

Eastern European students' motivations for pursuing an education in Denmark

Why do some students opt for an education outside the borders of their home country – thereby going against the dominant trend? Elizabeth Murphy-Lejeune (2002) argues that international mobility is not given to everyone but has to be learned and socialised. We are not born with the desire to cross borders; it is not in our DNA, rather, it is something that we acquire and develop throughout our upbringing. Personal or familial experiences of international mobility therefore increase the probability of taking an education abroad. Sören Carlson (2013) similarly underlines the importance of focusing on a broader range of factors that may play a role in spurring students' mobility, thereby challenging the assumption that student migration is the outcome of deliberate and rational decision making. International mobility, he claims, is rooted in a complex process that takes off long before students even begin to think about educational mobility. 'The role of previous mobility experiences, the impact of the students' social embeddedness, and the timing of specific events' are all important factors which, according to Carlson (2013, p. 170), should be explored when investigating the roots of their mobility.

In line with the studies above, this chapter explores some of the multifaceted factors that have ignited the Eastern European students' 'desire to circulate' (Raghuram, 2013, p. 138) as well as their specific choice of Denmark. It departs from the assumption that students' international mobility is connected to their previous life trajectory in combination with more present societal and personal circumstances (Brooks and Waters, 2010; Carlson, 2013; Murphy-Lejeune, 2002). Essentially, the research subjects in this book have all come of age in post-socialist societies. Throughout this chapter, I highlight the importance of situating the students' mobility 'within the broader economic, cultural and social environments wherein these decisions are formed' (Van Mol, 2014, p. 40). Particular attention is devoted to the ways students relate their ontological narratives (stories that social actors use to make sense of themselves and their relationship to the world) and their choice to study abroad within a broader metanarrative of the West. I also discuss how we should understand the role of economic considerations (free education and scholarships) in their choice of Denmark. The next section explores how the socio-cultural context, characterised by unprecedented opportunities to move, and the narratives of previous generations appear to be imperative when seeking to grasp *how* students from post-socialist countries have cultivated a taste for a life outside the national boundaries (see also Ginnerskov-Dahlberg, 2021).

Travelling narratives

The period of communism constitutes an essential part of the students' collective memory and continues to affect how they experience the present – even in the absence of any direct personal experience with life during communism (Roberts, 2009). Narratives circulate between generations and carry the impetus of the past into the present and dreams for the future (Liechty, 2003). During interviews and conversations, my interlocutors would frequently address the restricted mobility of previous generations. Obviously, mobility is always a matter of scale and individuals are never truly 'immobile' (Cresswell, 2006). Hence, when referring to the 'immobility' or restricted mobility of previous generations, this predominantly involves the inability of travelling freely internationally during the period of communism to destinations in the West. The students' parents might have moved around inside national contexts and there are, for instance, examples of students from Georgia and Moldova telling me about how their parents during communism studied in Moscow (i.e. within the Soviet Union). However, the vast majority of my interlocutors foregrounded an interpretation of their parents feeling extremely confined during their youth in terms of international travelling to particularly the West. Legal restrictions and the lack of money turned border crossing into a nearly impossible quest for Olga's parents during communism:

> Well, they were born basically when the Soviet Union still existed, so when they were in their 20s they could not just go abroad because of those restrictions from Russia and from the government in Poland. They could not do this. That was one reason. Another reason was that even if they could, there was always the financial matter because they did not come from wealthy families.
>
> (Olga, Poland)

In addition to travel restrictions, the quote underlines that a shortage of money may also have complicated aspirations of international travelling – something highlighted by several students. The travel restrictions and curtailed desires during communism appear to have turned the mere act of travelling into an intrinsic value for the geographically restricted individuals. Mobility bears many meanings that circulate widely (Cresswell, 2006). Hana Horáková (2010, p. 64) similarly argues that new possibilities for tourism following the fall of communism 'embodied the symbol of

post-communist "freedom," a symbolic transition from the time of isolation, moral darkness to the hope that people might start to live their lives
in dignity and light.' Essentially, this narrative of travelling as an intrinsic
value appears to have been passed on to those generations growing up in
the aftermath of communism. Tales of travel restrictions were also central
for the students' ontological narratives, who often described themselves as
fortunate for having grown up in a generation released from the national
borders. As have been established, narratives guide action (Somers, 1994).
This positive narrative of travelling and the students' ontological narratives
as 'fortunate' seemingly spurred their eagerness to cross borders. Even prior
to Denmark, many of the students had impressive 'travel records.' Due to
the large wage difference between Western and Eastern Europe, students
had taken advantage of opportunities, such as high-school exchanges or the
Erasmus programme, to explore the world on a limited budget.

The students connected their parents' troublesome relations with border
crossing during communism (and in some cases after) as pivotal to inspiring
their own wanderlust. They recalled how their parents actively sought to
plant little seeds that eventually would make them go abroad. For instance,
Christina's mother placed her in an international language school as a child
so that she would get the optimal possibilities for creating a life outside
the borders of North Macedonia. From a very early age, she thus had a
keen awareness of an alternative life away from her immediate and familiar
surroundings. Adam explained that his parents 'always wanted to travel'
and that they 'genetically send [him] the wish also to travel.' Etel similarly
established a causal link between her parents' curtailed desires during the
years of communism and her yearning to cross borders:

> Because I'm from Hungary and you know when my parents were young
> they could not travel because of the regime, the socialist regime, because
> the borders were closed and everything. So, I think in the first place they
> were the ones encouraging me to go and travel as much as I can because
> they could not when they were young, so I kind of have this feeling that
> I must take the opportunity because I have the opportunity and it's a
> great thing.
>
> (Etel, Hungary)

Gojko had also been encouraged by his mother to join a Serbian folk troupe
with whom he – despite his family's limited resources – could explore
different parts of the world and broaden his horizon:

> I mean my mother has not travelled much because of like economy
> and stuff but she has always wanted to travel and with my brother and
> me. She was always really interested in us like wanting to travel and
> wanting to sort of broaden our views. She did not insist on it, but she

sort of suggested when we were young that we start with this folk troupe because it also provides possibilities for travelling and stuff.

(Gojko, Serbia)

The students made a clear connection between their own hunger for travelling and their parents' valuation of travelling. They described that their parents – in spite of their internationally restricted lifestyle – had remained highly oriented towards the global world (see also Krivonos and Näre, 2019) and actively encouraged their offspring to pursue what was denied to them during their youth. Murphy-Lejeune (2002, pp. 54–55) argues that parents' 'openness towards foreignness' may plant seeds for future mobility despite the lack of physical mobility. Thereby, people who have not had the opportunity to travel sometimes hand over their unfulfilled dreams of discovering other cultures to their children. This further indicates how a person's imagination may voyage to other places and other times, while s/he is not physically moving (Salazar, 2011). Indeed, the students' explanations suggest that their parents handed over a positive narrative of travelling to their children where the act of travelling – to the West – symbolised *the good life*.

While communist travel restrictions now belong to the past, some students described how the end of communism did not necessarily change their parents' travel habits fundamentally. Ada's well-educated parents remained strangers to border crossing despite the fact that nothing in theory hindered them from exploring the world outside the Czech Republic. She understood their continued immobility as a ghost from the past: 'Because the country was closed for many years, so I think that people just generally got used to life and travel within the country.' On one occasion, her father even declined a prestigious position in Sweden, estimating that moving abroad would be too overwhelming for their family. Moreover, as exemplified by Olga above, the lack of money continued to complicate travels, particularly to Western European destinations. Olga also drew attention to other barriers to travelling such as her parents' lack of English skills, which made them uneasy at the idea of visiting Anglophone countries.

While the majority of my interlocutors portrayed their parents as strangers to international mobility, even following the end of communism, there were also examples of students with parents (often their father) who, following the end of communism, engaged in labour migration typically to a Western European country. Georgi from Bulgaria, Anna from North Macedonia, Gojko from Serbia, Clara from Romania, and Anastasia from Ukraine all had parents who, during extended periods of their lives, had worked abroad. In addition, the East–West migration patterns that arose following the fall of communism appear to have installed an awareness in their minds of the possibility for a life abroad. Many students pointed out how relatives and people in their immediate social network took up jobs in Western Europe following

the end of communism. Christina described how Germany occupied a special place in her home country, North Macedonia, due to the high number
of people who had migrated there: 'We even have this joke: So, what are we
going to do when the end of the world comes? We will pack our suitcases
and go to Germany because Germany is the like the holy grail of countries.'
When I asked her to elaborate on the roots of this narrative, she explained:

> Because in the past I have also had friends who had uncles and aunts
> who went to Germany to work as housekeepers or building buildings –
> you know those kinds of blue-collar jobs, and they would still live very
> well and build houses in Macedonia. So, it's kind of that kind of thing.
> In Germany, you can go and work without an education and still get a
> decent life in Macedonia.

> (Christina, North Macedonia)

Macedonian migrants' positive stories of the 'easy life' in Germany thus
seem to have strengthened a narrative of the West as a desirable destination
for migration.

A powerful metanarrative of 'the West'

While international journeys may vary in scope and length, they are
almost always guided by historically laden and socioculturally constructed
imaginaries (Salazar, 2011). This section explores the narratives which appear
to have influenced the Eastern European students' motivation for pursuing
an education in Denmark and, in particular, how a dominant metanarrative
of the West is key to understanding the roots of their journey. To recap,
metanarratives refer to master stories with a global currency in which social
actors are embedded. Such grand narratives have often become naturalised
to the extent that people seldom question them. In her study of international
students in Australia, Hannah Soong (2014, p. 11) contends that they were
drawn to the 'conceptual space of the West, as a spatial desire of transnational imagination for modernity.' Despite the absence of a physical East–
West barrier, many of my interlocutors appeared to have an acute awareness
of a divided Europe from a very early age. At the core of nearly all interviews
was an understanding of the West as a highly dynamic, developed, and progressive entity (Sztompka, 2004). Elena from Romania deemed Western
Europe 'ahead' of Eastern Europe in almost all aspects: 'Financially first.
Then civilisation. The Western part is much more open in a way, really like
much more progressive, really much more progressive, I mean the way you
see it in music – everything!' Esmira from Bosnia and Herzegovina disclosed
a similar understanding of what she regarded to be an uneven power balance
between Eastern and Western Europe: 'Most of the Western countries are in
a better position than Eastern European countries. So, we see the West as a

light I guess.' Thus, in the students' narratives, the West represented a combination of geography and an idealised place that they believed could offer a greater range of possibilities for a more meaningful life and brighter future (Krivonos and Näre, 2019; Manolova, 2018).

The students' narrations indicate an upbringing characterised by a strong sense of a peripheral status vis-à-vis Western Europe and the idea of a 'gradually diminishing civilization toward the East' (Melegh, 2006, p. 2). Paul shared interesting recollections of 'Western imaginaries' from his upbringing in a mountain village in Romania. I spent several days with him in his hometown, where he had returned after running out of money in Denmark. To cut down on his spending, he moved in with his parents while writing up his master's thesis. During a long walk in the forest, he told me about his upbringing and the details surrounding his interesting journey to Denmark. Growing up in rural Romania, Paul welcomed every step of, what he interpreted as, Romania's transition towards becoming more 'Western-like':

> After the revolution, they introduced Western style garbage bins in my town, and I remarked as a kid that Romania is becoming a Western country. For me, it all began with comparing Western and Eastern garbage bins.
>
> (Paul, Romania)

Paul's childhood memories indicate that a particular positive narrative of the West, as a desirable and progressive place, influenced him from an early age and established the ground for his unwavering conviction that the West constituted the ideal template for social development for the entire Eastern European region. Therefore, it was with joy and excitement that he noticed the modern garbage bins in his town, which he interpreted as 'emblems of Westernness' (Dombos, 2008, p. 132). Paul's perception of the West also reflects his early understanding of his home country, Romania, namely as a country falling short on the modernity-scale. Modernity, in his narrations, was something distinctively Western and basically the direct antithesis of communism.

Borge, who like Paul grew up in rural Romania, also ascribed the West with positive qualities from a very early age. However, Borge's route to Denmark was strikingly different. As underlined by Parvati Raghuram (2013), students do not engage in educational migration solely for the purpose of studying but also go abroad in the name of love, for work, and so on (see also Lulle and Buzinska, 2017). Initially, Borge did not arrive in Denmark with the intention to study; rather, he came to Denmark from rural Romania with the help of a church to sing in the local Romanian church. In fact, it was not until he lived in Denmark that he decided to enrol as a master's student at a Danish university. For him, the narrative of the West as a promised land was a major factor in spurring his desire to migrate:

So, I think it's everyone's dream, especially people from poor countries from the East like Russia, Romania, Bulgaria. And it's everyone's
dream to study in an international university like this one, and I think
it's everyone's dream to have a little better life so to speak. I planned [to
go to the West] since I was seven.

(Borge, Romania)

When Borge met his girlfriend (now wife), he immediately informed her
about his dream of leaving Romania and pursuing a life in a Western country
and that there was no common future for them if she wanted to stay in
Romania. Borge was convinced that particularly Western Europe could offer
him a way of life that Romania was incapable of delivering. The dream of
settling in the West meant so much to him that he was willing to sacrifice
almost everything for it – even romantic relationships. When visiting France
with his school as a teenager, he even tried to run away with the intention
of staying permanently in France. While the attempt was unsuccessful, his
dream of going to the West remained intact. While elaborating on the roots
of his 'Western fascination,' he highlighted the impact of movies produced
in the West:

Well, I think about the first way to get this kind of dreaming to go abroad
comes from movies. After the 1990s, we had like a lot of influences, a
lot of new television and new channels and so on. Of course, people
they were very impressed, it was so nice to live in France or to work in
England or in Denmark or in yeah. In the beginning, I did not know too
much about Denmark, because it seemed to be a little country but a rich
one and with good conditions for life.

(Borge, Romania)

For Borge, media seemingly played a pivotal role in delivering a positive
narrative of the West – and therefore a convincing narrative of a competing
social model. Colourful images from television armed him with hope that
life could be markedly different from the one he was leading in Romania.
For Arjun Appadurai (1996), the media are pivotal when it comes to our
subjective understandings and imagined worlds – not least on peoples'
perception of how their society stands in relation to others. Media, thus,
represent a medium through which we can imagine alternative lives somewhere else, which may lay the foundation for migration.

In addition to highlighting the influence of media, the quote above also
accentuates Borge's limited knowledge of Denmark before his arrival to the
country. He imagined Denmark as a destination which, due to its wealth, societal development, and location in the global West, offered a different mode
of existence. Indeed, few students had a detailed knowledge of Denmark
prior to their departure but their choice of Denmark seemingly grew out of
an *a priori assumption* that the educational level in Denmark was advanced.

The students saw a close relationship between a country's positioning on the East/West scale and the perceived value of 'academic capital' (Munk, 2009). Etel was very 'Western-oriented' when searching for international master's programmes. She considered Western education pivotal for future career advancement and was convinced that a university degree from Denmark would be an advantage in the Hungarian labour market:

> Yeah I'm sure, I mean I'm very positive about this but I'm not saying that it's specifically because of [this university], but I'm saying that employers in Hungary will see that I went to Western Europe and I did a degree in English, so I must have a good level in English, and I was able to manage my life in Western Europe and I think it's very positive like very – something that I can stand out of the crowd with this.
>
> (Etel, Hungary)

For Etel, an education in Denmark was clearly a matter of distinction (Bourdieu, 1984) and the aspiration to obtain a qualification that would make her stand out from other graduates in the labour market (Holloway et al., 2012). Elena similarly regarded a Danish degree as more valuable than 'any Eastern European diploma' due to Denmark's status and reputation and she was convinced that the degree would open more doors for her than her Bosnian education. We find a similar logic in Georgi's reasoning:

> People in Bulgaria, employers, they appreciate people who have graduated in foreign universities. In Bulgaria, it's a common perception that studying abroad is always a better option than studying in Bulgaria. In European countries. In countries that we consider better than Bulgaria – more progressive, Western countries. We would not choose to study in countries like Moldova or Macedonia but we would go to Denmark, England, Western countries.
>
> (Georgi, Bulgaria)

Indeed, the categorisation of Denmark as a part of the global West often seemed to weigh more than the name and ranking of the university or the education. This belief in the superiority of a Western university degree has also been noted by other scholars (e.g. Brooks and Waters, 2011). In her study of East Asia's middle-class educational strategies, Johanna Waters (2006, p. 185) notes that 'Western academic credentials are assumed to represent far more than specific competences, "guaranteeing" a whole host of embodied characteristics tantamount to the possession of a "general culture" by their holder.' In fact, most of my interlocutors became aware of the ranking of the university only *after* arriving in Denmark. Their discovery of the relatively high ranking of the university functioned primarily as a confirmation of already existing notions of Denmark – a Western country, which by default constituted a good place to study – rather than a factor which independently brought them to Denmark.

In his study of Chinese students pursuing education in Denmark, Stig Thøgersen (2012) emphasises how students operated with sharp divisions between 'Chinese' and 'Western' education. The students were generally critical of Chinese education, which in their view was deprived of critical thinking but characterised by 'rote learning, strict discipline, teacher-centred teaching methods and constant exams and rankings' (Thøgersen, 2012, p. 81). In a similar manner, the Eastern European students saw a clear divide between Western education and the education available in their home countries. Many described the educational system in post-socialist countries as old-fashioned and, akin to the Chinese students in Thøgersen's study, highly attuned towards reproducing large chunks of textbooks, as Anastasia's reflections illustrate:

> While studying in Ukraine we are always taught this is the post-Soviet education system, on one hand it's the best because it's very structured, methodological, you know students are being forced into very heavy reading, heavy note-taking. A lot presence in the classroom compared to Western education. Because Western education for me is very liberal. We are also told that it's very old-style that it's something you know from the past, that our education system is this ghost, this legacy from the past that continues and continues in our post-soviet space and that the Western educational model is something that we want to aspire to. I think that people with Western education they are in general more open and they are also more self-critical, they are more enthusiastic and they are more willing to challenge themselves and challenge others to ask questions.
>
> (Anastasia, Ukraine)

In the quote, Anastasia juxtaposes 'Western' and 'post-Soviet' education: While post-Soviet education builds on an outdated pedagogic, attuned towards producing passive and obedient personalities, education in the West fosters critical thinkers and confident individuals. This spatial hierarchy established between the archaic East and modern West echoes Parvarti Raghuram's (2013, p. 144) point of how spatial comparisons among international students tend to be 'based on a sense of incommensurability between the two places – sending and receiving – as two places marked primarily by difference.' Indeed, Anastasia definitely believed that an education in Denmark could offer her something unattainable in Ukraine.

Escaping the ghost of communism

To understand the students' motivation for pursuing an education abroad, attention must also be paid to the social contexts they leave behind. This section specifically turns to the students' narrations of their home countries and the ways in which they weave these into metanarratives of Eastern and Western Europe. Following the discussions of the asymmetrical power-relationship between Eastern and Western Europe, the section explores how the conceptual entities are narrated and contrasted with each other in spatial as well as temporal dimensions (Péteri, 2010).

My interlocutors generally expressed a highly critical attitude towards the social conditions in their home countries and a distinct understanding of coming from a region which they deemed temporally 'behind' the West. Their critique of their home countries was not only a question of belonging to a society which they perceived as economically behind, rather, they interpreted this as a symptom of something fundamentally wrong with their respective societies. They saw communism as a harmful element imposed on their societies by external powers and which had led the countries down a wrong and socially unhealthy path. Even if the Iron Curtain lost its physical representation with the destruction of the Berlin Wall (Sztompka, 2004), the students experienced that communism had left a definite mark on their societies that is difficult to eradicate. While Clara expressed a great amount of pride and affection for her home country, Romania, she remained highly sceptical towards the political road that the country had embarked on following the end of the Cold War or, more precisely, the road that the country did *not* take post-1989. In Clara's view, there existed an undisputable thread between the structures of communism and Romania's current shape. This strong connection between the past and present stood out when she looked at Romania's current political scene: 'the politicians are getting from bad to worse every day. I mean, 25 years after communism, we actually have the same people there. And it's stupid. It's stupid.' Due to the protracted economic and political crisis in Romania, Clara had aspirations of returning to her home country following her graduation, in order to offer her help:

> I really, really want to help my country, and anywhere I'm going to work I want to be something related to Romania. And eventually for my perfect future would be actually going back to Romania and have a good life there, and, I don't know, helping my country more than others because I think Romania needs me more than others.
>
> (Clara, Romania)

Clara's narrations echo the findings by Pamela Abbott et al. (2010) of how young people in Moldova expressed a sense of loyalty towards the nation despite the fact that they felt alienated from the formal political system and the state more generally. In Clara's case, her loyalty to her home country ruled out long-term migration to the West. Before studying in Denmark, Clara was no stranger to international migration. Despite the fact that her parents had been married for many years, her father lived and worked in Dubai ten months of the year to support his family in Romania. It was also Clara's father who initially encouraged her to pursue an education abroad: 'Our country is going to go really bad the next couple of years and you should just think about something else.' According to Adam, who like Clara originated from Romania, encouraging one's offspring to go abroad represented the 'normal mentality' among Romanian parents. In fact, he argued that 'most parents want their children to leave because there is nothing to do in Romania.' The students' explanations of parental involvement thus strengthen the findings of Allan Findlay et al. (2017) that an international career and lifestyle for some international students may be strongly structured by parents (see also White, 2010).

Her father's advice to migrate to another country did not cause Clara to rule out the possibility of leading a good life in Romania. Dreams for her 'perfect future,' however, did not only revolve around her personal well-being but also on the well-being of her home country. Clara saw it as her 'patriotic duty' (Lulle and Buzinska, 2017, p. 1364) to create similar possibilities in Romania to those available for young people in the West (see also Holloway et al., 2012). To position Romania differently on the East–West slope, Clara perceived the knowledge and tools which she hoped to accumulate while studying in Denmark as fundamental. Generally, the students expressed a strong belief that improved 'societal health' in their home countries was achieved only by them moving ideologically further towards the West. Similarly, Paul hoped that time would bring Romania closer to a 'Western path.' He summarised the historical era of communism in one blunt sentence: 'Communism was a genocidal, inhumane cluster-fuck.' In addition to highlighting their home countries' depressing political climate, the students described how many fellow national citizens had internalised certain 'communist traits.' According to Jacob, many Hungarians showed symptoms of having a highly problematic relationship with the state, which he ascribed to their 'socialist mindsets.' They suffered, he claimed, from what in the literature has been described as a 'homo sovieticus complex,' referring to their inability to shake old mental habits from the era of communism and embrace a modern, post-communist reality (Buchowski, 2006; Mayblin et al., 2016; Melegh, 2006). Consequently, Jacob believed that Hungarians' mentality and actions constituted a bad fit with Hungary's official label as a liberal democratic state. Akin to Clara's and Paul's narrations, he presented communism as a foreign element, which had been forced upon his home country. In his view, it constituted the main reason for the continued societal divergence between Europe's eastern and western parts:

> I strongly feel that right now Hungary is in a really bad place mainly politically and culturally. [...] Like the Hungarian society really markedly shows the Soviet influences. I mean in Hungary the system change was in 1989 and the influences of that era, the half of decade that we spend in Soviet oppression, it definitely has huge influence on society

and people's ideas and beliefs. Cheating the system was actually something noble in Hungary in the sense that there was the Soviet system and you were cheating that system you were kind of resisting that system. That was kind of an acceptable thing to do because the system was the enemy. Therefore, people working against the system was not something bad. People not paying their taxes or trying to make a living, it was necessary first of all and it was not bad. So even now when the system is not really the enemy anymore, because we are supposed to be a liberal democratic state, people have this attitude that carried over that going behind backs and lying and trying to make your way and not paying taxes is acceptable – when it is really not. And this is something that any democratic country with an established class of citizens does not have. It is a sense of responsibility and I think it is exceptionally strong in Scandinavia. It is something that has attracted me that people post their tax reviews on the internet or some companies do. That is also a very marked difference between East and West, I think. [...] I find it fascinating the way that Hungarian people behave and how that it is affected by history and the Soviet influences and how the Western cultures are influenced by different things. The reason that I wanted to go to Western Europe is obviously because of financial reasons as well. It is just much easier to make a living and lead the kind of life that I wish with travelling.

(Jacob, Hungary)

Hungary's failed transition process and the incapability of 'catching up' with the West economically and culturally frustrated Jacob. He regarded the country's communist past as a factor that continued to exercise considerable influence on the mindsets of Hungarian citizens today and was critical of their relation to the system and that the distorted public–private relationship did not cease to exist with communism. Thus, in Jacob's narrations, 'the West' emerged as an antithesis to Hungary – a superior marker that elucidated the country's pitfalls.

This understanding of the West as a promised land and the belief that an education in Denmark, a country with a long history of a well-developed welfare system, would provide Jacob with the possibility to pursue a life that he felt denied of in his home country (also in a material sense) constituted the main motivation for him to study abroad. It is further interesting to note that Jacob paid remarkably little attention to the specific educational programme in Denmark while reflecting on his motivations for going abroad. When outlining the main factors for pursuing an education in Denmark, he mostly focused on broader societal conditions in Hungary that made it impossible for him to envision a life there. For Jacob, educational mobility to Denmark was less motivated by factors such as the academic quality of the educational programme, ranking, or the potential ways that the specific choice of education would affect his future career. Even though some students emphasised specific educational programmes as an important pull-factor, the political and cultural differences between Eastern and Western Europe always figured as an overriding reason for pursuing foreign education. Educational mobility, then, carried a strong wish of escaping certain post-transitional conditions and aspirations of long-term settlement in the West. The latter supports the findings of scholars (Baas, 2010; Luthra and Platt, 2016; Robertson, 2013; Robertson and Runganaikaloo, 2014; Valentin, 2012) who argue that goals of foreign education and migration have become increasingly intertwined.

In both Clara's and Jacob's ontological narrations linger a sense of being further up the 'East–West civilizational slope' (Melegh, 2006, p. 2) than many of their fellow national citizens. Both students were engaging in processes of distinction vis-à-vis failed post-socialist subjects who never managed to move beyond the socialist past. By drawing symbolic boundaries, we associate ourselves with desired groups and distance ourselves from those we find less desirable (Lamont, 1992; Lamont and Molnár, 2002; Sayer, 2005). Therefore, symbolic boundaries are instrumental in the narrative construction of social identity (Lamont and Aksartova, 2002). While all people engage in boundary work, it is particularly pronounced among individuals who are physically or socially near members of stigmatised groups (Copes, 2016; Sayer, 2005). There was a marked moral dimension in Jacob's evaluation of the ordinary Hungarian who, despite the official demise of communism, systematically continued to cheat the system. Drawing moral boundaries served to cement a narrative of Jacob as above 'the mass' and, indeed, highly geared towards a post-communist reality. In contrast to fellow national citizens who, in Jacob's eyes, were incapable of embracing European civilised values, he presented a narrative of himself as an individual who had managed to escape the mental chains of communism. Fundamentally, this understanding of oneself, as culturally and morally superior to fellow national citizens, was not exclusive to the narrations of David and Clara but a consistent theme in the students' ontological narratives. The next section explores this tendency more in depth.

Eastern European Westerners

The students were generally highly critical of the societal developments in their home countries following the end of communism. As emphasised in the previous section, they were furthermore eager to carve out both cultural and moral boundaries between themselves and 'the less progressive segments' of their home countries. This way of distancing oneself from fellow national citizens can be understood along the lines of what Milica Bakić-Hayden's (1995) has termed 'nesting orientalisms.' Bakić-Hayden's conceptualisation is an expansion of Edward Said's (1978) work on Orientalism and refers to a process whereby the image of the other is manipulated and where people who themselves are *othered* project the image of the other onto other groups:

The gradation of 'Orients' that I call 'nesting orientalisms' is a pattern of reproduction of the original dichotomy upon which Orientalism is premised. In this pattern, Asia is more 'East' or 'other' than eastern Europe; within eastern Europe itself this gradation is reproduced with the Balkans perceived as most 'eastern'; within the Balkans there are similarly constructed hierarchies.

(Bakić-Hayden, 1995, p. 918)

Michal Buchowski (2006, p. 466) accentuates how the phenomenon of nesting orientalisms increasingly occurs *inside* national contexts, where otherness is projected onto one's 'sisters and brothers.' As exemplified through Clara's and Jacob's narrations in the previous section, the students projected 'the other' towards their fellow national citizens. This *othering* of one's fellow countrymen and home country served to reaffirm one's own identity as progressive and modern (see also Thøgersen, 2012). The distinction made between themselves and others revolves around the extent that an individual is capable of embracing a post-communist reality. Moreover, the unambiguous appreciation of the Western path, interpreted as 'the modern way,' is essential to grasp the students' eagerness to highlight certain European attributes they possess (Wilken and Dahlberg, 2017). Following Somers, ontological narratives never arise in isolation. Instead, ontological narrations link to public and master narratives and are always interpersonal. Aligning their ontological narratives with the metanarrative of (Western) Europe served to underline certain personal qualities – one of the most important being a progressive mind fit for a life in the West. David was one of the most vocal students in his critique of his home country, Hungary. During our conversations, he highlighted a plethora of frustrations with what he called an 'Eastern European mentality,' which entailed a certain backwardness and deprivation of civilised manners:

I don't like this Eastern European mentality, I'm like running away from it big time and I get so irritated because of sometimes and all these stupid things they do and I just don't want to be a part of it a lot of times. It's not like I'm, I don't have this identity crisis because I did not like that in Hungary either when people were doing really Balkan stuff, I was like 'no!'

(David, Hungary)

In the quote, David portrays himself as intrinsically different from the typical Hungarian – involving the majority of his friends back home. In Hungary, he experienced a growing distance to the individuals around him and his decision to go abroad was partly motivated by the wish of wanting to cement a symbolic boundary between himself and the stayers (see also Carlson, 2013; Krivonos and Näre, 2019):

My friends back in Hungary were characterised by an Eastern European mentality. This trashing ourselves to complete drunkenness every weekend, this loud crappy music. But I see from my friends that no one really wants to leave that. They are like between 25 and 30 and they still go to the same stupid, smelly, awful places. Still crying about their own problems, instead of doing something to solve it. And also, when I was home for a week I met some of my friends and the only thing they could talk about was their problems and I was like 'ok, do you try to solve them maybe?' And then no.

(David, Hungary)

Following Goffman's (1990) notion of stigma, David regarded his Eastern European 'roots' as a discrediting feature – a symbolic inheritance that he wanted to distance himself from. His attempt to manage my impression of him during the interview situation was based on emphasising a stereotype of the 'stupid' Eastern European (and/or Balkan) mentality that he despised, not least since he connected it with lack of agency. By accentuating various discrediting characteristics of Eastern Europeans, David sought – in line with a Goffmanian logic – to distance himself from the 'tribe' to escape its 'tribal stigma.' Pursuing an education in Denmark was thus an attempt to effect-ively deal with a situation in Hungary that he found highly unsatisfactory. In light of his friends' passive behaviour, he interpreted international mobility as a progressive act. Interestingly, Polina Manolova (2017) highlights similar dynamics among Bulgarian migrants whom she interviewed before, during, and after migrating to the UK. The migration narratives of what she coins 'Bulgarian Westerners' (that is, self-proclaimed Western-minded and modern individuals) are highly similar to descriptions of the students in this study. The migrants in Manolova's study also emphasised their symbolic and cultural proximity to the West as one of the main reasons for looking for a life outside the national borders. Often, they portrayed themselves as having a mentality more suitable for Western European countries (see also Krivonos and Näre, 2019). Similarly, the above explanations by David accentuate how some students viewed the education in Denmark as an opportunity to locate themselves physically among Western individuals with whom they imagined they would share ideals and values. International mobility thus functioned as an 'identity-making project' (Benson, 2011, p. 484).

During my fieldwork in Romania, I engaged in several interactions with locals who shared views analogous to David's narrations. Some of them showed a sensitivity to the category 'Eastern Europe' and felt a need to emphasise a symbolic boundary between fellow national citizens and them-selves. For instance, Larry, a close friend of Bogdan, described a feeling of being marginalised in an environment he perceived inhabited and dominated by people very different from himself. In our conversations, he continuously highlighted various cultural traits that distinguished him from the 'common Romanian' as if he was trying to convince me that he was inherently different. When Larry introduced himself, he highlighted that his group of friends were 'atypical Romanians' and that their interest to a greater extent resembled the French (while perceiving France as the ultimate symbol of sophistication). Although Larry was an eager amateur photographer, he despised taking photos of Romanian weddings since their 'vulgar, over-the-top expression' encapsulated everything he detested about Romania. The combination of aversion towards Romania and his self-proclaimed symbolic and cultural proximity to the West made him keen on going to Berlin to study and eventually settle more permanently abroad.

When applying Goffman's dramaturgical model for understanding and explaining human action, we see how Larry engages in a particular type of impression management aimed at avoiding potential stigmatisations from me, that is 'the Westerner.' During the scenes played out in Larry's home, he played the role of an Eastern European individual in relation to the Western European researcher. Larry, not being pleased with the connotations attached to his role, presented a specific 'front' of himself where he emerges as an exception from the mass – a cultivated and Western-minded individual in a land characterised by regressive Eastern Europeans. To recap Goffman's point, people engage in impression management to define not only the particular interaction but ultimately also who we want to be in the eyes of others. During our encounters, Larry accentuated his sameness with me (a representative of Western Europe) while downplaying his affiliation with Eastern Europe.

A sense of existential stagnation

The students often expressed feelings of frustration when picturing a hypothetical future in their home countries. The choice of pursuing an education abroad was often entangled with aspirations of leaving a society, which they interpreted as a developmental void (Vigh, 2009). Earlier I described how Clara had plans to return to Romania following her graduation in order to assist the country's development in the 'right direction.' While few students saw it as their 'patriotic duty' to return to their home country, most interlocutors found it difficult to envision a bright future for themselves in their home countries. Many talked about physical movement as the best and sometimes the only solution for what Ghassan Hage refers to as 'existential immobility.' (Hage and Papadopoulos, 2004 , p. 112) The experience of existential immobility, Hage claims, gives birth to dreams of life somewhere else and, consequently, the hope that physical mobility will simultaneously induce symbolic mobility:

> Now to me, those we classify as migrants, people who engage in a specific mode of physical mobility, are often people who initially feel 'symbolically stuck' where they are or at least, they feel themselves moving 'too slowly.' They are not 'going places.' 'Nothing is happening here'

migrants often say when describing the place they are leaving, or 'I am going nowhere' here. In this sense, migratory physical mobility is a substitute of symbolic mobility. It is only when we 'feel stuck' symbolically that we start dreaming of moving physically. Often the physical spaces we try to move to are places that, we hope, will allow us to experience symbolic mobility once again. That is, physical space is only a launching pad for this symbolic movement we yearn for.

(Hage and Papadopoulos, 2004, p. 112)

In the quote, Hage draws attention to how most decisions of mobility or migration relate to the feeling of being symbolically stuck. In fact, Steff Jansen (2009) describes a similar dynamic among his interlocutors in Bosnia and Herzegovina – namely how there persisted a specific valuation of *moving forward* which they only perceived possible outside the national borders. Although the students in this study originate from different national contexts and social positions, they were united by a feeling of being 'stuck' while residing in their home countries. Existential stagnation was precisely what made David keen on pursuing an education in Denmark. From the moment he finished his bachelor's studies in Hungary, he was determined to settle down in a Western country. Accidentally, he had heard of the Danish tradition of folk high schools[1] from a previous classmate in Hungary and, following a successful application, he received a scholarship from the Danish government to pursue a one-year study at a folk high school. After having spent a year in Denmark, he worked as an au pair in Italy to save money following which he returned to Denmark to pursue a master's degree. David linked this pronounced hunger to go abroad to Hungary's chaotic environment:

And then, of course, the whole situation in Hungary is just going worse and worse, not just well I always say to the people who ask me, one thing is the economy and the political situation is really bad, but then, on the other hand, the people are really losing themselves; this complete social insecurity. I always read the Hungarian news at least one hour of the day, so I know that people are going crazy and more and more people are becoming poorer and poorer and that really affected me when I lived in Budapest. I had to take the underground in the morning and the only thing I saw was completely depressed and hopeless people and I just wanted to shoot myself in the head and that was really when I decided I don't need this [laughing]. Because I guess that things can work in the West.

(David, Hungary)

David painted a gloomy picture of a country in a state of normative chaos or what Émile Durkheim (1951) would have referred to as *anomie*. The moral decay that David associated with Hungarians filled him with an immense sense of frustration and made it difficult for him to envision a future in Hungary. It was due to such societal frustrations that an education in the West emerged as a promising opportunity for creating a better platform for himself and of leaving a state of existential motionlessness. In David's narrations, the West imbued hope of symbolic mobility and his proclamation, 'I guess that things can work in the West,' suggests that he considered the global West to be the optimal platform for offering a certain structure and order not realisable in his natal country. A master's degree in Denmark became a potential means for freeing himself from the societal restraints of his home country. Indeed, mobility can be understood as a 'technology of the imagination, [...] an act through which people come to imagine better lives in other times or places' (Vigh, 2009, p. 94). While the overarching aim for David was to travel to the West, the specific choice of Denmark grew out of a combination of having a social network from the folk high school and the absence of tuition fees for attending Danish universities. Esmira had initially been convinced that Italy was the ideal location but eventually applied for a master's programme in Denmark following the advice of her sister:

> And then I made a list of why would I want to go to some countries or why would I not go and I think that the thing that decided in favour of Denmark was actually my sister, because I was trying to decide between Italy and Denmark and she was just like, well she loves Denmark! I don't know why she is obsessed with it and she was like saying very strictly Denmark is a great country, full of possibilities and if you decide to stay there after your studies, you are more likely to find a job, than you are to find in Italy because even people who live in Italy cannot find jobs.
>
> (Esmira, Bosnia and Herzegovina)

Esmira's explanations underline how a trusted person in her immediate network 'passed on' a highly positive image of Denmark to her as a land of opportunities and an optimal place for creating a promising career for oneself following graduation. Essentially, this focus on job opportunities following graduation echoes Marcu's (2015) points of how many of the Bulgarian and Romanian students in her study saw student mobility to Spain and the UK as a life-course strategy for migration and to better position themselves in the competitive labour market. Marcu notes that the students studying in the UK especially believed that the greatest professional payback would be to remain in the country to work.

Erina had similarly felt troubled by a sense of stagnation while residing in Bosnia and Herzegovina – feelings which were accompanied by a yearning for symbolic movement and freedom from certain restrictions imposed by the Bosnian government and broader society. She came from a well-educated family and both her parents had good positions at the local university. Although she already had a master's degree, she was eager to supplement her educational repertoire with foreign education:

> I mean the reasons why I left there, there are so many layers, there are so many reasons, I mean, I cannot even count them. The whole atmosphere and corruption and nepotism and the lack of opportunities. The general atmosphere of apathy – even at an academic level. The academic level is pretty high there, it's pretty strict we have like high expectations of students and professors of students and vice versa. It's really a good academic environment to study and to learn but in some aspects, it's really hard to go forward – to go forward in your career. To upgrade your career. […] I also tried to apply for a job as an assistant professor and I was declined because there is a lot of corruption in my country, so it was a reality check for me. Previously, I was hoping that I would get a job there and I would continue my career in academia and everything would be fine, but it turned out to be very difficult to get there because of a lot of nepotism and corruption. Since then I just decided that I will go somewhere else where I will be appreciated, where my grades will be appreciated, my hard effort and so on.
>
> (Erina, Bosnia and Herzegovina)

Clearly, Erina found it difficult to set her life along a desired life trajectory in Bosnia and Herzegovina. She experienced a marked mismatch between the narrative of 'the good life' – including a continuous sense of moving forward – and her social reality. She was particularly focused on how high levels of nepotism and corruption hindered her from finding employment in academia. Good grades at the university, she claimed, did not guarantee employment that reflected her academic qualifications and she saw no other option than to pursue a life outside the national borders. Foreign education thus represented a 'ticket to leave Bosnia and Herzegovina.' For Erina, the feeling of stagnation was born out of the lack of possibilities for social advancement and her inability to achieve a desirable career. Isidora's story was very similar to Erina's. She also grew up in the EU's immediate outside in a family with well-educated parents. Yet, like Erina, she was unable to imagine a desirable future for herself in her home country:

> Everywhere, everywhere there is corruption. Like the overall picture is if you belong to the party maybe you will have a better opportunity to find a job and you won't be punished or charged with fees or anything. […] It's really hard and people are like hopeless. I have lots of examples of people who have their master's degree, who have their bachelor's degree and they are high quality students and they are very hard working. I mean they have all the perquisites to have normal jobs but they don't have it. They cannot find it anywhere. And what is left

for you is like is if you want to have some amount of money for yourself, you can just work something not related to your profession and that's all. Can you imagine how bad it is if my friends are working as waiters or like babysitters [abroad] with their faculty diploma instead of working in Macedonia. [...] If you go back to Macedonia with your diploma, it does not count. So, no matter what – you are a PhD, you are from Harvard, no matter how appreciated you were abroad they don't count it. It only depends on your friends and the people who can help you work somewhere. That was the main reason why I wanted to go abroad and experience some different things – try to find some job here or somewhere else. Everyone wants to live surrounded by friends and family but it's really difficult.

(Isidora, North Macedonia)

The quote accentuates how Isidora would have preferred to stay physically close to her immediate social network, yet she found herself blocked from *advancing socially* due to high levels of nepotism. In her eyes, a university degree from North Macedonia was worthless without the right social relations and she experienced a marked disconnection between her educational level and the possibilities for employment. Note how Isidora spoke of 'normal jobs.' Abnormality here relates to the fact that the jobs available are far away from her educational qualifications. Generally, the students viewed their academic diplomas from their home countries as insufficient and incapable of *moving them forward* without the right connections, which strengthened feelings of coming from a country that thwarted the possibility of realising their full potential. They resented the high level of corruption and nepotism, which, in their mind, characterised the vast majority of the national politicians in their home countries. National politicians, they claimed, did not serve the people but rather their own narrow, personal interests and those of their social networks. There is a striking similarity to the rationale presented by the Chinese students in Vanessa Fong's (2011) study for pursuing an education abroad. Akin to the descriptions given by my interlocutors, the Chinese students hoped that a foreign education would enable them to achieve a broad variety of desirable life conditions such as:

High-quality educational opportunities, jobs, healthcare, and promotions without having to rely on social connections, gifts, bribes, and favors [and thereby set them free from] the corruption, biases, and unchecked tyranny of the managers, supervisors, and low-level bureaucrats who often made their lives miserable in China.

(p. 167)

Since many of the Eastern European students – from countries inside and outside the EU – regarded student mobility as a window for long-term settlement abroad, they often described how going abroad was anything but a straightforward decision. The excitement of exploring a new cultural environment was, for Isidora, accompanied by the knowledge that long-term migration would entail a life far away from her family and friends. When reflecting on her primary motivation for pursuing an education in Denmark, Isidora mainly touched upon the long-term benefits that she hoped would arise from pursuing an education abroad. She had been keen on leaving North Macedonia ever since studying for her bachelor's degree when a fully funded scholarship in Denmark turned such aspirations into reality. For Isidora, Denmark was to a great extent an 'independence project.' In the following quote, Isidora touches upon a consistent theme among the students, namely the difficulties of gaining financial independence from one's parents in a North Macedonian context:

> I cannot see my future in Macedonia, because it's very difficult to find a job and it's very difficult to maintain a family in Macedonia. Everything in Macedonia is cheap but the average salary is 200 euro, so that's really low. Usually with that amount of money you cannot do anything. If you are a student, you cannot imagine living alone and working – that's just not possible. Usually, until they are the age of 30 are without work and without a job and living with their parents because they don't have a choice. […] I really wanted to go somewhere where I can live alone, I mean it was not that my parents were bad or something happened, but I really wanted to be like independent. I really felt like I can handle myself all by myself. I really did not need parents any more, but the thing is from a financial perspective I could not do anything.
>
> (Isidora, North Macedonia)

Isidora had found the road to independence complicated in North Macedonia and emphasised an emotional tangle between wanting to stay physically close to friends and family and aspirations of providing for herself. Generally, students hoped that a foreign education would 'liberate' them from their parents' money. Smiljka Tomanović and Suzana Ignjatović (2006) note how young people in Eastern European countries find the paths to adulthood long due to their financial dependence on older generations. Their parents often have a central role when it comes to financial support during education, providing housing, support in establishing an independent household, and childcare (Tomanović and Ignjatović, 2006, p. 271). In fact, Peter from Hungary hoped that he eventually could provide not only for himself but also for his family. Having left his home country with a feeling of there being limited opportunities left for him, he became deeply saddened by the thought of embarking on a life in a different country than his loved ones: 'I had to do this. There was no choice. So it's sad and hard. But there was no choice.' Peter's narrations thus indicate how aspirations of migration produced mixed emotions (Halfacree, 2004). Indeed, educational migration was often embedded in aspirations of social mobility within a complex web of contradictory expectations and demands (Olwig and Valentin, 2015).

The above testimonies stand in contrast to other accounts from the literature on student mobility between Western destinations, where youth mobility is portrayed as an activity that assists the individuals involved in keeping adulthood at bay (Waters et al., 2011). For instance, in Vered Amit's (2010, p. 67) study on Canadian middle-class travellers, she makes an overarching description of youth mobility as a 'time out' from adult commitments. The relatively privileged backgrounds of the Canadian travellers imply that there – contrary to cases of more traditional labour migration – is 'limited risk' involved for them: 'If it is an adventure, it is a fairly safe one' (Amit, 2011, p. 87). The narrations of my interlocutors, however, suggest a different story. Echoing the narrations of aspiring labour migrants (Vigh, 2009), study abroad was for some students connected with the hope of providing patronage for family and friends and their journeys were often without a known expiration date. Thus, student travelling in this case is not detached from the phase of adulthood but rather deeply entangled in adult commitments and grown-up aspirations.

A yearning for normalcy

Taking into consideration the students' narrations of their home country as stagnant, I will further suggest that their decision to pursue an education abroad can be understood as a yearning for 'normalcy.' According to Barbara Misztal (2001), the concept of normalcy both refers to the present, average, or factual on the one hand, and to a desirable state, on the other hand. Misztal draws attention to two different yet interdependent modes of normalcy. First, a taken-for-granted mode of normalcy where the predictability, reliability, and legibility of social order constitute the synthetic criteria of normality. Second, a desirable state on a more conscious level that emerges when this taken-for-granted mode of normalcy becomes erupted. The student migrants described how they, before their arrival to Denmark, would contrast the societal conditions in their home countries with 'the normal life' that they saw elsewhere – particularly in the West. This section explores how 'thirst' for normality emanated from their experience of having grown up in societies deprived of the components 'predictability, reliability, and legibility.' As will be discussed, many students blamed their home countries' 'abnormal' societal conditions for blocking their ability to *move* at a desirable pace.

Scholars have increasingly employed 'normalcy' as an analytical prism for understanding the developments in post-socialist countries (Eglitis, 2002; Galbraith, 2003; Greenberg, 2011; Jansen, 2014, 2009; Kennedy, 1994). Daina Eglitis (2002) accentuates how there persisted a strong desire for a normal mode of life among ambitious post-socialist societies following the fall of the Soviet order. Focusing specifically on Latvia, Eglitis argues that Latvians understood normalcy as something 'non-Soviet' or 'non-Communist,' yet the exact recipe of normalcy remained an object of dispute. For some groups, normalcy referred to the conditions prior to the Soviet period, while others regarded Western Europe as the incarnation of normalcy and the optimal template for bringing Latvia on a 'normal path.' However, common for these groups was that normalcy represented an ideal societal state.

Aspirations of normalcy also play an important role in migration from Eastern to Western Europe (Gałasińska and Kozłowska, 2009; Lopez Rodriguez, 2010; Manolova, 2018; Polkowski, 2017; Rabikowska, 2010). Marta Rabikowska and colleagues claim that Western Europe has become an aspiration *and* a desired embodiment of normality for many people living in Eastern Europe (Rabikowska, 2010, p. 288). Nicola Mai (2001) also describes how young Albanians' aspirations of migration to the West following communism were interwoven with aspirations of leading a normal life. For the individuals in Mai's study, the notion of normality was predominantly established through comparison. When craving a 'normal life,' the young Albanians were longing for the (imagined) lifestyle of young people in the West. Western youth thus functioned as a yardstick by which they measured their own lives. Therefore, perceptions of normality were closely related to notions of societal progression, and 'normalcy' involved the ability to lead what they – from a distance – perceived to be a modern lifestyle. Contrary to Eglitis' (2002) study in Latvia, which revolves around aspirations of restoring normalcy in one's immediate society, this strand of literature points towards migration to Western European countries as influential for installing a sense of normalcy in one's life.

While the students in this study are not labour migrants in the traditional sense of the word, there are interesting overlaps between the abovementioned studies and the students' narrations. They too often made references to normality as a basis of *social critique* (Jensen, 2014). The sense of abnormality was rooted in the experience of coming from countries aloof from what they deemed to be 'normal' societal development. Therefore, 'normalcy,' as talked about by the student migrants, was above everything a normative category related to what life ideally should be like (Manolova, 2018). We sense this very clearly in the quote by Esmira:

> People are running away from a system that they have been stuck in for a long time. It's like an episode of The Walking Dead: People are dead inside but they are technically still alive. That's the climate that I'm personally feeling in this country and I think I'm not the only one. People are leaving the country to find a better life abroad. That is the better solution they see – to run away. For a long time I believed that the politics of this country does not concern me. That I can somehow be above all that. And I think that many young people felt the same, that you can lead a rather *normal life* for yourself without being affected

by the political situation. Now I know that this is not a possibility. In Denmark, a citizen does not have to be afraid that if my child gets sick I do not have to think about raising money to treat my sick child, because there is a system that will provide healthcare for that baby for instance. Also, all Danish citizens can get a scholarship to study at the university. That's a huge thing. They have the possibility to be the best version of themselves. They do not have to fear the system. All the things that are essential to a *normal life* are not functioning here.

(Esmira, Bosnia and Herzegovina)

Ivana Spasic (2012) has traced how, in Serbia, references to the 'normal life' are often made to describe what citizens feel they are denied in terms of material prosperity, social security, and chances for employment. Indeed, Esmira's narrations illustrate how she felt deprived of essential components for leading a normal life and viewed migration as the only solution to 'regain vitality' and obtain 'the ability to render one's desires or commitments into an actionable truth' (Greenberg, 2011, p. 93). In his writings just following the end of communism, Michael Kennedy (1994, p. 4) notes that people residing in a post-socialist context 'wish to be who they "really" are, or who they ought to be. In short, they want to be something inconsistent with the system they recently overturned and the social relations it produced.' Similarly, Esmira's reflections exemplify how the students' migration narratives were marked by aspirations of becoming who they ought to be – the best version of themselves – outside the restraints of their countries of origin. This entailed the possibility of living their lives in a context where they could *perform* in accordance with their desired roles (Goffman, 1956).

The previous section highlighted how the absence of 'normal jobs' filled Isidora with a sense of frustration. In addition to lacking a sense of social security, Isidora's statement highlights how students felt at a distance from their 'normal activities' such as international travelling and embarking on a desirable career path. Hence, the lack of opportunities to create predictable futures under the precarious labour market conditions in their home countries was often emphasised (Bygnes and Erdal, 2017). The students thus hoped that educational mobility would facilitate better conditions for controlling their present and plan their future. Ania, for instance, felt restricted from acting on her inner yearnings when living in Poland and she remained critical towards the high level of nepotism in Poland since it had restrained her from embarking on certain career paths. Earlier in life, she had been eager to pursue a career as a pianist. However, she gave up such aspirations completely when she turned 15 following the advice of her mother:

But then my mother thought it's not going to be a very easy job, because it's obvious that beginners struggle and especially in Poland everyone needs a good network to become an influential artist.

(Ania, Poland)

For Ania, yearning for normalcy was a question of uniting her desires with her social reality. Aspirations of a normal life had made Ania keen on establishing herself in Scandinavia on a more permanent basis. In high school, she had gone on exchange to Norway and participated in Erasmus exchange to Denmark as a part of her bachelor's studies. During the latter stay, she became romantically involved with a Danish man. Romantic love can act as a powerful factor in making people cross borders (Mai and King, 2009; Riaño, 2015), and it was also one of the reasons why she returned to Denmark to pursue her master's degree. However, above everything, it was the high level of social safety in Scandinavia which appealed to her:

> First and foremost, I think the Scandinavian countries are friendly places to *normal people* and if I should explain now what I mean, I think that in Poland it's not always the one who possesses the knowledge but the one who has the network who gets ahead. And I think Scandinavia works very good – like not only the ones in government but even the bus drivers speak English. Like everyone is well prepared and educated to do their job and even in the government I think there are people, I believe them to be also well prepared and suited to give people a chance – not only people who are making money. It might sound aggressive but it's what is going on in Poland. […] I was still thinking it's so cool in Denmark and because I started to read about Danish culture, I watched some movies, I don't know it appeared for me as this angel. It seems like it is kind of a *normal country,* I mean in a positive way because it's also important for me to know that I will be well in the environment.
>
> (Ania, Poland)

Ania's experience of Poland being deprived of 'predictability, reliability and legibility' (Misztal, 2001) clearly informed her perception of Denmark as a 'normal country.' In her mind, an appealing future in Poland was far too dependent on having the right connections and money. Thus, the discouraging job market in Poland was instrumental for Ania's labelling of Poland as 'abnormal.' Aleksandra Gałasińska and Dariusz Kozłowska (2009) demonstrate how perceptions and aspirations of 'normalcy' among Polish migrants in the UK were closely interwoven with hopes and expectations of a job market that could lead to a more fulfilling life outside work. The migrants considered a satisfying job key to obtaining a 'normal life.' Such expectations were rooted in the view of Poland having an 'abnormal' labour market due to local employers' amoral practices and the importance of informal social networks, which consequently complicated possibilities for finding a desirable job.

In many ways, Gałasińska's and Kozłowska's empirical findings echo my interlocutors' presentations of their home countries. The students viewed a master's degree abroad as an attractive option for taking control over one's future and locating 'normality.' Note how Denmark, in Ania's descriptions above, emerges as an 'angel' and a potential saviour. For Ania, the notion of normalcy encapsulated aspirations for the capitalisation of meritocratic opportunities (see also Lopez Rodriguez, 2010). She hoped that the Danish government would provide equal redistribution of material and social resources to each based on their personal merits – regardless of race, gender, and social networks. For the students, the attraction of meritocracy lies not only in the opportunity of getting a free master's degree and the Danish state stipend but it is something more profound. Education in Denmark symbolised a possibility to acquire agency and getting a chance in life, which they felt denied of in their home countries. It was a question of creating an environment for themselves in line with perceptions about normality and well-being (see also Lopez Rodriguez, 2010). In this sense, Denmark symbolised a hope of being appreciated for one's talent rather than the quality of one's social connections.

If returning to Ania's proclamation of Denmark as 'a friendly place to normal people,' it is important to note that she, in addition to framing Denmark as a normal place, simultaneously inserts herself into the category of normal people by drawing a firm moral boundary between herself and, in her eyes, the abnormal conditions and people in Poland. I previously discussed how Goffman (1963, p. 15), in his work on stigmatised individuals, differentiates between 'discredited people' and 'normals.' Following this line of thought, one could argue that Ania subtracts herself from the stigmatised while locating herself among 'normals' – thereby enforcing the stigmatisation of her fellow national citizens. Contrary to the attitude, which she considered prevalent among fellow national citizens, she was interested in a society where people get ahead due to their human qualities rather than the quality of their social networks. In the students' explanations lingered a feeling of being a hostage of abnormal societal conditions, yet they managed to keep oneself normal against all the odds. As highlighted in the previous section, David explained how the subjection to poverty and the lack of a social safety net had caused people to go 'crazy' in Hungary – suggesting a loss of a 'moral compass' (Greenberg, 2011, p. 89). In David's eyes, the moral deterioration imbued all levels of society – from the political to the individual level.

An affordable study destination in the West

How should we understand the students' specific choice of Denmark? This section moves further into this question and the role that especially free education plays in shaping my interlocutors' choice of study destination. In the politically charged Danish media discourse, free education has been portrayed as the main attraction for Eastern European students in Denmark. As emphasised, some politicians have expressed concern that students from EU member states take advantage of the generous welfare system only to return to their home countries shortly following their graduation. Scholars have also suggested that sensitivity to free education or significantly lower fees offered by the Scandinavian countries and other European nations, such as the Netherlands, may function as an important impetus for circulating students (Brooks and Waters, 2011). In addition, a higher ratio of per capita income in a particular destination country to a particular source country may act as a deterrent on student flows from (comparatively) poorer countries (Perkins and Neumayer, 2014).

While one cannot reduce the student migration to a question of rational cost-benefit calculation (as accentuated in the previous sections), the choice of Denmark was for the vast majority of both non-EU 'scholarship-students' and EU movers entangled with the possibility to receive free education. Tuition fees and higher ratio of per capita income in Western European countries meant that financing a master's degree in this region was out of the question with the money at their disposal. For instance, Erina drew attention to the paradox of having lived a 'normal life' in Bosnia and Herzegovina (in a material sense) but that it would be impossible for her to study outside the borders of her home country without financial aid. Thus, a scholarship was a necessity for leaving the country. Essentially, this resembles the situation of the Kazakhstan students in Sarah Holloway et al.'s (2012) study who, despite coming from comfortably well-off families, only could afford to study in the UK with state help.

The huge salary differences between North Macedonia and Western European countries also entailed that Isidora, despite the fact that both of her parents had relatively well-paid jobs in their local context, was completely dependent on a fully funded scholarship for studying abroad. She would have preferred to study in the UK but opted for a Danish university because the destination came with a scholarship. Especially for the non-EU students, the choice of Denmark often seemed rather accidental and to a great extent a matter of where the money brought them (see also Ginnerskov-Dahlberg and Valentin, forthcoming). Few appeared to have a very detailed knowledge about Denmark prior to their arrival. Ivan from Belarus expressed a particular interest in the study program he enrolled in at the Danish university since it was banned in his home country due to censorship. He nevertheless underlined that 'Denmark is a very random choice, because it depended on the scholarship.'

Most EU citizens similarly mentioned the prospect of no tuition as paramount for choosing Denmark. While Elena from Romania initially was attracted to a specific educational programme in Denmark, it would not have been possible if she had to pay for it: 'I would never have gone to a country where I'm supposed to pay tuition fees because I can't, no I can't do that.' However, like Ivan, Elena had been very focused on the specific academic programme and the possibilities she hoped it would bring about in terms of her future career. Through acquaintances in Romania, she heard that Denmark offered high-quality education. Peter from Hungary seemed almost surprised by the, in his eyes, high academic level in Denmark: 'So it turned out that the university is very good. And the education is free, which was one of the most important parts.' Clearly, his knowledge of Denmark and the specific university had also been very limited but his concern had been predominantly a question of finding a Western European university without tuition fee. Although free tuition allowed Peter to study in Denmark, he was drawn to the idea of a new beginning in Scandinavia. It would, despite the students' emphasis on free education, be a mistake to reduce education in Denmark to a question of economy. As outlined earlier, many hoped that mobility to a Western European country would induce a sense of symbolic mobility and make it easier to create a desirable future for themselves. Moreover, aims of improving one's skills and obtaining an academic degree coexisted with long-term aspirations of settling down (Ginnerskov-Dahlberg and Valentin, forthcoming).

My conversations with Adam similarly illustrated the complexity surrounding the issue of money and free education. He had been focusing on educational programs outside the borders of Romania since the beginning of his academic journey. His undergraduate studies took place within a so-called offshore bachelor's programme offered by a highly ranked UK university located in Greece.[2] It would have been financially out of reach for him and his family to pursue a 'classic' bachelor's programme in the UK. At a much more favourable price, he had received a bachelor's diploma that indicated affiliation to a prestigious university. Adam's parents had financed his studies, although he hoped that a master's degree in Denmark, that is, a university without tuition, would make him less dependent on his parents' financial goodwill. While the prospect of free tuition was important for Adam, the master's programme had to be located in a country of certain development level. For Adam, this ruled out 'Arabian countries' regardless of their status as economically developed:

> I just studied on the Internet – countries where you can study for free and I found that in Arabian countries you can get paid if you study there but I don't want to go to Arabian countries. It's too hot and I did not feel like there were a lot of opportunities to get a job over there because they are still in development and Denmark seemed like a country which ... you already made it. I mean you are already developed, you are not a developing country, you are a developed country. You got it! So that is why I wanted to go there and I was going to prove them that I'm a great guy and I deserve to be a part of this society and I can do it.
>
> (Adam, Romania)

As evident, the notion of societal development was of pivotal importance for Adam's choice of study destination. Adam's choice of Denmark was related to a wish of becoming an integrated part of the Danish society and on a broader level the 'developed world.' Hence, there was much more to Adam's choice of Denmark than free tuition. While Adam's explanations underline the importance of free tuition, the choice of Denmark was also linked to an imagined global hierarchy of countries and the metanarrative of Western superiority. This observation strengthens the earlier findings presented by Valentin (2015, 2012) of Nepalese students who navigate the global land-scape following an imagined hierarchy of countries and the Chinese students in Fong's (2011) study who aspire to become citizens of the 'developed world' through the means of education abroad. In line with Adam's narrations, there were certain countries and regions with an imagined lower position in a global hierarchy of countries that students generally were eager to avoid. Gojko from Serbia was determined to avoid 'underdeveloped countries' – at least if it was a question of more permanent migration. In addition to the fully funded scholarship, his choice of Denmark was influenced by broader societal concerns such as lifestyle factors and the Scandinavian value system, which he connected to democratic core principles such as 'efficiency' and 'transparency.' Paul specifically pinpointed Russia as the country with a societal model to be avoided at all costs:

> First of all, there is this cultural thing again – it's the big bear, you don't want to go to the big bear. And then you feel that all our aspirations of becoming a prosperous nation are somehow in contradiction with the Russian model, this autocratic whatever, I would not want to go to a country that is regressing in these terms and importantly acute social problems. I'm not going to trade my own little socially impaired country for another one – switch to another disaster. [...] There are very good schools of psychology for instance in Russia so I'm not laughing at their scientific level or whatever, it's only so many people in Romania would not imagine themselves going to Russia or that sort of places.
>
> (Paul, Romania)

It was not only free tuition that influenced Paul's decision. The quote accentuates how he ascribed Denmark's social model a great importance for his choice of study destination and how he did not want to pursue an educa-tion in a country that he deemed to be on a lower or a similar development level as Romania. In his narrations, Russia symbolises the dark past and a social model that Romania desperately had been trying to distance itself from following the end of communism. This made the high academic quality of Russian educational programmes insignificant to Paul. Interestingly, many underlined that Denmark would not have been their first pick, if they could have chosen freely among all study destinations. Despite the fact that the students could not afford the tuition fees required by prestigious universities in the UK and the US, they were convinced of the academic superiority of these institutions when viewed through a global lens, as exemplified by Clara:

> Well, the fact that you don't pay [...] to study here. It's pretty attractive because usually, you want to go to [...] the best and that is England by

far [...] you go to the UK and Cambridge and I don't know which one more Oxford or Stanford. Or is Stanford in the US [...]? Of course, USA would be the best of the best, but England is closer so that would be the first [choice], but for that, you need to make either a loan or to have enough money to pay your tuition fee. So, after that you try to find other places that you can pay less or you don't have to pay at all. Denmark is the only one where you don't have to pay at all.

(Clara, Romania)

Clara's descriptions suggest a hierarchy of study destinations *within* the overarching category of the West. As evident, she would have preferred to study in the UK or the US if she had the necessary funds. Despite the fact that Denmark was not on top of Clara's imaginary ranking of Western destinations, the country represented the most attractive option in light of the money at her disposal. More generally, the specific combination of free tuition or a funded scholarship and the sense of going to a developed country with a high educational level appeared to be fundamental for the students' choice of Denmark.

Conclusions

This chapter drew attention to the complexity that underpins the Eastern European students' choice of pursuing a master's degree in Denmark. I showed how the meanings that the students attached to 'the material environment' (Szewczyk, 2015, p. 154) – that is, the socio-economic, historical, and political context – to which the students were embedded during their upbringing are imperative when seeking to understand *why* they pursue a master's degree in Denmark. The students' narratives suggest that previous generations' forced immobility and resentment to the international travel restrictions imposed during the communist era influenced their wanderlust. Narratives of involuntary immobility have given rise to a narrative of travelling as an intrinsic value – a possibility that new generations, by all means, should exploit.

This chapter also accentuated how the students held the period of communism responsible for, what they described as, disturbing conditions in their home countries. They juxtaposed the lack of development, corruption, and passivity conditions, which in their eyes characterised their home countries – with the stability, prosperity, and progress they saw in the West. Hence, student migration was encouraged by historically laden imaginaries and, in particular, a dominant metanarrative of the West as the incarnation of civilisational advancement. They furthermore saw a close relationship between countries' positioning on the East–West scale and the value of a master's degree and were convinced that they would be positioned more favourably with a 'Western degree' upon their graduation. In their ontological narratives, they evoked a particular story of themselves as 'Eastern

European Westerners,' that is, individuals fit for a Western and modern reality. While narrating their personal stories, they carved out cultural and moral boundaries between themselves and the (in their eyes) less progressive segments of their home countries. I interpreted this tendency as an act of impression management that served to distance the student migrants from the discredited image of the *homo sovieticus*, that is, a person unable to shake old mental habits from the era of communism and embrace a modern, post-communist reality.

While some students saw it as their patriotic duty to return to their home countries, the majority did not foresee an expiration date to their journey and hoped that a foreign education would function as a stepping-stone towards more permanent settlement in the West. Such goals of long-term migration were born out of the absence of a stable and meritocratic economic and political system in their home countries, which they claimed obstructed their ability to achieve different personal goals. This included employment, which reflected their educational level and, more generally, the possibility to act upon curtailed desires. As such, expectations of future unemployment in their home countries functioned as a main impetus for going abroad and seeking out countries with more 'fair' labour markets (see also White, 2010). In their narratives, Denmark – with its well-developed and all-embracing welfare system – signified the direct antithesis to their home countries. Migration was perceived to be instrumental in integrating a sense of symbolic movement and a state of 'normalcy' into their lives, entailing a synergy between their desires and social realities. Hence, motivations for studying abroad often exceeded aims of formal education.

In contrast to the media's portrayal of Eastern European students as 'benefit tourists' taking advantage of the generous Danish welfare system, I elucidated how the student migrants' specific choice of Denmark is the result of a complex interplay between economic and 'non-economic' factors. While factors such as free education and English-medium programs made Denmark accessible, they do by no means explain the students' migration on their own. Indeed, the choice of Denmark was also embedded in the narratives of a global hierarchy of countries and in particular a dominant metanarrative of Western superiority. The perceived 'development level' of Denmark seems particularly important when viewed in light of the students' aspirations of long-term settlement.

I have previously argued that there has been a tendency to treat study abroad as a 'light variant' of migration. The empirical findings presented in this chapter suggest that the boundaries between student mobility and other forms of migration (such as labour migration) have become increasingly blurred – at least when looking at students' initial aspirations. As will be accentuated in the upcoming chapter, plans, ambitions, and narratives of countries are, nonetheless, not static and often shift following actual experiences of residing and studying abroad. The next chapter explores the complex relation between expectations and the students' narrations of their lived realities in Denmark.

Notes

1 A folk high school is a non-formal residential school offering learning opportunities in almost any subject. Most students are between 18 and 24 years old and the length of a typical stay is 4 months. It is a boarding school, so you sleep, eat, study, and spend your spare time at the school. There are no academic requirements for admittance, and there are no exams.
2 For a more detailed discussion of off-shore branch campuses see Waters and Leung (2013).

References

Abbott, P., Wallace, C., Mascauteanu, M., Sapsford, R., 2010. Concepts of citizenship, social and system integration among young people in post-Soviet Moldova. J. Youth Stud. 13, 581–596. https://doi.org/10.1080/13676261.2010.489605

Amit, V., 2011. 'Before I settle down': Youth travel and enduring life course paradigms. Anthropologica 53, 79–88.

Amit, V., 2010. The limits of liminality: Capacities for change and transition among student travellers, in: Rapport, N. (Eds.), Human Nature as Capacity. Berghahn Books, New York.

Appadurai, A., 1996. Modernity at Large: Cultural Dimensions of Globalization. University of Minnesota Press, Minneapolis.

Baas, M., 2010. Imagined Mobility: Migration and Transnationalism Among Indian Students in Australia. Anthem Press, London.

Bakić-Hayden, M., 1995. Nesting orientalisms: The case of former Yugoslavia. Slav. Rev. 54, 917–931. https://doi.org/10.2307/2501399

Benson, M., 2011. The movement beyond (lifestyle) migration: Mobile practices and the constitution of a better way of life. Mobilities, 6, 221–235.

Bourdieu, P., 1984. Distinction: A Social Critique of the Judgement of Taste. Harvard University Press, Cambridge, MA.

Brooks, R., Waters, J., 2011. Fees, funding and overseas study: Mobile UK students and educational inequalities. Sociol. Res. Online 16. https://doi.org/10.5153/sro.2362

Brooks, R., Waters, J., 2010. Social networks and educational mobility: The experiences of UK students. Glob. Soc. Educ. 8, 143–157. https://doi.org/10.1080/14767720903574132

Buchowski, M., 2006. Social thought & commentary: The specter of orientalism in Europe: From exotic other to stigmatized brother. Anthropol. Q. 79, 463–482.

Bygnes, S., Erdal, M.B., 2017. Liquid migration, grounded lives: Considerations about future mobility and settlement among Polish and Spanish migrants in Norway. J. Ethn. Migr. Stud. 43, 102–118. https://doi.org/10.1080/1369183X.2016.1211004

Carlson, S., 2013. Becoming a mobile student – a processual perspective on German degree student mobility. Popul. Space Place 19, 168–180. https://doi.org/10.1002/psp.1749

Copes, H., 2016. A narrative approach to studying symbolic boundaries among drug users: A qualitative meta-synthesis. Crime Media Cult. 12, 193–213. https://doi.org/10.1177/1741659016641720

Cresswell, T., 2006. On the Move: Mobility in the Modern Western World. Routledge, London.

Dombos, T., 2008. 'Longing for the West': The geo-symbolics of the ethical consumption discourse in Hungary, in: Luetchford, P., Neve, G.D., Pratt, J. (Eds.), Hidden Hands in the Market: Ethnographies of Fair Trade, Ethical Consumption and Corporate Social Responsibility. Emerald Group Publishing, Bingley.

Durkheim, É., 1951. Suicide, a Study in Sociology. Free Press, Glencoe, IL.

Eglitis, D.S., 2002. Imagining the Nation: History, Modernity, and Revolution in Latvia, Post-communist Cultural Studies. Pennsylvania State University Press, University Park.

Findlay, A., Prazeres, L., McCollum, D., Packwood, H., 2017. 'It was always the plan': International study as 'learning to migrate.' Area 49, 192–199. https://doi.org/10.1111/area.12315

Fong, V.L., 2011. Paradise Redefined. Stanford University Press, Stanford, CA.

Gałasińska, A., Kozłowska, O., 2009. Discourses of a 'normal life' among post-accession migrants from Poland to Britain, in: Burrell, K. (Ed.), Polish Migration to the UK in the 'New' European Union. Routledge, London and New York.

Galbraith, M., 2003. 'We just want to live normally': Intersecting discourses of public, private, Poland, and the West. J. Soc. Anthropol. Eur. 3, 2–13. https://doi.org/10.1525/JSAE.2003.3.1.2

Ginnerskov-Dahlberg, M., 2021. Inherited dreams of 'the West.' Eastern European students' paths to Denmark, in: Cairns, D. (Ed.), The Palgrave Handbook of Youth Mobility and Educational Migration. Palgrave Macmillan, Basingstoke.

Ginnerskov-Dahlberg, M., Valentin, K., forthcoming. Unpredictable mobilities: Post-graduation trajectories of international students in Denmark.

Goffman, E., 1990. Stigma: Notes on the Management of Spoiled Identity. Penguin Books, Harmondsworth.

Goffman, E., 1963. Stigma: Notes on the Management of Spoiled Identity. Prentice-Hall, Englewood Cliffs, NJ.

Goffman, E., 1956. The Presentation of Self in Everyday Life, University of Edinburgh Social Sciences Research Centre monographs; 2. University of Edinburgh Social Sciences Research Centre, Edinburgh.

Greenberg, J., 2011. On the road to normal: Negotiating agency and state sovereignty in postsocialist Serbia. Am. Anthropol. 113, 88–100. https://doi.org/10.1111/j.1548-1433.2010.01308.x

Hage, G., Papadopoulos, D., 2004. Ghassan Hage in conversation with Dimitris Papadopoulos: Migration, hope and the making of subjectivity in transnational capitalism. Int. J. Crit. Psychol. 12, 95–117.

Halfacree, K., 2004. A utopian imagination in migration's terra incognita? Acknowledging the non-economic worlds of migration decision-making. Popul. Space Place 10, 239–253. https://doi.org/10.1002/psp.326

Holloway, S.L., O'Hara, S.L., Pimlott-Wilson, H., 2012. Educational mobility and the gendered geography of cultural capital: The case of international student flows between Central Asia and the UK. Environ. Plan. Econ. Space 44, 2278–2294. https://doi.org/10.1068/a44655

Horáková, H., 2010. Post-communist transformation of tourism in Czech rural areas: New dilemmas. Anthropol. Noteb. 16, 59–77.

Jansen, S., 2014. On not moving well enough: Temporal reasoning in Sarajevo yearnings for 'normal lives.' Curr. Anthropol. 55, S74–S84. https://doi.org/10.1086/676421

Jansen, S., 2009. After the red passport: Towards an anthropology of the everyday geopolitics of entrapment in the EU's 'immediate outside.' J. R. Anthropol. Inst. 15, 815–832. https://doi.org/10.1111/j.1467-9655.2009.01586.x

Jensen, A.M., 2014. Borderland Cosmopolitans – Normalcy and Europe among Youth in Bosnia. Aarhus University, Aarhus.

Kennedy, M.D., 1994. An introduction to East European ideology and identity in transformation, in: Kennedy, M.D. (Ed.), Envisioning Eastern Europe. Postcommunist Cultural Studies. The University of Michigan Press, Michigan.

Krivonos, D., Näre, L., 2019. Imagining the 'West' in the context of global coloniality: The case of post-Soviet youth migration to Finland. Sociology 53, 1177–1193. https://doi.org/10.1177/0038038519853111

Lamont, M., 1992. Money, Morals, and Manners: The Culture of the French and American Upper-middle Class, Morality and Society. University of Chicago Press, Chicago.

Lamont, M., Aksartova, S., 2002. Ordinary cosmopolitanisms – strategies for bridging racial boundaries among working-class men. Theory Cult. Soc. 19, 1–25. https://doi.org/10.1177/026327640201900400

Lamont, M., Molnár, V., 2002. The study of boundaries in the social sciences. Annu. Rev. Sociol. 28, 167–195. https://doi.org/10.1146/annurev.soc.28.110601.141107

Liechty, M., 2003. Suitably Modern: Making Middle-class Culture in a New Consumer Society. Princeton University Press, Princeton, NJ.

Lopez Rodriguez, M., 2010. Migration and a quest for 'normalcy': Polish migrant mothers and the capitalization of meritocratic opportunities in the UK. Soc. Identities 16, 339–358. https://doi.org/10.1080/13504630.2010.482422

Lulle, A., Buzinska, L., 2017. Between a 'student abroad' and 'being from Latvia': Inequalities of access, prestige, and foreign-earned cultural capital. J. Ethn. Migr. Stud. 43, 1362–1378. https://doi.org/10.1080/1369183X.2017.1300336

Luthra, R., Platt, L., 2016. Elite or middling? International students and migrant diversification. Ethnicities 16, 316–344. https://doi.org/10.1177/1468796815616155

Mai, N., 2001. 'Italy is beautiful': The role of Italian television in the Albanian migratory flow to Italy, in: Russel, K., Wood, N. (Eds.), Media and Migration: Constructions of Mobility and Difference. Routledge, London.

Mai, N., King, R., 2009. Love, sexuality and migration: Mapping the issue(s). Mobilities 4, 295–307. https://doi.org/10.1080/17450100903195318

Manolova, P., 2018. 'Going to the West is my last chance to get a normal life': Bulgarian would-be migrants' imaginings of life in the UK. Cent. East. Eur. Migr. Rev. 8, 1–23. https://doi.org/10.17467/ceemr.2018.01

Manolova, P., 2017. On the Way to the Imaginary West: Bulgarian Migrations, Imaginations, and Disillusionments. (Unpublished thesis). Department of Political Science and International Studies, Birmingham University, Birmingham.

Marcu, S., 2015. Uneven mobility experiences: Life-strategy expectations among Eastern European undergraduate students in the UK and Spain. Geoforum 58, 68–75. https://doi.org/10.1016/j.geoforum.2014.10.017

Mayblin, L., Piekut, A., Valentine, G., 2016. 'Other' posts in 'other' places: Poland through a postcolonial lens? Sociology 50, 60–76. https://doi:10.1177/0038038514556796

Melegh, A., 2006. On the East-West Slope: Globalization, Nationalism, Racism and Discourses on Central and Eastern Europe. Central European University Press, New York.

Misztal, B.A., 2001. Normality and trust in Goffman's theory of interaction order. Sociol. Theory 19, 312–324.

Munk, M.D., 2009. Transnational investments in informational capital: A comparative study of Denmark, France and Sweden. Acta Sociol. 52, 5–23. https://doi.org/10.1177/0001699308100631

Murphy-Lejeune, E., 2002. Student Mobility and Narrative in Europe: The New Strangers, Routledge Studies in Anthropology. Routledge, London.

Olwig, K.F., Valentin, K., 2015. Mobility, education and life trajectories: New and old migratory pathways. Identities 22, 247–257. https://doi.org/10.1080/1070289X.2014.939191

Perkins, R., Neumayer, E., 2014. Geographies of educational mobilities: Exploring the uneven flows of international students. Geogr. J. 180, 246–259. https://doi.org/10.1111/geoj.12045

Péteri, G., 2010. Imagining the West in Eastern Europe and the Soviet Union. University of Pittsburg Press, Pittsburg.

Polkowski, R., 2017. Normality unpacked: Migration, ethnicity and local structure of feeling among Polish migrant workers in Northern Ireland with a comparative perspective on Scotland. J. Ethn. Migr. Stud. 43, 1–17. https://doi.org/10.1080/1369183X.2017.1299621

Rabikowska, M., 2010. Negotiation of normality and identity among migrants from Eastern Europe to the United Kingdom after 2004. Soc. Identities 16, 285–296. https://doi.org/10.1080/13504630.2010.482391

Raghuram, P., 2013. Theorising the spaces of student migration. Popul. Space Place 19, 138–154. https://doi.org/10.1002/psp.1747

Riaño, Y., 2015. Latin American women who migrate for love: Imagining European men as ideal partners, in: Enguix, B., Roca, J. (Eds.), Rethinking Romantic Love: Discussions, Imaginaries and Practices. Cambridge Scholars Publishing, Cambridge, pp. 45–60.

Roberts, K., 2009. Youth in Transition: Eastern Europe and the West. Palgrave Macmillan, Basingstoke.

Robertson, S., 2013. Transnational Student-migrants and the State: The Education-Migration Nexus. Palgrave Macmillan, Basingstoke.

Robertson, S., Runganaikaloo, A., 2014. Lives in limbo: Migration experiences in Australia's education–migration nexus. Ethnicities 14, 208–226. https://doi.org/10.1177/1468796813504552

Said, E.W., 1978. Orientalism. Pantheon Books, New York.

Salazar, N.B., 2011. The power of imagination in transnational mobilities. Identities 18, 576–598. https://doi.org/10.1080/1070289X.2011.672859

Sayer, A., 2005. Class, moral worth and recognition. Sociology 39, 947–963. https://doi.org/10.1177/0038038505058376

Somers, M.R., 1994. The narrative constitution of identity: A relational and network approach. Theory Soc. 23, 605–649. https://doi-org.ezproxy.its.uu.se/10.1007/BF00992905

Soong, H., 2014. Transnational Students and Mobility: Lived Experiences of Migration. Routledge, London.

Spasic, I., 2012. Yugoslavia as a place for living a normal life: Memories of ordinary people in Serbia. Sociologija 54, 577–594. https://doi.org/10.2298/SOC1204577S

Szewczyk, A., 2015. 'European generation of migration': Change and agency in the post-2004 Polish graduates' migratory experience. Geoforum 60, 153–162. https://doi.org/10.1016/j.geoforum.2015.02.001

Sztompka, P., 2004. From East Europeans to Europeans: Shifting collective identities and symbolic boundaries in the New Europe. Eur. Rev. 12, 481–496. https://doi.org/10.1017/S1062798704000420

Thøgersen, S., 2012. Chinese students' great expectations: Prospective pre-school teachers on the move. Learn. Teach. 5, 75–93. https://doi.org/10.3167/latiss.2012.050305

Tomanović, S., Ignjatović, S., 2006. The transition of young people in a transitional society: The case of Serbia. J. Youth Stud. 9, 269–285. https://doi.org/10.1080/13676260600805648

Valentin, K., 2015. Transnational education and the remaking of social identity: Nepalese student migration to Denmark. Identities 22, 318–332. https://doi.org/10.1080/1070289X.2014.939186

Valentin, K., 2012. Caught between internationalisation and immigration: The case of Nepalese students in Denmark. Learn. Teach. 5, 56–74. https://doi.org/10.3167/latiss.2012.050304

Van Mol, C., 2014. Post-industrial society and European integration, in: Van Mol, C. (Ed.), Intra-European Student Mobility in International Higher Education Circuits: Europe on the Move, Palgrave Studies in Global Higher Education. Palgrave Macmillan, London, pp. 23–39. https://doi.org/10.1057/9781137355447_2

Vigh, H., 2009. Wayward migration: On imagined futures and technological voids. Ethnos 74, 91–109. https://doi.org/10.1080/00141840902751220

Waters, J., Brooks, R., Pimlott-Wilson, H., 2011. Youthful escapes? British students, overseas education and the pursuit of happiness. Soc. Cult. Geogr. 12, 455–469. https://doi.org/10.1080/14649365.2011.588802

Waters, J., Leung, M., 2013. Immobile transnationalisms? Young people and their *in situ* experiences of 'international' education in Hong Kong. Urban Stud. 50, 606–620. https://doi.org/10.1177/0042098012468902

Waters, J.L., 2006. Geographies of cultural capital: Education, international migration and family strategies between Hong Kong and Canada. Trans. Inst. Br. Geogr. 31, 179–192. https://doi.org/10.1111/j.1475-5661.2006.00202.x

White, A., 2010. Young people and migration from contemporary Poland. J. Youth Stud. 13, 565–580. https://doi.org/10.1080/13676261.2010.487520

Wilken, L., Dahlberg, M.G., 2017. Between international student mobility and work migration: Experiences of students from EU's newer member states in Denmark. J. Ethn. Migr. Stud. 43, 1347–1361. https://doi.org/10.1080/1369183X.2017.1300330

4 'Thrivers' and 'dead guys'

The lives of Eastern European students in the West

The previous chapter focused on the Eastern European students' motivations for pursuing post-graduate studies in Denmark and how they connected a Danish master's degree to hopes of existential movement and aspirations of achieving a state of (personal and societal) 'normalcy.' It accentuated how a sole focus on financial incentives is insufficient for capturing the complexity of the students' mobility, but that the specific social context of the students' home countries and dominant metanarratives of Eastern and Western Europe constitute vital components for understanding the attraction of an education in Denmark. By shedding light on the students' narratives of living and studying abroad, this chapter seeks to highlight how narratives are shaped, changed, and transformed in the process of student migration. Particular attention is devoted to students from European Union (EU) countries and their narrations of selfhood in relation to the material and symbolic boundaries they encounter in Denmark. The comparison between narratives of non-EU students funded by scholarships and (predominantly) self-financing EU students serves to illustrate the ways that structural factors, such as the money at one's disposal, affect students' experiences of studying abroad. Thus, the empirical findings discussed in this chapter accentuate how the EU integration process positions student migrants differently abroad depending on their home country's EU membership status and, fundamentally, their possibilities for receiving financial support.

An unprecedented level of precariousness: finding a job (fast!)

I have already emphasised how the Eastern European students found their agency curtailed by the prospect of limited jobs upon graduation and low-income levels in their home countries, which in turn strengthened their dependency on the financial support of their parents. Since this financial support model often ended upon their arrival to Denmark, many were – potentially for the first time in their lives – economically on their own. While there is a growing awareness of the multiple roles that international students fill abroad (Raghuram, 2013), their experiences as workers while studying have been neglected in the literature (Gilmartin et al., 2020). For the students in this study who did not receive any economic support from a scholarship or from their parents, employment played a fundamental role in their ability to sustain themselves in their new country of residence. Finding a job thus constituted a top priority upon their arrival to Denmark and it was often a question of getting a job or returning to one's home country. Their situation is highly similar to the Eastern European migrants interviewed by Violetta Parutis (2014) following their migration to the UK:

> When they arrive in the United Kingdom, the migrants' first concerns relate to finding a source of income on which they could survive. Therefore, they search for 'any job' that would pay their living and subsistence costs in London.
>
> (p. 41)

Like the migrants in Parutis' study, my interlocutors were basically interested in finding 'any job.' In light of their dependence on a stable income abroad, it is hardly surprising that they experienced the job search as highly stressful. Etel and Maria gave almost identical accounts of the at-times nerve-wracking process:

> I came to Denmark with very little money and I came in August, you know my study program started in September and I knew that I had just enough money to pay the deposit and the two months' rent. So, I knew that if I did not find a job until the end of October, I knew that my money is over and I had to go home.
>
> (Etel, Hungary)

> Well, I arrived in the middle of August and I started looking for something in the end of September. I had planned that I could pay the rent and eat for I think up to three or four months, so I knew that I needed to get a job or something.
>
> (Maria, Estonia)

Both students depict a time characterised by a high degree of insecurity with just enough money to cover their basic needs. Even though Maria and Etel had been aware of the necessity of getting a job, they were completely taken off guard by the few jobs available in Denmark – despite their openness to 'any job.' A lack of social network, limited knowledge of the Danish language, and limited work experience mean that international students generally have a limited range of jobs to choose from (Wilken and Dahlberg, 2017).

There was a noticeable difference between the level of stress experienced by students from the EU and those from non-EU countries. While the latter group was comparatively financially secure abroad due to their scholarship (some even managed to send some money to their families at home), most

EU movers were from the get-go worried if the lack of money would constitute a potential barrier for their studies in Denmark. This pressure was
aggravated by the fact that they did not want to burden their parents. Akin
to the international students in Erlenawati Sawir et al.'s (2009, p. 468) study
in New Zealand, my interlocutors described a 'moral obligation' to support
themselves abroad. Sawir et al.'s findings highlight how students sponsored
by their parents are particularly exposed abroad due to their lack of financial means (see also Pan, 2011). As Paul noted, relying on financial support
from your parents is never an optimal situation: 'If you have the money
from your parents it's a bad situation because you are depending on other
people.' In fact, many of my interlocutors initially regarded Denmark as an
optimal opportunity to break with patterns of intergenerational financial
dependence. Ania had aspirations of becoming entirely reliant on herself
while studying in Denmark to avoid placing additional financial pressure
on her parents. Prior to her departure, her parents had already found themselves in a financially challenging situation and, in line with the students'
descriptions above, she was acutely aware that she had to find a paid job to
continue studying in Denmark:

> I was saying to myself I will manage. I think I'm kind of self-confident
> and kind of decided that I, for a certain period of time, I will have to
> cope in a difficult situation and I was aware that I'm going to work and
> study and yeah if I decide to do that, it was clear for me, like I knew it,
> I knew that I'm going to find a job because otherwise I could not study
> in Denmark. And it was actually why I was fighting – it was to maintain
> my studies.
>
> (Ania, Poland)

Ania described her first time in Denmark as a period characterised by financial and emotional struggling, where she more or less had to manage on her
own. The high level of stress weakened her health and she even started to
lose her hair (see also Maury, 2020). Her deteriorating mental and physical health, she claimed, was the result of her precarious situation and not
knowing whether or not she eventually would have to 'throw in the towel'
and return to Poland without a Danish master's degree. Her experience of
hardship was intensified by the fact that she initially came to Denmark to
live with her Danish boyfriend whom she had met as an Erasmus student.
However, just before Ania's arrival to Denmark, he had ended their relationship and she decided to move into the apartment of a Polish friend who
lived in a smaller town approximately 30 minutes away from the city centre
and the university. Ania estimated that she sent out between 150 and 200
job applications during her first months in Denmark before finally managing
to get a job in a smaller city one hour away from her residence. Due to the
geographical distance between her home and first job, she eventually found
employment as a temporary worker, meaning that she often on very short

notice was asked to perform different job tasks (mostly cleaning). Despite the poor working conditions, she described the job as an 'injection of relief' since it facilitated the possibility to get the Danish student stipend.

Despite the fact that students from EU countries enjoyed the privilege of being EU 'free movers,' few seemed prepared for the precarious life conditions that awaited them abroad. While Denmark initially represented an independence-making project, most of the students experienced the range of new responsibilities facing them abroad as overwhelming. In their study of young Romanian return-migrants, Dumitru Sandu et al. (2018) note how their research subjects were challenged by the unprecedented levels of freedom from parental interference while living in Western European countries. For the young Romanians, these unforeseen levels of independence affected their integration into the new societies negatively and eventually prompted the return of many. Certainly, for the student migrants in this study, the level of insecurity they encountered in Denmark stood in sharp contrast to the social security that they initially expected to find in a country with a strong welfare state. Before pursuing a master's degree in Denmark, Ania connected Scandinavia to high living standards and a place where 'people are just very relaxed and everything pretty much secured.' It was almost as if Ania believed that the protection offered by the Danish welfare state would smoothen the transition from her parents. However, in spite of her rough beginning, she remained hopeful that she was heading towards the secure and peaceful lifestyle that in her mind characterised the lives of Scandinavian citizens. According to Michaela Benson (2011, p. 226), migrants' initial motivations for moving – that is, their pre-migratory imaginings and quality of the lives that they sought – constitute essential components for understanding their justification for their continued presence within a destination. In line with Benson's observation, Ania stuck long to the belief that the struggle and hardship were temporary and that the situation only would last 'for a certain period.' Thus, the students' pre-mobility aspirations continued to play a significant role in framing their expectations of life in Denmark irrespective of initial start-up difficulties.

In no-job-land: Peter and Adam

I met Peter during the introduction weeks for international students and hung out with him on a frequent basis during his first months in Denmark. We often went to the city centre and participated in various social events mainly targeted at international students. Yet, towards the end of the first semester, I increasingly lost track of his whereabouts. In August 2014 – approximately one year after our first meeting – I met up with Peter at a café in Copenhagen where he had moved to pursue a new master's programme at Copenhagen University. He enthusiastically revealed that he had just gotten a room at a very good and central dormitory. A while into our conversation, I asked him more specifically about his experience of being a student and living in Denmark. He told me that he had felt very lonely and isolated during much of the time in Denmark. Despite the fact that we had been close during this period, I had seemingly missed important nuances of his stay in Denmark and the depth of his worries. He hoped that the new dorm in Copenhagen would constitute a window for socialising and creating a broader social network of local students.

Our conversation in Copenhagen predominantly focused on his initial struggles in Denmark, and he painted a bleak picture of his time abroad. According to Peter, these struggles were primarily rooted in financial problems and the fact that he had been unable to get a job in Denmark. The situation had at times made him incapable of getting up in the morning and he explained how often he would 'just lie in bed without being able to move.' After running out of money, Peter went back to Hungary to live with his parents for a while but eventually returned to Denmark with the help of his grandmother. With an awkward smile, he explained that he had received the money that his grandmother had saved for her own funeral – something which made him even more determined to make it in the West. Despite the fact that his initial attempt to establish a life in Denmark had failed, he remained hopeful that his second attempt abroad would be successful.

For Peter, who dreamed about being able to support both friends and family from a financially secure platform in Denmark, the pressure to succeed in Denmark was substantial. Similar to Marcu's (2015) study on Eastern European students in Spain, which accentuated how educational mobility was a part of a collective aspiration of securing financial stability for the entire family, it was not only Peter's well-being and dreams which were at stake but the well-being of his immediate family. There is a striking resemblance between Peter's and Adam's narrations. In Chapter 3, I highlighted how Adam had been focused on going from Romania to a 'developed country' while he, by all means, wanted to steer clear of 'Arabian countries.' Like Peter, Adam had also planned for longer-term settlement in Denmark:

> I wanted to live in Denmark, contribute to Denmark, pay my taxes, pay my everything and just be a part of it. I wanted to stay with my family abroad, it was 100 per cent for me. I mean you may or may not believe me but my whole intention was just to be a part of Denmark.
>
> (Adam, Romania)

However, contrary to Peter, who resided in Denmark due to the financial assistance of his grandmother, Adam returned to his parent's house in Romania without completing his master's degree after only six months abroad. Like many of my interlocutors, he was completely caught off guard by the high cost of living in Denmark. Even though his father gave him 3000 euros to manage during the first months, he quickly realised that the money was not going to last long in a country with the highest price level of consumer goods and services in the entire EU. While Adam initially remained enrolled at the university in Denmark, he officially dropped out when he found employment in Romania. Before our conversation, I had only heard casual stories about him from students who attended the same educational programme as him. Several referred to him as 'this Eastern European guy' who was desperate to find a paid job and who seldom showed up to class at the university. Moreover, his classmates were unaware of what had happened to him. The fact that his peers neither knew his name nor current whereabouts provided a further indication that he had not been an integrated part of the social environment at the university. My relation to Adam was different from most other interlocutors in the sense that I did not talk to him until *after* he physically had left Denmark. I met him on Skype shortly after he had moved back to his home country, where he painted a dreary picture of his brief encounter with Denmark:

> It was a hard period. Actually, it was the saddest period of my life. I was so depressed and angry all the time because of the job thing, so I was always having fights with my parents and with my girlfriend. I did not have a depression – that is a really bad thing, but I was depressed, I had depressive symptoms. I did not have a lot of classes – once or twice a week – so I had five days a week to look for jobs. I remember going with my CVs to bars and cleaning companies, anything, I was so desperate. I wanted to do anything just to make some money.
>
> (Adam, Romania)

Adam described how he, in Denmark, became increasingly frustrated with the failed attempts of finding a job and the Danish employers' unwillingness to hire him. He was continuously informed that familiarity with the Danish language was a requirement for getting a job. Similar to Peter's descriptions, the feeling of constant failure and rejection made him increasingly despondent:

> During that period, I did not find any reason to wake up in the morning. I woke up at seven o'clock, I had classes and I just felt that there is no reason for me to go to classes so I just kept on sleeping to twelve. For example, I had days when I told my dad I'm going to look for a job but I told him that and after that I just went back to bed. I just did not have any hopes anymore and was lying to my parents that I was still trying but I actually was not trying any more. When I was trying, I told you I was going around with printed CVs, I actually tried to get council help from the university, someone who specialised in making CVs, he gave me some tips, I followed the tips, I modified my CV, but still nothing. I gave the CV to managers for bars, cleaning companies, anywhere but no luck nowhere for six months. I tried but nothing ever happened.
>
> (Adam, Romania)

Adam's explanations illustrate how he felt entirely outside the Danish society during his short period in Denmark. The day he decided to leave the country was the same day he called the Danish study stipend office to ask for their financial assistance. When they turned his desperate plea down, Adam decided that it was time for him to return to Romania:

> The day I decided to leave was the day I called the SU office and of course I knew that I had a stupid question – they were not willing to give me money without having a job – but I asked them: 'What do I need to do in this situation, I don't have any money, I'm a student so I belong to this university, and I literally don't have any money, can you help me in any way.' And they just told me: 'We never had this situation before; we just don't have any procedures for this. This never happened to us, so, we don't know what to do. Bye bye.' I just cried after I had this phone conversation. I just started crying on the street. I realised that I'm not going to make it in Denmark, I'm a dead guy, I cannot make it. I called my dad and I told him: 'Dad, I've lost, I cannot do it.' It was really bad. I'm proud that I passed that moment, I'm so sorry that I have sad memories about living in Denmark because I really like Denmark, it's a really nice country, but the system was not prepared for a guy going there with no more than 3000 euros in his pocket.
>
> (Adam, Romania)

Denmark was nothing like Adam had imagined from afar and aspirations of becoming a full-blown member of the Danish society never materialised. The stories by Adam and Peter provide an honest window into how being in a financially unstable situation affect students' overall well-being and sense of self tremendously. As indicated, financial instability was a particularly prevalent life-condition among students from EU member states.

A discrepancy between past and present

During an interview with Francesca, an Italian master's student studying in Denmark, she highlighted the financial dissimilarities in the student body and the particularly precarious situation of Eastern European students. In contrast to most of her Eastern European classmates, Francesca's parents continued to support her on a monthly basis during her stay abroad and when I asked whether she planned to get a job, she laughingly replied:

FRANCESCA: No, not at all. Not at all.

METTE: But is it your impression that some students have a harder time financially?

FRANCESCA: Yeah, yeah, yeah, yeah. Especially the students from Eastern Europe, they have I guess way more problems...

METTE: How do you sense that?

FRANCESCA: Well for example when we go out for drinks you always have someone who says 'but that place is way too expensive' or 'I cannot afford spending 50 kroner for just one beer' or 'I mean 50 kroner is way too much so let's go to another bar.' Or people that don't go out at all because they cannot afford it, so yeah.

METTE: Do you find that uncomfortable?

FRANCESCA: Well, it's not uncomfortable but it's like … it's weird when you don't have the money issues and someone else does, it's always weird, I guess.

(Francesca, Italy)

Francesca was not reliant on finding a job nor pressured by the thought of receiving money from her parents. Even though Francesca had moved to a new country, her every day still has more or less the same tempo and structure as in Italy: It predominantly revolved around life at the university such as going to classes and socialising with friends and classmates. In noticeable contrast, Francesca's classmate Paul experienced a significant discrepancy between his life in Romania and his new realities in Denmark. As the majority of Eastern European students, Paul was fully supported economically by his parents while studying in his country of origin. Both of his parents were well educated, had good jobs, and could offer a comfortable upbringing for Paul and his sibling. While residing in Romania, he was not dependent on an income from a job next to his studies but was, like Francesca, mostly preoccupied with activities related to his studies and hanging out with friends. However, His accustomed lifestyle was put to a test abroad when confronted with an unprecedented focus on money abroad. While Paul had lived a more or less carefree life in Romania, he quickly discovered that the money he got from his parents only covered fundamental needs in Denmark. Moreover, his parents could only offer him financial support at the beginning of his stay. In one of our conversations, he reflected on his financial situation in Denmark versus life in Romania:

PAUL: I was not used to counting every penny I had.

METTE: You did that in Denmark?

PAUL: Yes, I was counting my money – sometimes even during class. I would just [count] for a matter of five or ten seconds, which would not go on for a half an hour, but I would know if I go shopping in the afternoon then I have that very, very small amount of money.

(Paul, Romania)

Paul's explanation accentuates the discrepancy between his life in Romania and Denmark. In Denmark, he suddenly had to think carefully and strategically about how to spend his money. The tight budget left him with limited room for engaging in costly social activities such as going to bars and restaurants in the city centre. The quote above indicates how financial concerns would occupy his mind even while attending classes at the university. The mental pressure from being in a precarious situation also manifested itself in physical ways:

> And also, there is a physical thing in it, because I was really losing a lot of pounds and at some point, I called [a friend] and I asked her: 'Do you think I'm really thin? Do you think I'm really thin? Tell me am I terribly thin! Do you look at me on the street and think: That guy, oh, how thin he is?' So, I'm telling you the financial thing is quite complex and it leads to all sort of stuff.
>
> (Paul, Romania)

Paul's explanations suggest a case of what Michael Bury (1982, p. 169) calls a 'biographical disruption' – entailing a situation whereby the structures of an individual's everyday life and the forms of knowledge which underpin them become disrupted. Aside from worries related to making ends meet, Paul felt troubled by the thought of burdening his parents financially by studying in Denmark. His sentiments are highly similar to those described by Susan Thomas (2017) in her study of Indian students in New York. She uses the term 'educational debts' to capture the different forms of indebtedness that structure these young people's educational migration, one of the pronounced sense of indebtedness being towards their parents (Thomas, 2017, p. 1881). To halt his parental dependence and ease the sense of indebtedness, Paul opted for a job as a newspaper deliverer during the night during his second year in Denmark.

Elena had also calculated on a stable income from a part-time job in Denmark when she initially decided to pursue an education abroad. She had been confident that the job hunt would be successful due to her multifaceted experience from previous work – after all, she had worked for several years after obtaining her master's degree from a Romanian university. The greater the surprise, when she discovered that previously acquired merits and skills appeared to be of little help in finding a job:

ELENA: Yes, I actually thought that I could find a job – definitely that was my plan. In the beginning, I knew that if I wanted to do something that I like, I'm supposed to work, right, but in the end, I had to live with quite little. You know, just think about my rent mainly and then do program stuff, I mean, to make a very strict schedule what I'm doing and what I'm wasting or spending, because in the end, my parents paid for my rent.

METTE: But do you think it's very difficult to get jobs in general?

ELENA: Yes, it's very difficult. I mean, I did not imagine, I thought: 'Okay, I have some work experience.' I think for everybody it's quite annoying, which is, I don't know, it's not fair.

(Elena, Romania)

Despite unemployment, she could stay in Denmark with the financial help from her family in Romania – money which barely covered rent and food. Since she had been working full-time in Romania, life in Denmark presented itself as very different from the one she left behind: From having been a financially independent woman with a (comparatively) good salary, she became entirely reliant on the financial goodwill of her parents. As emphasised, many students were attracted to the idea of gaining a newfound sense of independence by moving abroad. However, Elena's narrations suggest a case of a reversed 'independence narrative', since foreign education did not result in increased *independence* but rather brought her to a stage of almost complete financial parental *dependence*. The fact that she was incapable of finding a job in Denmark entailed that she, like Paul, had to choose both wisely and strategically when deciding to spend her money – or rather, as she explained, how *not* to spend:

> I'm really, like, trying to live with little, little, little – that's the thing, I'm saving. It's sometimes too much to say that I'm saving, I'm actually trying not to spend [laughing]. Saving seems to me like something that you add up but that does not happen and yeah, I'm trying… I mean I have been applying for jobs, nobody wants to get me but it's fine.
>
> (Elena, Romania)

Although Elena did not find her previous job in Romania intellectually stimulating, it was rather well paid and allowed her to lead a comfortable life *inside* the borders of Romania. Moreover, back then she was not confronted with the burdensome sense of guilt from burdening her parents financially with *her* choice of studying abroad. While drinking a cup of coffee at the university canteen, she told me how the feeling of living on a 'day-to-day' basis and not knowing if she would have enough money to pay the next month's rent filled her with anxiety. I felt her frustration very clearly when, during one of our interviews, she broke down in tears when explaining me about her life conditions. In line with the student narrations discussed in the previous section, she developed a depression-like condition and it became increasingly difficult for me to get in contact with her. One day I noticed that she had uploaded a photo on a social media platform stating: 'All your dreams have been cancelled' and shortly after this I discovered that she had returned to Romania.

One could argue that Paul and Elena were privileged in the sense that they both received small sums of money to cover their basic needs from their family. Nonetheless, both students expressed how they felt completely worn out by their situation in Denmark, especially towards the end of their studies. They increasingly condemned themselves to what Polina Manolova (2017, p. 224) has referred to as an 'ascetic lifestyle,' which means that they cut back on expenses not directly related to their subsistence while subjecting themselves to material privation and social isolation. In

Manolova's study of young Bulgarians migrating to the UK, she accentuates how this life condition affected the migrants' physical and psychological well-being enormously. As I will return to, my interlocutors' modest life-style created, akin to Manolova's descriptions, the foundation for a sense of loneliness when alienating them from the environment around the university and more broadly the Danish society. While the previous chapter showed how many of the students experienced a sense of stagnation in their home countries due to the socio-political milieu they had to navigate in on a daily basis, their frustrations were in most cases not caused by the lack of money. Although the students found the low salary level in their home countries discouraging, they did not have an everyday characterised by economic deprivation or struggling. Elena's previous salary in Romania was low when compared to Danish standards, but it was, nonetheless, of a similar level to most Romanians in the same social fraction. The shift, when it comes to the nature of the students' frustrations, is essential in order to understand their experience of their new realities in Denmark. The following section delves further into the EU movers' process of coming to terms with an imposed alternation of their ontological narratives.

Coming to terms with new ontological narratives

It has already been established how many of my interlocutors from EU countries became dependent on low-skilled employment (often as cleaners, bartenders, or as newspaper deliverers) next to their studies in order to sustain themselves in Denmark. Often these jobs represented their first encounter with physical labour and the level of exhaustion that accompanied this type of work caught many by surprise – not least the extent that it complicated their ability to keep up with their studies (see also Gilmartin et al., 2020; Pan, 2011). For Ania, the manual labour was so tiresome that she lacked the motivation to study after work. This realisation made her conclude 'that it's not so easy to combine both studies and physical work.' Thus, the cleaning job – her only financial lifeline in Denmark – conflicted with her ability to keep up with her studies at the university. Maria from Estonia and Bogdan from Romania painted almost identical pictures of how their level of concentration suffered from the substantial time that they invested in their part-time jobs. The many hours of work every day negatively affected Maria's ability to concentrate and she would often prepare for classes on the bus. Sometimes she even had to skip classes because of her demanding work schedule. As a consequence of her realities in Denmark, she went on an Erasmus exchange to another EU country with a markedly lower cost of living to 'breathe' and rekindle with her studies far away from the pressure of a demanding job and assisted by the financial aid from an Erasmus scholarship. Eventually, the unsatisfactory study conditions caused Maria to end her studies in Denmark before graduating.

Similar to the students' descriptions above, Bogdan explained how his daily routine of 'working, sleeping for two hours now, waking up and doing something and then sleeping again' made him feel dizzy. While a diligent student in Romania, he had to lower his ambition levels considerably in Denmark and felt obliged to postpone several of his exams. A Danish master's degree has an estimated duration of two years, yet for Bogdan, it took more than four years to graduate. His master's thesis was the only written exam for which he had received the top grade (12) and he added that this was the only time where he did not work during the night while writing and preparing the paper. Juggling the roles of 'university student' and 'manual labourer' simultaneously constituted a demanding task for many students. The low-skilled work kept them at bay from their studies and their wish of becoming the student they initially aspired to be or used to be before moving to Denmark. According to Suzanne Huot and Debbie Rudman (2010), migration from one country to another often entails a shift of a particular physical, economic, political, social, and cultural context for another. This shift of contexts may pose a challenge to people's possibility to sustain their accustomed occupations – that is, the everyday routines and interactions that were commonplace in the initial setting. As Somers (1994,1992) notes, narrative identities are never complete but moulded by the context. Indeed, the results of this study suggest that physical mobility may challenge people's ability to keep up with certain ontological narratives and accustomed roles central to these narratives.

To get a better comprehension of Bogdan's frustrations in Denmark, it is important to understand his dedication to playing the role that he associate with the narrative of an intellectual – a role which, in his view, did not harmonise well with the role of a manual labourer. In Romania, his every day mostly revolved around reading and writing and, before departing to Denmark, he had just published his first book. During my visit to Romania, I followed him to one of his poetry readings in an old theatre in his hometown. While he read a collection of his poems aloud to an enthusiastic and engaged audience, I thought about the marked contrast between the surroundings and people at the theatre and the Danish newspaper central's inane environment. I wrote the following in my field notes: 'In a way it is absurd that the man who delivers newspapers during the night in Denmark also is a skilled and locally renowned poet in Romania.' Seeing Bogdan in his accustomed milieu accentuated how far away life in Denmark was from his 'old' self in Romania. It offered me a deeper understanding of why he frequently drew attention to the enormous gap between his then-current realities and the life he initially had imagined when applying for the master's programme. At times, he felt like a *stranger* to the ontological narrative his current circumstances forced upon him. As Goffman (1956, p. 22) reminds us, we tend to invest our egos in specific routines and some roles are more important for us than others. Moreover, divestment passages – entailing a separation from one's accustomed status for an uncertain duration – involving the identities most dear to us seem to have the most deleterious effects on our sense of self (Ezzy, 1993). For Bogdan, educational mobility led to a 'biographical shift' from 'a perceived normal trajectory through relatively predictable chronological steps to one fundamentally abnormal and to some extent inwardly damaging' (Bury, 1982, p. 171).

There appear to be several reasons why the job as a newspaper deliverer affected Bogdan's mental health negatively. First, the job was physically draining. As underlined in the quote above, the lack of sleep made him feel dizzy and low-spirited. During one of our encounters, he described a feeling of not existing during the days and that his bleak situation caused his consumption of cigarettes to escalate dramatically. Secondly, Bogdan's performances made it difficult for him to uphold certain ontological narratives but installed the sense in him of having a diminished self. Identities require continual legitimation (Ezzy, 1993; Goffman, 1990; Huot and Rudman, 2010) and although Bogdan perceived himself as an intellectual, there was an alarming mismatch between his ontological narrative and his everyday performances, which paved the way for a discordant relationship between his internal and external realities. Bogdan's experience strengthens Douglas Ezzy's (1993) point that failure to sustain a meaningful life may have a direct impact on an individual's psychological integrity.

The inability to engage in social involvements conducive to the performance of valued identities and roles also affected Paul's well-being, especially towards the end of his studies. Akin to Bogdan, he presented an ontological narrative of himself as a diligent student during his bachelor's degree in Romania. Paul, however, became increasingly filled with despair when the lack of money in combination with a time-consuming job as a newspaper deliverer denied him the possibility to perform the roles central for upholding a positive ontological narrative:

> So, in the month before I got the newspaper delivery job, I knew that my parents are not sending me any more money and that month I had the exams – the summer exams – and so I was looking for a job and doing the exams and I only completed one exam out of three. So, I always had the feeling that I'm screwing up my whole academic education because of my financial situation. And then, I remembered that I went through the re-exams when I already had the job in newspaper delivery. And I went to the re-exam and I could not do the exam, so I picked out a subject and I did not know too much about it and I remember that I was quite in shock that I was in a situation where I was clueless about the exam because I was working during the night and it was really difficult to study. And I was thinking, well this is a wonderful situation. This is truly wonderful! The whole situation is completely pointless you know.
>
> (Paul, Romania)

Paul became increasingly frustrated and saddened by his situation in Denmark and the sense that what previously had felt like a promising academic career was slowly but steadily slipping through his fingers. The sense that his days were dominated by an uninspiring part-time job in combination with a constant focus on money gradually paved the way for a complete 'disconnection' from his university studies:

> Rather it was sort of a physical depletion that leads to sort of an emotional and motivational depletion, so I did not really care too much about my studies when then the third semester started. I was sort of disconnected from the whole thing and I was saying that the only reason for this whole disconnection was this financial fiasco.
>
> (Paul, Romania)

Paul's depictions of his everyday life in Denmark revolved around a plethora of negative emotions and, in particular, the ways his mental health had suffered from his precarious situation abroad. The feeling of not knowing where his academic journey would end filled him with anxiety and made him question the logic behind having gone to Denmark. As argued by Huot and Rudman (2010), the range of occupations people engage in directly contributes to, confirms, and re-affirms people's identities over time as they form daily routines and interact with others on an ongoing basis. Paul's situation, and the sense that his life was deprived of any meaningful 'performances,' was also the reason why he eventually returned to Romania to write up his master's thesis from his parents' house despite initially being against the idea.

Dirty, dull, and dangerous jobs

Previous studies (Campbell et al., 2016; Pan, 2011; Robertson, 2013) have drawn attention to the financial vulnerability that surrounds the lives of some international students. This life condition abroad turns student migrants into easy prey for crafty employers, who may offer wages considerably below that of the average citizen as well as other unfavourable work conditions. As accentuated in Chapter 1, a report from 2017 on the working conditions of Eastern European students in Denmark suggested that their job dependence makes them particularly exposed to labour market exploitation (Scheuer, 2017). In fact, several of my interlocutors told me stories of how employers knowingly had exploited their desperation for employment – thereby taking advantage of workers whose residence depends on their access to paid work, using them as a source of cheap labour (Maury, 2020). While drinking a cup of coffee together at the university canteen, Borge told me that he and his wife, who recently joined him from Romania, were involved in a legal trial against his previous Danish employer who consistently had paid him considerably less than the hours he had worked. According to Borge, he had consistently been underpaid, entailing that his salary did not accurately reflect the hours he had spent cleaning. Etel, who came to Denmark with limited money in her pocket, found herself in a similar situation. Like Borge, she was subjected to exploitation at work:

> At first, I had two jobs; one was a bartender job without a contract and [...] one was a cleaning job at a hotel and in that hotel there were only international students and international people working. [...] no Dane would ever take such a job [...]. So only the boss was Danish. All the workers were international [...]. I had to clean rooms but for every room, I got like 12 minutes to clean – that was the system. So, if I cleaned 10 rooms it meant that I got paid for 120 minutes. I got paid for two hours' work. But nobody cared if I spent one hour in one room because it was so messy; still I got paid 12 minutes per room.
>
> (Etel, Hungary)

Regardless of the poor working conditions, which confronted Etel on an everyday basis, she remained an employee at the hotel for much longer than she would have preferred due to a lack of viable alternatives. A university degree in Denmark was for her synonymous with 'humiliating working conditions,' where she felt deprived of the possibility of saying 'no' because she feared that she would be forced to return to Hungary. Maria from Estonia described a similar situation. After discovering that her Danish employer did not pay her commensurate with the hours she had worked, she wanted to resign. Her dependency on some income, however, hindered her from doing so: 'People don't understand that it's not a possibility to quit the job. I mean, you really need the money.'

Stories of students being exploited at the workplace appear to be indicative of an employment pattern, where Danish companies offer students from EU countries contracts of 10–12 hours of work per week, which enables them to get the SU, but which in reality requires that they work more (Scheuer, 2017; Wilken and Dahlberg, 2017). Some worked without an official contract, which positioned them in a legal grey zone despite their – in theory – privileged status as EU movers (Simola, 2018). For obvious reasons, illicit employment conditions were a difficult subject to discuss with students, since they dreaded the potential repercussions of having taken up semi-legal employment in Denmark. Adam, for instance, only confided to me years after he had left Denmark that he had worked without a contract in Denmark.

Etel's characterisation of the staff at her workplace was very similar to the environment I encountered when accompanying Bogdan to the newspaper central – namely a workforce dominated by foreign workers. Etel experienced a marked difference between her situation and Danish citizens, whom, she believed, would never have accepted a job on similar premises. In her study of

Chinese students in Ireland, Darcy Pan (2011) shows how her interlocutors were subjected to discrimination at work ranging from bullying and harassment to poor pay conditions. Pan contends that there was a racialised dimension to Chinese students' experience, which in turn had a negative impact on their interaction within the Irish society. Focusing on the experience of post-socialist migrants, Barbara Samaluk (2016) similarly argues that the orientalisation of Central and Eastern Europe legitimises local employers' unequal treatment of these individuals. Indeed, the student migrants in this present study had a strong sense of being employed on markedly different terms than locals. Etel felt as if she was confronted with a European hierarchy at work, since it in particular was the Eastern European workers who were doing the 'dirty, dull and dangerous' work (Favell, 2008, p. 704). Akin to Pan's (2011) descriptions, the sketchy jobs fostered a sense of alienation towards the Danish society when Etel had to accept certain employment conditions that other (i.e. Western) people, in her mind, were unwilling to subject themselves to. This sense of gradual alienation was enforced by other incidences such as Danish employers consistently offering Etel a lower salary – a pattern she attributed to her Eastern European 'heritage':

> I have this experience because they see that I'm coming from Eastern Europe, so I'm coming from Hungary, Romania something like that which they mix in their minds – that's why they offer me a lower salary.
> (Etel, Hungary)

At other times, Danish employers had mistaken Etel for being a third-country national rather than an EU citizen using her legal right to mobility. In line with the point from the previous sections, her explanations accentuate how selves are produced and moderated through social interaction and the ways that the specific context and practices we engage in dictate the range of narratives we can tell of ourselves (Goffman, 1990; Somers, 1994). Essentially, the external categorisation of her stood in sharp contrast to her ontological narrative. She underlined how she always thought of herself as a 'European kid' and a firm believer in 'European values' – thereby presenting herself as a progressive individual. Yet, this previously undisputable narrative seemed less evident in a Danish context. As discussed in Chapter 3, like Etel, many of my interlocutors presented themselves as 'Eastern European Westerners' when narrating their position in the home countries, indicating a sense of *a priori* belonging to the global West. This also accentuates why Etel was surprised by the alienation confronting her in Denmark, where she felt that she was not approached as an equal. She clearly saw an antagonistic relationship between her ontological narrative as a progressive, European, and Western-minded individual and the categorisation of her as a non-European immigrant. We see a similar reasoning in Jacob' reflections:

I was surprised because I was treated as an Eastern European immigrant but I never thought of myself as an immigrant. Well, I guess I work here, I pay my taxes here, I live here, so I guess I am an immigrant. But I never really thought of it that way before because I am just moving to a different city within the EU and I am just doing a higher education.

(Jacob, Hungary)

Like Etel, Jacob felt *othered* by being grouped within a broad and anonymous immigrant category. He clearly saw a status hierarchy between the categories 'EU citizen' and 'immigrant' (see also Manolova, 2020). Where an EU citizen signalled something *internal* to Europe, a voluntary act of movement, the status of immigrant denoted, in Jacob's view, something forced and external that he wanted to distance from himself. Yet, his European citizenship and student identity, which he previously had treasured highly, offered little assistance in what he experienced as a degradation in a symbolic power cartography. Later in this chapter, I will go further into my interlocutors' experiences of being weaved into a discrediting public narrative of Eastern Europe in Denmark.

Financial freedom to choose

Until now, this chapter has mostly focused on the narrations of student migrants from EU countries. This section, however, goes further into the experiences and life conditions of the students from non-EU countries. As highlighted previously, the Eastern European students from non-EU countries in this study were all sponsored by scholarships. I will especially point out how differences between having a relatively stable income (due to the financial assistance from a scholarship) and being without a financial safety net appear to produce very different lived realities for students abroad, not least in terms of the possibilities for engaging with one's studies, socialising with other student communities, and in pursuing extra-curricular activities. In contrast to the insecure and economically vulnerable conditions which characterised the lives of many of my interlocutors from EU countries, the students from non-EU countries generally found their scholarships sufficient to cover their living expenses, as highlighted by Christina:

Like my scholarship is 1000 euros per month, which is like completely ok to survive here – well not survive, but live normally, I guess. It's definitely more than what Danish students get like with the SU and stuff.

(Christina, North Macedonia)

Due to her scholarship, Christina was not only able to pay for essentials such as food and rent but could, for instance, go out with friends to bars and restaurants. Indeed, as she underlines, the scholarship made it possible for her to lead *a normal life* in Denmark. In line with earlier discussions of 'normality' in this book, Christina's sense of leading a normal life involved the sense of having a proportionate balance between one's desires and the possibility to act upon them (Greenberg, 2011). In marked contrast to my interlocutors who were utterly dependent on paid work, she even deemed her economic situation *better* than that of the average Danish student. Of the ten students financed by scholarships in this study, Christina was the only student with a (paid) part-time job as a babysitter in a family. This employment made it possible for her to save money for the Green Card application following her graduation, which at the time (2014) was the relevant legal scheme for international students' labour market transition after graduation. The babysitting, however, only amounted to a few hours per week and the job did not conflict with her ability to focus on her studies. Thus, Christina could lead a life with a similar structure as in North Macedonia and, following Goffmanian terminology, continue to play the accustomed role of a university student after having moved to Denmark. Her narrations exemplify how scholarship students were less exposed to 'biographical disruptions' (Bury, 1982) caused by markedly different lived realities abroad and in their home countries.

Most scholarship students were not opposed to the idea of getting a job. However, it was not the attraction of money *per se* that constituted the primary motivation but, rather, the possibility to obtain valuable experiences related to their future career field. The students generally regarded jobs and internships related to their studies to be advantageous, which should be viewed in the light of extra-curricular activities increasing importance for post-graduation trajectories (Lehmann, 2009). Some months into her studies in Denmark, Isidora from North Macedonia was keen on getting a part-time job. She explained that it was especially the prospect of 'testing herself' to see if she could manage to work while studying at the university which appealed to her. With the help of contacts in her social network, she found a job as a bartender in the city centre where she was promised 50 DKK per hour 'under the table.' After only one evening at the bar, she nonetheless concluded that this type of job was below her standards and decided to quit immediately. Instead, she wanted to dedicate her time entirely to her studies in Denmark. After all, the university was the main purpose of going abroad in the first place. It is important to notice how her relative financial freedom entailed that she did not have to subject herself to a job that she disliked and that she could prioritise her studies if she wanted to do so. In contrast to Etel, who felt deprived of the possibility of saying 'no' to unacceptable working conditions when fearing that the lack of income would force her to give up her studies and return to Hungary, the scholarship gave Isidora the liberty to choose. In addition, the EU scholarship 'freed' her from relying on parental support and feelings of financial indebtedness (Thomas, 2017).

The thought of getting a job next to her studies also appealed to Alma from Montenegro. With much spare time next to her studies, she was eager to utilise her time in a more instrumental way to further enhance her future career path. Alma was very particular when pinpointing the type of part-time jobs she sought. Ideally, she preferred to work for an NGO specialising in international projects. In sharp contrast to the EU movers, she was not interested in 'any job' but specifically work that complemented her educational profile. When asked if there were jobs that she was reluctant to take, she underscored that she was 'way too lazy' to consider jobs involving cleaning and that she wished to focus on jobs that also 'require mental skills.' Thus, Alma's aspirations of getting a job were not born out of economic necessity but rather the wish to acquire first-hand experience with NGO work while simultaneously developing useful contacts to utilise following the completion of her studies. The prospect of a strong and multifaceted CV was also the main reason why Gojko from Serbia wanted to find a volunteer job during his second year in Denmark. He was similarly not driven by the prospect of paid work but was keen on work tasks that matched his academic interests and which could facilitate an international network. Gojko, therefore, hoped to find a position as a volunteer at a peace organisation or at least a position that would put him in contact with people from all over the world. However, during the course of his studies, he developed a greater interest in research. In line with his new career aspirations, he became employed as a research assistant at the university. Work, in this sense, did not directly conflict with Alma's and Gojko's possibilities to study and play the role of an international student but rather constituted a form of preparation for the future stages of their pending professional careers.

The non-EU students' narrations demonstrate how their relative economic freedom allowed them to engage in various activities that potentially could turn out to be crucial for their future career paths. In addition to the stories above, there were examples of students doing internships in Brussels or in high-profiled companies in the capital Copenhagen. Students with scholarships were clearly less restrained from pursuing extra-curricular activities related to their field of study than those reliant on work next to their studies. This pattern supports Wolfgang Lehmann's (2009) observation from a Canadian context that students with fewer financial hindrances have better possibilities for gaining experiences outside the university in order to build their CVs. The considerable differences in terms of living conditions between students with and without a scholarship were not unknown to the students, as is shown in the following quote by Erina:

> While living here I have a scholarship and for me life here is more or less easy. But I'm really also amazed why some students are coming here and sacrificing so much. I mean I could understand theoretically that they need better jobs, they need better opportunities but I don't know … sometimes it's too difficult. I think just a couple of people succeed and they just have to be like really, really strong focused or they have like some personal issues. For example, I had no idea that the motivation

for people to come here is so different, I mean most of them from the European Union they are the same, they want to find a job.

(Erina, Bosnia and Herzegovina)

According to Erina, life with a scholarship was 'more or less easy' and her explanations do not indicate any evident discrepancy between past and present. While the students with scholarships could continue to act in accordance with their more or less accustomed roles central for their onto-logical narratives, students who were dependent on jobs to support them-selves were forced to prioritise activities directly related to their subsistence, which for example entailed that they had less time to build an impressive CV. The latter group, furthermore, exhibited a higher level of stress due to diffi-culties of making ends meet financially and the uncertainty of not knowing whether the lack of financial means would obstruct their studies. While this present section has highlighted how the narrations of non-EU students set them apart from most EU movers, their (comparatively) privileged situation and experiences of life abroad also differ from the non-EU students in Olivia Maury's (2020, 2017) study from Finland and the non-EU students in Karen Valentin's (2012) study from Denmark. In both studies, the vast majority of the students were – like the self-financing EU students in this study – dependent on a regular income from a job while studying in Finland and Denmark. In addition, their working lives were further shaped by the limits and requirements of the student permit. As such, this indicates that important nuances also exist within the category 'non-EU students.' In the following section, I delve further into how various degrees of economic restraints also affect students' social networks and sense of belonging.

The influence of social networks on student migrants' sense of belonging

Our identity is moulded by our surroundings – not least through our relations and interactions with others, which shape the narratives we can tell about ourselves (Somers, 1994, 1992). International migration challenges the relations we have with emplaced configurations of people and events (Conradson and Mckay, 2007). According to Shanthi Robertson (2018), we should not underestimate the importance of international students' social networks abroad since they play a vital role in the (re)construction of self and sense of belonging. As my fieldwork progressed, it became increasingly clear that structural inequalities offered students vastly different perquisites for forming friendships and taking part in various social groupings. For instance, Bogdan's part-time job played a determining role in the constella-tion of his social network in Denmark. His dense working schedule meant that he barely was a part of student clusters at the university. In response to the question of how his work affected his social life, he laughingly replied,

'I don't know if I have a social life.' Bogdan had initially imagined that he through his studies automatically would become a part of a vibrant, cosmopolitan environment with students from all over the world (see also Beech, 2018); yet, his dense schedule put an abrupt end to such aspirations. In sharp contrast to previous imaginaries, he resided in a 'Romanian bubble' in Denmark where his main circle of friends were uneducated low-skilled workers from his home country. He admitted that he used to look down on manual labourers but that he had gotten a more nuanced view of people from other social groupings through his job as a newspaper deliverer. Clearly, the structures and conditions that underpinned his everyday life abroad made it difficult to draw boundaries between himself and the Romanian migrant community and cultivate an ontological narrative of himself as being 'different.'

Bogdan's descriptions of his circle of friends in Denmark stand in contrast to a dominant notion among researchers that international students tend to socialise within tight groups consisting mainly of other international students (Amit, 2010; Beech, 2018; Gomes, 2015; Murphy-Lejeune, 2002). For instance, in a study of international students in Australia, Catherine Gomes (2015, p. 52) writes: 'Having other international students as friends allowed participants to fill the huge gap that has been left because of their separation from not only their homeland but more significantly from family and friends.' In contrast to the above studies, the constellation of Bogdan's social networks was similar to those sometimes described among low-skilled labour migrants, where ethnic-specific networks act as a gate-keeper into the host society (Ryan, 2011; Ryan and Mulholland, 2014). Polina Manolova (2017) shows how Bulgarian migrants in the UK were drawn into the confines of the Bulgarian immigrant community despite being firmly against it before their arrival. The migrants' marginal position abroad made them highly reliant on assistance from fellow Bulgarians when looking for a place to stay, when seeking legal advice, for job recommendations, and general information on life in the UK. In many ways, Manolova's descriptions resemble the experiences of students like Bogdan who also found himself immersed into a national community upon his arrival to Denmark despite initially having aspirations of becoming a part of a cosmopolitan network of university students. Instead, he became a member of a social group with whom he previously did not identify or feel that he had anything in common with. In line with Manolova's findings, Bogdan's identification with other Romanian migrants seemed related to their common marginal status in Denmark.

In the previous sections, I discussed how Bogdan's everyday routines in Denmark differed significantly from those that characterised his life in Romania. Essentially, this also included his social circles, which in Romania mostly consisted of intellectuals from the university. There was thus a marked discrepancy between his social groups at home and abroad (see also Ryan, 2011). Bogdan's new circle of friends seemed to play a role in his sense of alienation from the milieu surrounding the university. Following the assumption that migration provides opportunities for new forms of subjectivity and emotion to emerge (Conradson and Mckay, 2007; Huot and Rudman, 2010; Robertson, 2018), Bogdan increasingly embraced an ontological narrative as a religious man in Denmark. While a convinced atheist in Romania, his Christian faith gradually strengthened in Denmark and he spent much of his waking hours in the community surrounding the local Romanian church. The times I visited the Romanian church, I was surprised by how secluded the community felt from the Danish society. Stepping into the small church seemed like a step into an unknown world characterised by profoundly different customs, practices, smells, and sounds. In addition to the spiritual dimension, the church also functioned as a meeting place for people of predominantly Romanian origin. When I arrived in the church, I was received in an incredibly warm manner and with curiosity despite the fact that I was the only Dane who participated in their Sunday service. The church visits provided me with an additional insight into how Bogdan in many ways lived his life parallel to the Danish society while studying in Denmark. The fact that he mainly interacted with Romanian migrants undoubtedly strengthened his identification with his 'Romanian roots.' At one point he stated, 'I used to hate Romania, but now I have fallen in love with the country all over again.' In Denmark, he thus experienced a newfound attraction to his home country – the place he previously had been so eager to escape. In fact, there were several examples among my interlocutors of cross-border mobility seemingly enforcing a sense of national belonging instead of weakening it. This resembles the findings from Genova's (2016) study of Bulgarian student migrants in the UK, where their lived realities abroad triggered a marked sense of patriotism.

Elena similarly found comfort in the religious circles surrounding the local Romanian church. In addition to the spiritual dimension, the church offered her a place to meet familiar faces. In contrast to Bogdan's descriptions, it was not a tight work schedule that exempted her from interacting with other university students. As she explains in the following quote, it was predominantly her lack of money:

ELENA: Well, I have very few friends, I mean I used to go out. The Ukrainian girl she left, I mean, and the other ones not that much, I mean, who else … there is this Romanian guy, this Spanish guy, then there was this Dutch guy, yeah, I mean, [we are] just talking in the library. I mean, friendship here it means talking about school.

METTE: Do you think that friendship has a different meaning here than in Romania?

ELENA: Yeah of course, I mean it's normal, I mean of course. There is a big difference between old friends and new friends. I know that because, yes, I cannot go out that much because I don't have money, so how can you be social? And I accept that: 'Ok, let's try to be good and not spend money.' I'm trying to stay cool and not overdo because I know that at some point if I do it, I will lose control. So yeah, yeah, it's about money mainly and friendship apparently – yeah being social costs.

(Elena, Romania)

For Elena, the lack of money gradually paved the way for social isolation. She claimed that the sporadic encounters with classmates at the library mostly revolved around 'superficial topics' connected to their mutual studies and she felt a pronounced reluctance from their side to engage in more personal matters. According to Marco Antonsich (2010), our sense of belonging to a place is strongly contingent on our social relations. Essentially, 'weak ties' are not sufficient to generate a sense of connectedness to others on which belonging relies. In Elena's case, 'weak ties' appeared to be one of the main reasons why Denmark was characterised by a marked sense of loneliness and, indeed, distance from the Danish society. Despite the fact that Elena was physically present in Denmark, her primary group of friends remained her 'old' social network in Romania. Therefore, her struggle to establish 'meaningful ties' in Denmark was accompanied by the continuation of strong emotional ties to people in Romania.

While both Elena and Bogdan are examples of students who felt alienated from the social environment surrounding the university, there were also students from EU countries who gave a radically different account of their social life in Denmark. The year spent in a Danish folk high school prior to his university studies meant that David from Hungary primarily socialised with a tight-knit group of mostly local students. In contrast to Elena's descriptions, David's social ties to people and places 'back home' had weakened considerably during his time abroad and he had become increasingly critical towards everything involving Hungary. In Denmark, he was actively avoiding communities mainly consisting of native Hungarians:

DAVID: I knew a lot of Hungarians who had financial problems because on Facebook there is a group for Hungarians in Denmark [but] I refused to be a part of it.

METTE: Why don't you want to be a part of the Facebook group?

DAVID: I was screwed up by Hungarians way too many times. Yeah, it's like if you meet a Hungarian abroad you need a good reason to talk to that person, and I met three really nice people at Learn Danish [Lær Dansk] and the other Hungarian guy at my workplace is also a really nice guy and I really like them and it's fun to hang out with them but that is just the minority. And also, in Denmark, also in the States, also in Italy I met so many Hungarians who just want to take advantage of you. It's like no, no, no, no – I don't need that. […] And when I checked out this [Facebook] group, immediately I felt this attitude – 'we are Hungarians,' 'we have to stick together,' 'we have to do stuff together' – and immediately I could feel this mental shutdown. I don't need that – that I should be a part of it just because they are Hungarians, I don't feel that I need that. That's what my mother could not understand: 'Why don't you hang out with Hungarians?' Just because they are Hungarians, they can be just as bad as anyone else. And of course, when I have positive examples that is really good and that's nice. And also, I hear it from other Hungarians – you better avoid them!

(David, Hungary)

There is a straight line between David's wish to avoid Hungarians in Denmark and his motivation for leaving Hungary in the first place. He was tired of the 'Eastern European mentality,' which, in his mind, characterised most of his fellow national citizens. Instead, David felt increasingly attached to Denmark and convinced that he wanted to stay in the country after having completed his studies. His many local contacts seemingly nurtured a sense of local belonging (see also Robertson, 2018). While there are obviously various reasons for why David's social network differed markedly from the students discussed above, one factor appeared to be that David had a more stable economy and a job that allowed him to be social. In contrast to Bogdan, he did not rely emotionally on the support of a mono-national immigrant community but could delineate symbolic boundaries of 'the average Hungarian' while presenting an ontological narrative of himself as morally and culturally superior. In fact, he was one of the few working students who expressed an overall satisfaction with his part-time work, since he managed to maintain a 'healthy' work–study balance, where he worked around 10 hours per week during the weekends as a dishwasher. This further meant that he worked enough hours to meet the requirements for getting the Danish study stipend. As a result, David experienced a high degree of financial freedom in Denmark despite not receiving any financial support from his parents:

Yeah, like this is for me like heaven. I don't know, like, I study, I meet smart people, I work in a really good team, I have a lot of extra benefits and have money, I can go out and that's how I could go to London and that's how I can invite my parents here.

(David, Hungary)

In contrast to the explanations provided by many of the working students from EU countries, David connected Denmark to a level of financial freedom previously denied to him in his home country. He therefore considered Denmark as an upgrade from his earlier lifestyle where activities such as international travelling were complicated due to the lack of money. In fact, there is a great similarity between David's situation and the students sponsored by a scholarship. While most of the scholarship students did not have an impressive local network as David, their circles of friends were predominantly composed of other university students. Their social networks did not mainly consist of individuals of similar nationality nor did they actively seek out social groupings outside the university. They also appeared highly committed to the activities taking place at the university campus such as student symposia and university bars, which facilitated a strong sense of attachment to the university. Since they were not constrained by the lack of money or an overwhelming workload from a low-skilled job, they seemed considerably freer than most of the EU-movers to socialise with other students.

My interlocutors' explanations suggest that structural differences such as economy and working conditions affected students' possibilities for socialising and forging meaningful relationships with individuals inside and outside the university. Their financial situation abroad appeared to dictate their memberships of particular social constellations. For instance, Elena's narrations suggest that her lack of money played a vital role in her *inability* to build a network of students in Denmark while exacerbating a sense of alienation to the university and, more broadly, the Danish society. In contrast, relative economic freedom increased students' possibilities to engage actively in the social communities at the university. As emphasised, students who were financially secure displayed a much stronger sense of belonging to the university. For example, David's ability to maintain a local social network was highly dependent on having the time and the means for doing so. His robust local social network in Denmark placed him in a position where he could reject a network of Hungarians, which in turn made it easier for him to further cultivate an ontological narrative of himself as being culturally and morally superior – an 'Eastern European Westerner.'

An 'aura of calmness' and the moral advantages of hardship

The international students with whom I spoke during the beginning of their stay in Denmark were all highly focused on making Danish friends, not least because a local network in their eyes constituted the ideal platform for diving into Danish culture, as explained by Gojko:

> I want to get Danish friends in the sense that I want to feel if I was here for like two years and if I go home without any Danish friends, I would feel it was sort of a waste. If you are coming somewhere you sort of have to, you know, get to know the culture and adapt yourself and stuff, so you can't do that without actually meeting people from [Denmark].
>
> (Gojko, Serbia)

As their studies progressed, many students realised that this quest was more difficult than initially expected. They often told me that my open attitude towards 'foreigners' and interest in socialising with international students made me a 'special' and 'different' Dane. While I am uncertain if the Danish students were extraordinarily closed or if they rather had a more extensive local social network which made them less attentive, most of my interlocutors nonetheless felt a certain distance from their Danish classmates.

This local/international gap is in itself not a unique insight: Scholars working with international education have for a long time highlighted how international students and local students rarely mix (Beech, 2018). More than 20 years ago, Simone Volet and Grace Ang (1998, p. 5) characterised the lack of interaction between Australian students and international students from Asian backgrounds as 'one of the most disturbing aspects of the internationalisation of higher education in Australia.' In her study of Canadian students, Vered Amit (2010, p. 62) similarly observed how international students were eager to socialise with locals but that the latter group already had their own established social networks. This meant that local students were less likely to take the time away from familiars to invest in getting to know new people who had a short expiration date. Therefore, the international students primarily formed close relations with other internationals in similar circumstances.

While these insights are valuable, there is, to my knowledge, very little research on how structural factors, such as different socio-economic backgrounds, affect the integration of students into the international student body. While a demanding and time-consuming job may intensify the sense of alienation to the environment surrounding the university and more broadly the Danish society, this section discusses how economic marginality also enforced international/local divisions by accentuating the sense of living in a reality parallel to that of the local and Western European students. There was a tendency for students who were most pressured financially to present a narrative of Danish, and more generally Western European students, as privileged. Bogdan, for instance, identified a clear difference between the economic situation of Western and Eastern European students:

BOGDAN: [International students] will feel more confident if they had a contract and they would pay taxes. Ok, you give me free education and I will pay taxes – that's ok by me so nobody complains. But if you need to work, I don't know, in the bazaar or some kind of slavery job like – there are a lot of students who also do that and the cleaning companies which have different approaches to immigrants – that's not the sort of thing I usually like.

METTE: Is this the same for all international students? Do you know that? Having difficulties finding jobs and not having enough money?

BOGDAN: As far as I know non-European internationals, they already have a scholarship, I don't know if [the scholarship] is from Denmark or the state, but usually Eastern Europeans [are the ones who are having difficulties finding jobs and not having enough money]. I don't know, maybe people coming from France, Belgium, England they would like to find a job because that would be easier for their parents but it's not that they don't have somebody to sustain them.

METTE: Ok, so they have parents who can support them?
BOGDAN: Yeah, in need, if needed. But they would also like to find a job – a normal kind of job.

(Bogdan, Romania)

In Bogdan's view, Eastern European students were more exposed to 'slavery jobs' in Denmark, whereas he saw Western European students as privileged in the sense that they either had someone to support them or that they at least could find 'normal jobs.' Contrary to Western European students' relative economic safety, Eastern European students resided, according to Bogdan, at the margins of Danish society. They were viewed and treated as second-class citizens and due to their shady jobs, they were hindered from paying taxes, which prevented them from becoming 'fully-fledged' members of the Danish society. In the previous chapter, I accentuated how students talked about their abnormal situation in their home countries and how they often hoped that educational mobility would function as a way to integrate a state of normality into their lives and thus a sense of 'predictability, reliability, and legibility' (Misztal, 2001). In stark contrast to such aspirations, Bogdan's narrations suggested a feeling of residing outside a normal context in Denmark by being deprived of the financial safety in his eyes enjoyed by local and Western European students. The exposed situation of Eastern Europeans in Denmark infuriated Olga:

> Well, it was hard because we do not get any scholarships. It's like you are basically on your own. If you are from Eastern Europe, mostly your parents can't support you financially, so you are sort of alone. If you want to live in Denmark, you have to work for it and study at the same time. Well, I don't know, depending on where you live and how much money you need, you would work typically at least 12 hours per week. Not because you have to save up for a vacation, but simply you have to survive. I don't know if people realise that some people just have to work. It's not their choice. You can't just sit home and study all the time.
>
> (Olga, Poland)

When Olga speaks of 'surviving,' she is not talking about life and death but about being able to continue with her studies in Denmark. Olga was one of the more vocal students in terms of venting critical opinions of her Danish classmates. In the quote, she indirectly compared her situation to that of her Danish peers who she deemed to be privileged due to their favourable financial situation. She found that local students were surrounded by a degree of freedom that she herself was denied. Contrary to Olga, Danish students could save money for a vacation and invest all of their energy into their studies. Their Mac computers, Olga claimed, bore witness of the profound inequalities that permeated the international study environment:

It's visible. Like first of all the Macs, the computers, it just a distinguished thing about Danes [laughing]. Yes, that they can afford to have the like Apple on the desktop, on their desk during the lectures, what I have never ever seen in Poland. Yeah, yeah, yeah. This is an obvious fact that, yeah, Danes they have very good study conditions.

(Olga, Poland)

Olga's and Bogdan's stories constitute excellent examples of how there appeared to be general awareness among the students from EU countries of being in a markedly different situation than local students. The experience of finding oneself in an unjust situation affected their impression of the Danes in a negative way (see also Maury, 2020). They had been seduced by a narrative of Denmark and Scandinavia as a place where people are particularly 'calm' and 'relaxed' because of the impressive welfare levels and yet discovered that this easiness was reserved for their Danish peers. Ania used to perceive Scandinavians as 'very relaxed' where 'everything is pretty much secured' by a generous welfare state, but her life in Denmark instead became synonymous with precariousness and uncertainty. Akin to Ania's narrations, many of my interlocutors found that Danish students displayed a certain calmness that they themselves were deprived. This desirable personal attribute was, in Paul's mind, a direct result of the welfare system:

You sense that [the Danish students] are calm you know this aura of calmness around them, like 'the state is taking care of you' and 'you can just focus on your studies' or whatever. Or at some point you always have the option, so you can always give up your studies. There is a safety net idea in the social system in Denmark where you don't fall on solid ground and you are somehow safe in that system.

(Paul, Romania)

The 'aura of calmness,' which Paul linked to Danish students, stood in contrast to his own situation in Denmark where he felt the opposite of calm due to his reliance on his parents' financial goodwill. Thus, the feeling of being without a safety net in Denmark clearly shaped Paul's impression of Danish students. Elena presented a similar rationale:

I mean, we need to struggle with the fact that we don't get the SU [the Danish study stipend] and that makes us a bit more aware sometimes. What I see people doing, they are just contracting some loans if they cannot get help from parents or work manual jobs and again once you work a few hours per day physical work you cannot study that much and so on and this is what international students do. But Danes, the ones that I know, they don't work manual jobs anymore and yeah, they have time for their private lives and they don't worry too much. People around here are pretty relaxed about things.

(Elena, Romania)

Elena interpreted the Danish students' situation as markedly different from her own. Their relaxedness stood in contrast to her ongoing 'struggle' and, contrary to many Eastern European students, Danish students could avoid manual jobs. For both Elena and Paul, their own chaotic situation functioned as yardsticks against which they judged and measured local students. Despite being physically close to Danish students, Elena felt alienated from them – as if she belonged to a different world characterised by constant struggling. To confront the Danes' 'social myopia' (Lamont, 2000, p. 2) and enlighten them about how it felt to be in her shoes, she wanted Danish students to settle in a foreign country over a longer period:

I would really be sooo happy to hear more about Danes leaving and coming back. [...] To struggle to find a place, to struggle to a place to stay, to find some friends or not, to do something that you would never think of.

(Elena, Romania)

It was not only the Danes' relaxedness that captured Elena's attention; she also expressed a moral aversion to their careless practices, which, in her opinion, was a direct result of having been morally damaged by the Danish welfare system:

In the beginning, I really appreciated [the Danish system], I mean I thought this is perfect [...] you just get paid for [studying]. And then I realised [...] I mean they don't finish in time – their degrees, and they just, you know, it gives them more time [...] to drink and do drugs and do something that is not good for their own lives.

(Elena, Romania)

As opposed to Paul, who primarily described the Danish welfare system in favourable terms – a 'safety net' that can catch a person from falling on 'solid ground' – Elena was predominantly sceptical of 'the Danish way' since it, in her mind, kept students at bay from the real world, which confronts inter- national students in Denmark. While Danish students had the upper hand financially, there were, according to Elena, significant *moral advantages* born out of hardship (Lamont, 2000, 1992; Lehmann, 2009; Sayer, 2005). For instance, she was convinced that she possessed a stronger work ethic than Danish students as well as higher levels of maturity, independence, as well as first-hand experience with the real world. Elena's descriptions carry an interesting resemblance to Michèle Lamont's (2000) observation of how people from the working class dissociate socio-economic status from moral worth, thereby locating themselves above the upper-middle class according to a standard to which they attach overarching importance. Similarly, Lehmann (2009, p. 640) highlights how Canadian working-class students were convinced that 'maturity and responsibility develop through (at least moderate levels of) hardship, as opposed to being handed everything in life.' Indeed, the struggling students often narrated the negative social circumstances as something that ultimately led to a positive personal outcome, as accentuated by Etel:

> Well, I think if you have these kinds of pressures in your life, I think it's good because then you really have to stand up and do something. So, I think that if I had come to Denmark with ten times more money, I think I would not experience as much because then I would just say to myself: 'Okay I have money, okay I will figure something out.' But in my case, it was pretty urgent and I knew that I must do something and thinking back now I think it was a good thing.
>
> (Etel, Hungary)

Etel regarded her financial struggles in Denmark as something that ultimately turned her into a stronger person and capable of handling similar situations in the future. Etel's narrations can be understood along the lines of what Ezzy (2000, p. 123) refers to as 'heroic job loss narratives' whereby the loss of a job – that is, a divestment passage – is constructed as something positive and empowering by the narrator (see also Wilken and Dahlberg, 2017). In a similar manner, my interlocutors would construct their struggles as something empowering – a *super power* that their Danish peers were without due to their privileged situation.

Ghetto-living

Contrary to universities in countries like the US or the UK, universities in Denmark do not have a tradition for on-campus housing. Instead, students typically live in student halls of residences situated some distance from the campus, or in private accommodation of their own. The city where most of the fieldwork was conducted is like many cities with a booming student population notorious for its shortage of housing. The municipality offers a public housing guarantee to incoming students, entailing that they are guaranteed one housing offer if they sign up for a waiting list preferably six months in advance. If students do not accept the housing offer, they are removed from the list. In principle, this entails that they have very little to say about the location of their housing. Moreover, students typically apply for housing prior to their arrival, meaning that they have to make housing choices based on very limited knowledge of the city. Since it may take up to six months before being offered accommodation, some students – including several of my informants – initially lived in 'caravans,' with only three square meters of privacy. The caravans are a temporary solution set up by the municipality at the beginning of each semester and cost approximately 14 euros per night.

When signing up for housing, international students can choose between a range of accommodations in different parts of the city. They are, however, encouraged to 'apply broadly,' which essentially means that they should consider areas that have been labelled unattractive in the public media discourse and by previous tenants. Thus, newly arrived students are strongly advised to give up potential dreams of living in the heart of the city centre. The webpage for housing singles out two specific dorms as places (in this study they have been given the fictive names 'Inter Dorm' and 'Nordskov community'), which students should take into consideration when filling out their housing applications. Both dorms are located in the outskirts of the city in a part of the town known for its 'super-diversity' (Vertovec, 2007). The area is characterised by the absence of a dominant ethnic group, as well as the proliferation of differentiation according to national origins, languages, religious backgrounds, and socio-economic backgrounds. The dorms are adjacent to an infamous housing area, which figures on the Danish government's notorious 'ghetto-list.' The list includes areas in Denmark which score high in factors such as the concentration of unemployed people, crime rates, and inhabitants from non-Western countries. As such, the area generally had a bad reputation and received much negative media coverage. In the attempt to counter the negative connotations linked to the two dorms, the housing webpage states in bold letters that the residences are not subjected to higher crime rates than other dorms in the city.

Like many newly arrived student migrants, my interlocutors were offered and, in most cases, accepted a room at the 'Inter Dorm.'[1] The dorm is located seven kilometres from the university and which, due to its capacity to host more than 1000 students, is the largest dorm in the city. Every time I visited students at the Inter Dorm, I became surprised by its distance from the city centre and that it took me approximately 40 minutes to get there by bus. While this might not be an overwhelming travel distance in cities like New York or London, it did feel quite far away in light of the actual size of the city where the students lived. The dorm was built in the latter half of the 20th century and consists of numerous grey concrete buildings. Many buildings appeared to be worn down by the many years that had passed without any proper renovation. As indicated, the dorm was rarely the first pick for local students. In addition to its geographical location and physical condition, the dorm also had problems with burglaries and was known for its unsafe atmosphere. The Inter Dorm has been called a 'transit-dorm' due to the short time people usually stay there. While searching on the Internet, I encountered several sites with students debating with previous tenants whether to accept a room at the dorm.[2] While some highlighted the dorm's tight-knit social community of students as a positive aspect, the debates were generally characterised by marked negativity. One previous tenant advised all students 'to stay FAR away from the place'; another specified why the place could only be considered 'the last stop before the street' listing four critical points: the geographical location, the old concrete buildings, the high crime rate, and its proximity to the ghetto.

In my larger sample of students (involving students from all over the world), I noticed that none of the Danish students lived at the Inter Dorm. Instead, their rooms or apartments were usually located in the city centre. Paul also observed a tendency of markedly different living conditions between 'Internationals' and 'Westerners,' which he connected to the financial inequalities in the student body: 'Many Westerners have more money to get a better place or that sort of stuff. I'm living [at the Inter Dorm] somewhere next to a ghetto.' In line with Paul's observation, I noticed a consistent pattern that students with less money typically had a room or even a shared apartment at the Inter Dorm. Some even shared rooms intended for one person to save money despite this being against the official rules. Contrary to the dorm's status as a transit-dorm, the most financially pressured Eastern European students usually stayed there throughout their entire master's degree due to the costs (such as the start-up deposit) involved in moving. At first, many residents were startled by the condition of their accommodation. Paul, who came from 'a rather emancipated part of what they generally regard as a Romanian town, not one of those ghetto types of places,' recalled the shock going through his body when the bus dropped him off in front of the grey concrete walls:

> There are always going to be some cultural differences that are going to be sticking at the beginning and it's really strange. You know, there is always the ghetto experience, you are thinking that you are going to Denmark this, for Eastern Europeans Denmark is, of course, this wealthy modern European country, and you are suddenly parachuted to this strange place. You know, it's always a tangle between your expectations and what is actually there.
>
> (Paul, Romania)

Clearly, the narrative of Denmark as a modern and progressive country, which Paul adhered to prior to his arrival in Denmark, was inconsistent with the physical realities he encountered. Moreover, as scholars remind us, living in deprived areas may have negative consequences for one's sense of self and enforce feelings of marginalisation (Wacquant, 2008). In her study of Nepalese students in Denmark, Karen Valentin (2015) shows how experiences of being unwanted immigrants (contrary to students contributing with intercultural diversity) were nurtured by living in areas densely populated by immigrants. While many of the Nepalese students aspired to move to 'supposedly safer areas of Copenhagen with fewer foreigners' (Valentin, 2015, p. 327), such aspirations rarely materialised due to the lack of available housing. Some of my interlocutors were also affected negatively by their housing situation, as suggested by Jacob:

The housing situation in [the city] is terrible and it's impossible to get an apartment and it's really hard to get an apartment as a foreigner, so I was forced to live [at the Inter Dorm] with four other students. So, we were actually six students living in this big apartment which I think was actually only for four people, so I was like supposed to do things I did not want to do and it was not a convenient situation but I just... And finding an apartment took a really long time even after I had the financial means. [...] This experience of having to live in a ghetto where your apartment is broken into and things like that really make you feel that you are living on the outskirts of society.

(Jacob, Hungary)

Clearly, Jacob was not satisfied with his initial living situation in Denmark and only stayed at the Inter Dorm due to a combination of housing insufficiency and the lack of money. The rough neighbourhood and the territorial marginalisation appeared to strengthen his sense of alienation from the Danish society. Moreover, Jacob was not the only student who recalled incidents of 'unwanted visitors.' Ivan and Peter both told me about how their apartments had been broken into. To avoid the stigmatising category of 'regular immigrants,' Jacob accentuated the cultural dissimilarities between himself and other national groups living in the multicultural area:

It is also really interesting that the people who live in [the ghetto] automatically are associated with Eastern Europeans even though there are huge cultural differences between the people of Iran and the people from Hungary.

(Jacob, Hungary)

Jacob's narrations illustrate how we, when our intrinsic identity is at stake, seek to distinguish ourselves from those belonging to different groups (Lopez Rodriguez, 2010). In the quote, Jacob seeks to escape a 'territorial stigma' (Wacquant, 2008) by nuancing the understanding of people living in the ghetto and drawing cultural boundaries between people from Iran and Hungary. Overall, the students' narrations of their living conditions suggest the importance of paying attention to living conditions as a factor, which may enforce a sense of marginalisation. In the following sections, I go further into the students' experiences of being confronted with an Eastern European stigma in Denmark.

Becoming Eastern European in the West

The merging of narrative with identity, as proposed by Somers (1994, 1992), entails an analytical focus on the aspect of *time*, *space*, and *relationality*. Social categories such as race and gender are never to be treated as fixed entities in the singular. While in Denmark, my interlocutors were confronted by a repertoire of public narratives to which they previously had little direct exposure and many felt that they automatically became woven into a discrediting public narrative of Eastern Europe. Indeed, various qualitative studies have highlighted that Eastern European migrants are subjected to discrimination in Western European countries – from the workplace to everyday interactions (Fox et al., 2015; Lopez Rodriguez, 2010; Samaluk, 2016). Micheline van Riemsdijk (2010) has shown how Polish nurses in Norway are confronted with various stereotypes connected to their country of origin and ultimately constructed as 'less white' by their Norwegian employers and co-workers. Since my interlocutors, in their ontological narrations, would emphasise their European attributes and cultural proximity to the West, many were caught off guard by what they experienced as an unprecedented focus on their 'Eastern European roots.' Vedrana Veličković (2019, p. 5) argues that the label 'Eastern European' casts doubts about one's European status. Veličković's reasoning thus enhances our understanding of why Ania was surprised when realising that people in Denmark would classify her as a person of Eastern European origin. Especially when taking into account that Ania grew up with a narrative of her home country, Poland, as geographically (and symbolically) located at the heart of Central Europe.

> Yes, actually for the first time I heard that I'm from Eastern Europe when I came to Denmark, because I was taught in the high school that Poland is placed in Central Europe and such a thing like Eastern Europe is further away East, like Russia or something like this. And now I'm fighting this 'Eastern Europe,' but I don't care. I know it bears maybe some social stereotypes and I don't really care about it. It's just funny, yeah.
>
> (Ania, Poland)

Ania's ambivalent emotions towards being labelled 'Eastern European' relate to the term's symbolic connotations and the notion of somehow being 'lesser European' (Marc, 2009). As we sense in the above quote, Ania initially tried to give the impression that she was not affected by this categorisation. If dissecting the interview situation with assistance from Goffman's analytical tools, one could argue that Ania regarded belonging to an 'Eastern European tribe' as something discrediting and immediately engaged in stigma management by subtracting the entity 'Poland' from the overarching category 'Eastern Europe.' Through this manoeuvre, she detached herself from the discredited 'tribe' at the expense of countries 'further away East, like Russia or something.' At the same time, Ania distanced herself from the stigma she faced and downplayed its effect when stating, 'I don't really care about it. It's just funny.' As the interview progressed, Ania, however, confided to me how she felt that Danes would glance at her sceptically when shopping and talking in Polish at the local supermarket, which paved the way for feelings of insecurity. Despite initial attempts at writing off the Eastern European stereotypes as 'funny,' she was clearly affected by what she experienced as alienation from the Danish community and, more broadly, *othering* from the metanarrative of Europe as progress and civilisation. While Ania used to dream about being a part of a meritocratic society founded on a core principle of inclusion, she did not feel that people in Denmark approached her as a 'fellow European.' Thus, she often wondered if she would gain acceptance on a longer-term basis. A main concern, which stuck with her throughout her stay in Denmark, was if she ever would be able to find skilled employment since her accent revealed that she was not a native Dane. Thus, she feared that she would remain trapped in low-skilled jobs 'reserved' for a foreign workforce.

Many students found that people in Denmark would homogenise Eastern European countries (Samaluk, 2016). As the logic of stigma goes, they felt as if the complexity of their actual social identity was reduced to a stereotypical characterisation. On several occasions, Etel encountered people who automatically presumed that coming from an Eastern European country was synonymous with fluency in Russian:

> Because a lot of time they were asking me if I speak Russian and 'Oh my God, why would I speak Russian?' I have never seen a Russian person in my entire life. And they kind of have these stereotypes if I speak Russian, if I use the Russian alphabet. Listen, I have never seen the Russian alphabet in Hungary in my entire life but still from a Western perspective they have these kinds of questions.
>
> (Etel, Hungary)

In the quote, Etel signals a marked unwillingness of being placed in the same stall as Russia – the country that students generally interpreted as furthest down the civilisational ladder on the East–West slope. Etel's reflections suggest a sense of powerlessness of being fixated into a narrow narrative of Eastern Europe, which she found uncomfortable, unfamiliar, and discrediting. The surprise and, at times, irritation of feeling that an Eastern European stamp overshadowed the complexities of one's persona was also evident in Paul's explanations, who similarly felt that his nationality attracted a great deal of negative attention. He recalled an incident where a girl asked him to verify if he was in fact from Romania since he seemed so different from all the 'straight up crazy Romanians' she had encountered in the past. Such comments made Paul feel that his nationality stole too much focus from more important facets of his 'actual social identity' and that the negative narrative linked to Romania and Eastern Europe often became *the one* that people focused on in certain social situations:

> Because I'm Romanian, I have to give extra explanations about where I'm from and why the situation is such and you can make a list of all the social issues in Romania. I always felt, not necessarily during student

presentations, but during social events that it's expected of me to defend Romania or give explanations of different issues in Romania rather than speaking about my intellectual projects or academic projects. I have to go on and on about gipsy kids in Paris and I don't care about that too much – of course I care about it, but I cannot keep on discussing this subject and of course, everybody asks. You already know the words and what to say and actually if you also mention that you are sort of ethnically Hungarian then you get another pile of work to do because Hungary now is so fascist and whatever.

(Paul, Romania)

For Paul, the negative categorisation and the *expectation* of being received with scepticism due to his nationality and ethnic background meant that he, for instance, was hesitant to apply for PhD stipends in countries such as the UK and Italy following his graduation because he wanted to avoid the 'antagonistic preconceptions' of what a Romanian is. He said: 'Imagine if you are doing your PhD and there is all this negative energy about you being from somewhere, and that is the reason why you are getting these negative energies and for no other reason.' Although initial suspicions would fade away after people got to know him, Paul experienced the negative narrative attached to Eastern Europe as stigmatising since it reduced the complexity of his personality to a stereotype about what people from that region 'ought to be like.' In the attempt to fight off the dominant narratives, he engaged in stigma management by offering counter-narratives of himself and staging counter performances where he strongly accentuated his intellectual capabilities and academic interests. Paul's reflections highlight how many of my interlocutors shared the feeling of constantly having to prove oneself as a decent human being who deserves to be a part of a progressive and civilised society. Somewhat ironically, it was when leaving Eastern Europe physically that the students first experienced Eastern Europe, both as a cultural entity and as an ascribed identity. The meaning of this 'Eastern Europeanness' was, according to the students' narrations, predominantly constituted by the negative prejudices they imagined Western Europeans carried, into which I will delve in depth in the following section.

Fearing stigma

In different ways and to a different extent, most of my interlocutors experienced their 'Eastern Europeanness' as a discrediting attribute – a tribal stigma transferred through the linages of previous generations (Goffman, 1963). As outlined, they engaged in stigma management aimed at mystifying the stigmatising consequences of originating from Eastern Europe. As the students felt more comfortable around me, they talked more openly about unpleasant encounters in Denmark and fears of racialised gazes from locals. There is an analogy between their experiences of stigmatisation and

Frantz Fanon's analysis of the psychology of colonialism. Fanon (2008, p. 4) suggests that colonial subjects are characterised by a marked 'inferiority complex,' which refers to an inner condition born out of economic subjugation and the internationalisation of the cultural and intellectual supremacy of the white man. In the foreword to Fanon's classic *Black Skin, White Masks* (2008), Ziauddin Sardar writes:

> When the black man comes into contact with the white world he goes through an experience of sensitization. His ego collapses. His self-esteem evaporates. He ceases to be a self-motivated person. The entire purpose of his behaviour is to emulate the white man, to become like him, and thus hope to be accepted as a man.
>
> (Sardar, 2008, p. xiii)

In the book, Fanon (2008, p. 15) shows how black men from the French Antilles became offended when mistaken for a Senegalese since a person from the Antilles is considered more civilised than the African due to their symbolic proximity to the colonisers. Despite their seemingly privileged position as 'ethnic white Europeans' (Andreouli and Howarth, 2019) – entailing less blatant differences between the Eastern European visitors and the host society population – there seems to be similar power dynamics at stake as pinpointed by Fanon (see also Manolova, 2018). Like the colonial subjects' fight for recognition, the Eastern European students' narrations suggest that they also strove to gain acceptance as members of the 'European club.' In Denmark, many, however, felt that their 'Eastern Europeanness' functioned as a reminder of their 'incomplete Europeanness' (Mishhova and Kostadinova, 2018). Thus, the feelings of inferiority and sensitivity captured in Fanon's writings also lingered in the students' explanations. Often, it was not actual comments that spurred feelings of insecurity, but many were *prior* to encounters with locals preoccupied with the potential discrediting stereotypes attached to them. The Balkan referent always lingered in Gojko's mind during encounters with Western Europeans outside a Serbian context:

METTE: Do you ever think about your nationality in any sense while being abroad?

GOJKO: I do, I do, I definitely do [whispering]. I'm sort of always aware of it in the sense that I'm … I don't know, like, it might be a bit paranoid, but like whenever, someone ask me where I'm from and I say it, like there is this part of my mind that sort of thinks: 'What is this person going to think of, like, me? Saying that I'm from Serbia or, like, is this person going to judge me about where I'm from or stuff like that?' So, there is always that part in my mind, unfortunately. It's really weird for me, you know it sounds really tacky like when you say: 'Oh, I'm not like a typical person from Serbia.' But I really think I'm not – at least from the people I know from Serbia and from the typical people I know.

METTE: What prejudices do you fear people have?

GOJKO: Like, I can't say that I have been on the receiving end of any direct prejudices. It's just like that when you sort of see but you are not sure that someone's behaviour changes when you say that you are from the Balkans – that is the only prejudices I guess I faced more or less directly. But I have luckily never received any assaults.

METTE: So, it's more a feeling within you?

GOJKO: Yeah, yeah. It's mostly like my own thing.

METTE: Where do you fear meeting these stereotypes?

GOJKO: Wherever, I mean whenever I meet someone that is not from the Balkans. Like not only Denmark – wherever I sort of, you know you meet someone who, I guess, like Western Europe or such. You never know what people are going to think.

(Gojko, Serbia)

One could draw a parallel to Fanon's (2008) colonial subjects since it was only when confronted with the Western gaze that the Gojko was reminded of his 'cultural blackness' (Kovačević, 2008, p. 1). As evident in the quote, his anxiety was predominantly triggered by the ways he *imagined* people would perceive him rather than actual comments from 'Westerners.' This further-more made him highly aware of his accent and he explained how he, in an attempt to cover up his Eastern European roots and 'be accepted as a man' (Fanon, 2008, p. xiii), tried to imitate an American accent while speaking. In the quote, Gojko also performed stigma management that evokes a 'self-colonial logic' (Samaluk, 2016, p. 107). By distancing himself from 'typical Serbians' and portraying himself as 'different,' he detaches himself from the non-Western space that he associates with the Balkans. The stigmatisation of others – in this case, people from the Balkans – thus becomes an attempt to manage his 'spoiled identity' and redeem his self-worth (Goffman, 1963).

Due to Romania's high rates of emigration and the negative stereotypes attached to Romanian citizens in Western European press (Cheregi, 2015), Romanian students seemed particularly worried about sceptical looks when 'revealing' their nationality and regional belongings. Bogdan, for instance, experienced a systematic pattern when interacting with Danes, namely that their discovery of his Romanian roots would make them lose interest in him – or at least he attributed their loss of interest to his stigmatised national identity. To avoid this scenario, he often referred to himself as 'Latin.' Indeed, Bogdan's experience supports Goffman's (1963, p. 69) assumption of how discredited individuals often find themselves in a state of uncertainty in terms of what 'to display or not to display; to tell or not to tell; to let on or not to let on; to lie or not to lie.' Thus, to be on 'the safe side' Bogdan often avoided revealing his actual nationality. Even though Adam never experienced any direct discrimination on the basis of his Romanian nationality, he still felt uncertain of locals' perception of him:

> Nobody ever told me something directly negative to me because I'm Romanian, but I do feel like it matters [when interacting with locals]. Maybe it's just my inner feelings speaking. I never felt discriminated because I'm Romanian. Maybe I felt discriminated because I'm from the Balkans. Maybe. Because that is how Romania and Bulgaria are seen. But I have never been denied service or something like that specifically because I'm from Romania.
>
> (Adam, Romania)

The negative associations with her Romanian heritage were also the reason why Clara expected that locals would meet her with a considerable portion of distrust:

CLARA: I expect people to look at me at least a bit different because I say that I am Romanian.
METTE: Really?
CLARA: Yes.
METTE: In what way?
CLARA: Not trusting me from the first second but then they get to know me and things loosen up.
METTE: That must be a bit tough?
CLARA: It is, but at a student level you can barely feel it. On a student level, it's more about 'you know more than I do' or 'you know less than I do' or 'you know other things.' At this level it's different, it's so much easier to form a community.

(Clara, Romania)

In Clara's case, it was primarily outside the university walls that she expected that people would treat her differently whereas her nationality meant less when socialising with other university students. This echoes Elena Genova's (2016, p. 401) findings of how Bulgarian students in the UK felt a marked difference between the 'inclusiveness, belonging, equality, and safety guaranteed by the multicultural university environment' and their experiences outside the university walls. While this section focused on my interlocutors' experiences of their 'Eastern Europeanness' as a discrediting attribute, the next section goes further into the students' (narrative) attempts of managing a spoiled identity (Goffman, 1963).

Managing a spoiled identity

While some students strongly believed that they were subjected to discrimination on the basis of their Eastern European heritage, there were also examples of students arguing that the discrimination they experienced in Denmark was not directed towards Eastern Europeans *per se* but rather symptomatic of Danes' problematic relationship with foreigners. Borge, for instance, emphasised that discriminatory practices are ingrained in human nature and in some sense 'natural.' He believed that the poor treatment he received, while employed as a cleaner in Denmark, was rooted in a general fear of foreigners rather than directed at him personally or Romanians as a group. He gave the hypothetical example of how he probably would have acted in a similar manner had he been an employer in Romania choosing between a Chinese and a Romanian worker: 'Of course, I would choose a Romanian instead of a Chinese.' According to Jon Fox et al. (2015), denying racialised discrimination can function as a means of stigma management. Claiming discrimination 'entails association with beleaguered (and racialised) victims of discrimination' and therefore 'endorsing a racial order that places the discriminated in a dominated position' (Fox et al., 2015, p. 743). Denying discrimination may thus constitute a useful narrative strategy for migrants to subtract themselves from dominated groups. Indeed, by labelling Danes' discriminatory behaviour 'natural,' Borge accentuates certain sameness with the dominators – thereby seemingly making it easier for him to cope with the role as the victim of discriminatory practices.

Another way of managing a 'blemished identity' may be through offering alternative narratives. For instance, Karen Fog Olwig (2018) shows how Caribbean migrants residing in Denmark actively tried to challenge the negative images often associated with the immigrant category. The migrants, Olwig (2018, p. 166) argues, claimed a positive migrant identity by offering counter-narratives of themselves as 'adventure travellers, curious, open-minded and eager to explore the world,' that is, human qualities that are admired and respected in the Western world and that challenge their classification as immigrants from the socioeconomically disadvantaged part of the world. In line with Olwig's findings, Borge was determined to nuance, challenge, and change the negative narratives of Romanian migrants and contribute to the emergence of a positive counter-narrative by performing various kind gestures:

BORGE: I'm fighting for my people to be seen a little different by others. I had a colleague, a Danish one, a girl from Copenhagen, we have been in Rome together with the school, with the master's programme, and I bought two coffees, one for me and one for her. Then she said 'I want to pay the coffee' and I said 'No, your country has given me a lot of things, I can give you a coffee for free.'

METTE: How did she respond?

BORGE: She said: 'Oh that's very impressive, why do you have this mentality?' And I said 'I'm working to change the impressions of Danish people regarding Romanians from my level and as much as I can.'

(Borge, Romania)

The quote exemplifies how Borge engaged in stigma management when interacting with local Danes. Clearly, he was focused on presenting a particular *front* to his Danish classmate. By offering to pay for their coffee, Borge aimed at performing a role in accordance with the moral criteria valued by the host society (Lamont and Aksartova, 2002; Olwig, 2018) and to steer the impressions of locals in a direction that would re-affirm his social identity as a natural part of the host society (Huot and Rudman, 2010). Borge also recalled another episode where he invited a total stranger (of Danish origin) into his apartment for coffee right after that same person unrightfully had accused him of stealing his bike. Through such performances, he actively sought to challenge entrenched hierarchies of domination but also to distance himself from discrediting narratives unjustly assigned to him.

In their study of the working-class men's strategies for bridging racial boundaries, Michèle Lamont and Sada Aksartova (2002) disclose how North African workers in France build bridges towards the French by providing what they refer to as *evidence of personal goodness*. This strategy involves abstracting oneself from one's race/nation/religion in order to show that a member is not necessarily defined by the group to which s/he belongs or that judgments about a group cannot be extended to each of its representatives (Lamont and Aksartova, 2002, p. 13). By offering a cup of coffee to strangers and displaying generous personal traits, Borge, similarly, sought to display evidence of his personal goodness, thereby confronting potential negative judgments. The fact that Borge felt obliged to prove his worthiness to locals by accentuating his *cultural sameness* and his proximity to 'Western values' suggests a latent inferior complex, similar to Fanon's analysis of colonial subjects.

Olga also focused on contracting the negative categorisations from popular conceptualisations of Eastern Europe in Denmark. Instead of hiding her Eastern European roots (or projecting them to other individuals and groups), she was determined to 'play with open cards' when it came to her country of birth. Olga believed that factors such as her own aura of 'coolness' steered locals' impression of Eastern European migrants and Eastern Europe more generally in a more positive direction:

> I'm a really proud Eastern European, I'm really proud saying I'm from Eastern Europe and I really don't like Polish people who claim 'I'm not from Eastern Europe, I'm from Central Europe.' I don't really like those people. And I really like emphasising that I'm from Eastern Europe, because if I in this way can make Eastern Europe look much cooler because Western Europeans like me and they are going to think ok if she is from Eastern Europe then Eastern Europe is a cool place. If I can do this then some people are going to view Eastern Europe in a different way. I am making changes in this way.
>
> (Olga, Poland)

Olga's reflections suggest a particular fixation on the *Western gaze*. While she presented an ontological narrative of herself as a person unaffected by people's opinion of her, the above quote underlines how Olga, at least to some extent, thought about Westerners' view of her as well as her compatibility with them. There were also students who predominantly focused on differences between Eastern and Western Europe by highlighting the advantages of coming from Eastern Europe and particularly the moral superiority they associated with people from Eastern European countries. I previously underlined how some students believed that their precarious situation paved the way for certain positive personal features such as stamina and independence. Following a similar logic, some interlocutors argued that post-socialist countries' economic struggles provided the region's citizens with moral advantages. Marcus, for instance, emphasised the value of family in Romania. Regardless of Western Europe's 'economic strength,' he believed that Eastern European countries had a strong upper hand in the more intimate sphere. It was especially within the domain of the family that he deemed 'Western culture' backwards. While Marcus had arrived in Denmark with *grand* expectations of settling in the country on a longer-term basis, he became increasingly convinced that he belonged in Romania. This is also the main reason why he had made plans to return to Romania and start a family following his graduation. In the next section, I go further into how these different narratives of 'home country,' 'Eastern Europe,' and 'the West' played central roles in the students' rationales for leaving Denmark.

Reclaiming one's heritage and the question of return

While migration to a Western country had been a dream for Borge since he was a young boy, he found himself increasingly attracted to the idea of returning to Romania after having spent several years in Denmark:

> I'm seeing my future in Romania because I think if you will have all the best conditions in another country, you will always feel like something is missing and especially in your heart or in your soul. And I think that's something like, I feel like a calling from my country. But I do have periods when I'm thinking just to stay here and then I have periods when I'm thinking of going back.
>
> (Borge, Romania)

For Borge, the thought of returning was characterised by a high degree of ambivalence. Although being emotionally drawn to his home country and 'his people,' he simultaneously feared that it would be complicated to build a life for himself and his wife in Romania due to the low wages. Indeed, several of my interlocutors who initially perceived a master's degree abroad as an important step towards more permanent migration to the West began to revaluate their original plans as time went by in Denmark. Even though most students previously had been highly critical of certain societal conditions in their home countries, many began to see the countries in a less clear-cut negative light as time went by. Borge's descriptions illustrate how the yearning to return was intensified by transnational ties to people in their home country (Snel et al., 2015).

Olga expressed a similar newfound sense of national belonging just a few weeks before she returned to Poland. During our conversation, she reflected on her time in Denmark and, in particular, her decision to return to Poland without having completed her master's degree. In Denmark, she worked extensively with jobs in the cleaning industry and the constant focus on money filled her with an increasing sense of fatigue. This situation, she claimed, could have been avoided with the financial aid of a scholarship. It was not only economic hardship that ultimately prompted Olga's return but, akin to Borge's descriptions, the emotional ties to family and friends back home grew increasingly important. Interestingly, Olga's ontological narrations suggest a stronger identification with her 'Eastern European roots' than was previously the case:

> It's more about not being among those people you most care about or that you used to care about. It is just time to go home. I'm just very Eastern European, I cannot really live in this country just because how different people are. You might not actually notice it, but we are extremely different from local Danish people. I feel those differences in behaviour, the way that people think, the way they prioritise – it's extremely different. I just prefer to live in a country where people act in a similar manner as I do.
>
> (Olga, Poland)

It is interesting to note that while Olga previously focused on accentuating sameness and compatibleness with Western European societies, she became increasingly preoccupied with the marked 'differences in behaviour' between herself, a 'very Eastern European' individual, and the Danish people. Olga ascribed feelings of alienation in Denmark to the 'inherent differences' between South-Eastern and Western European cultures. In her view, Danes were characterised by 'completely different temperaments' compared to people of Polish origin. In sharp contrast to Danes who speak quietly and who only use a few gestures, she considered herself to have a very 'dynamic' and 'very Italian' persona. At one point, Olga sarcastically noted that 'even my Italian fellows say I'm very Italian.' After having spent several years in Denmark, she longed to be among 'less Nordic' people, where she would feel more anonymous. In the interview situation, Olga displays a form of stigma management based on narrating stereotypical characterisations of Danes and North-Western Europeans, which she juxtaposes with Poles and South-Eastern Europeans. In contrast to earlier conversations, she now

presented her South-Eastern European roots as some of the most fundamental attributes for the person she had become while residing abroad.
Olga, furthermore, claimed that she has been 'verbally attacked' by Danes
questioning the reasonableness of her receiving a free education without
giving something back to the Danish society:

OLGA: Well, I definitely think that being abroad, well it's hard because you
        have to face some kinds of verbal attacks. Also, like, people attack you
        all the time. Like the people obviously, who you met and who like you,
        they won't attack – however, if you meet new people you always get all
        those questions: 'Why are you here?,' 'What are you doing here?' and
        'Why are you taking up our study spots?' and stuff like this.
METTE: Really?
OLGA: Really! Even university students ask like: 'Eihhh, but you are actu-
        ally taking our university place and then you don't want to stay in
        Denmark?' But then again, I don't want to stay in Denmark because I
        have no chance of a full-time job. It's really difficult for Arts students to
        get a full-time job here.

(Olga, Poland)

As evident in the quote, Olga felt that locals blamed her for taking advantage
of the Danish welfare system by returning to Poland instead of staying and
paying taxes to the country that provided her with free education. Olga's
narrations, furthermore, exemplify how the students' initial plans – which for
the majority had involved long-term settlement in the West – often changed
following their experience of living in Denmark. This follows Allan Findlay
et al.'s (2017) insights on how international students may find their long-term
desires and imaginary life mobilities disrupted by personal circumstances
encountered during the course of their studies. In addition, the quote by Olga
captures a more general tendency among the students – namely the discour-
agement that many described when talking about entering the Danish labour
market following their graduation as foreign graduates from interdisciplinary backgrounds in social sciences and humanities.

It is worth noting the relatively high number of students who did not
manage to complete their master's degree in Denmark. Out of the 27
interlocutors from Eastern European countries, 6 dropped out of their educational programs prior to graduation. Additionally, 4 students wrote their
master's theses while living at their parents' house due to lack of money.
Essentially, these 10 students all originated from EU countries, while all of
the 11 students, fully supported by scholarships in Denmark, graduated
from the university on time. Hence, these numbers indicate that the relative economic security during one's studies – the most marked difference
between the students with and without a scholarship – appears to have a
significant impact on international students' ability to finish their studies
whereas financial struggles constitute a significant barrier for graduating.

Conclusions

This chapter focused on the Eastern European students' narratives connected to living and studying in Denmark. Throughout the chapter, I drew attention to how structural differences – in particular (the lack of), money and reliance on part-time jobs – shaped the students' lived realities abroad. While I, in this book, group various post-socialist countries under the broad label 'Eastern Europe,' my findings indicate a marked difference between the narrations and experiences of non-EU students fully funded by scholarships and the students originating from EU member states. This difference revolves around the extent that their ontological narratives and accustomed roles are challenged by the act of cross-border mobility. While EU citizens enjoy greater mobility freedom than non-EU students, many EU movers ended up living under uncertain and economically vulnerable conditions in Denmark. Since parental support rarely was an option for these students, they were entirely dependent on finding paid employment to finance their lives abroad while studying. In Chapter 3, I discussed how my interlocutors initially saw Denmark as an opportunity to install a sense of 'normalcy' in their lives, involving predictability, reliability, and legibility (Misztal, 2001) and the ability to render one's desires or commitments into an actionable truth (Greenberg, 2011). Yet, in contrast to such aspirations, many EU movers were confronted with a new version of 'abnormality' when finding their lives characterised by an unparalleled level of precariousness and an unprecedented focus on money.

Those who succeeded in finding paid employment hoped that their new situation would bring more stability into their lives and put an end to their hardship. However, their employment as low-skilled workers often generated new and unforeseen challenges due to unmatched levels of exhaustion from the many hours invested in the demanding jobs. This situation gradually paved the way for a sense of having lost control over the pace and direction of their lives. Indeed, few EU movers seemed prepared for the unparalleled precarious life conditions that awaited them abroad. Their dependence on paid work – not least since a minimum of 10–12 hours of work per week is required to get the Danish state stipend – made them exposed to exploitation from local employers. In turn, humiliating conditions at the labour market created a feeling of alienation to the host society and their Danish peers and, as a consequence, the feeling of being second-class EU citizens. Moreover, the lack of money and the physical and mental pressure from their part-time jobs constituted a significant barrier to participate fully in various communities in Denmark. I argued that these students underwent a 'divestment passage,' entailing a negatively experienced separation from their accustomed ontological narratives and performances of uncertain duration. For some, the limited involvement in meaningful occupations seemingly paved the way for a 'disconnect' from their ontological narratives, which appeared to have an adverse effect on their overall well-being.

While the so-called EU movers played the 'lead role' in this chapter, the narrations of the students sponsored by scholarship served, among other things, to carve out the ways that structural inequalities may impact students' mobility experience. The relative financial security provided by a scholarship meant that these students enjoyed a higher degree of freedom to engage in activities they valued. They were relatively free to build their CVs through extra-curricular activities and getting involved in work related to their areas of interest. They could also choose not to work or engage in volunteer tasks that complemented their educational profile to position them more favourably in relation to the job market upon their graduation. As such, their lives were neither deprived of meaningful social networks with other students nor were they hindered from taking part in activities at the university campus. In contrast to many students from EU countries, they did not experience a 'biographical disruption' where the structures of an individual's everyday life and the forms of knowledge which underpin them become disrupted (Bury, 1982). While the non-EU students obviously were not immune to occasional feelings of loneliness or frustration, their performances and ontological narratives remained more or less stable and aligned during the course of study. Consequently, their narrations suggested greater satisfaction with life in Denmark. Overall, the empirical findings presented in this chapter accentuate how the EU integration process positions students very differently abroad depending on their home country's EU membership status and that EU movers are not necessarily in a privileged position abroad (see also Simola, 2018).

In Chapter 3, I highlighted how the students initially presented their *progressive, modern, and Europe-oriented* attitudes as a reason for leaving their home countries and setting sails 'West.' In this chapter, I, however, discussed how many, upon their arrival to Denmark, found their ontological narratives challenged by the negative public narratives attached to Eastern European migrants. Many students explained how they, even before encounters with people of Western European origin, were preoccupied with their 'Western gaze' and the discrediting narrative they feared to become entangled in. Student migration, then, may also involve 'struggles over identity' (Somers, 1994, p. 610) and I showed how my interlocutors, in their attempt to fight off dominant narratives, engaged in stigma management by offering counter-performances and counter-narratives of themselves. Even though the majority of the students alluded to feelings of 'incomplete Europeanness,' factors such as their economic situation, their housing arrangement, and their work-life in Denmark appeared to strengthen experiences of stigmatisation and alienation from an overarching narrative of Europe.

Finally, the chapter discussed how many of the students began to rethink their initial plans for the future in light of their lived realities of Denmark. I showed how students, who previously had been highly critical of the social conditions in their home countries, began to see these in a somewhat different and often more positive light. As time went by, many became attracted to the idea of returning or at least changing geographical location. By following my interlocutors consistently over a longer period, I was thus able to track important changes in their narratives and ideas about their future. Aspirations of returning to their home countries often represented a considerable deviation from the students' initial plans of long-term settlement in Denmark and the West.

Notes

1 To keep the anonymity of the participants in this study, the name of the dorm is fictional.
2 My own translation from various Danish debate forums on the Internet.

References

Amit, V., 2010. The limits of liminality: Capacities for change and transition among student travellers, in: Rapport, N. (Ed.), Human Nature as Capacity. Berghahn Books, New York.

Andreouli, E., Howarth, C., 2019. Everyday cosmopolitanism in representations of Europe among young Romanians in Britain. Sociology 53, 280–296. https://doi.org/10.1177/0038038518777693

Antonsich, M., 2010. Searching for belonging – an analytical framework. Geogr. Compass 4, 644–659. https://doi.org/10.1111/j.1749-8198.2009.00317.x

Beech, S.E., 2018. Negotiating the complex geographies of friendships overseas: Becoming, being and sharing in student mobility. Geoforum 92, 18–25. https://doi.org/10.1016/j.geoforum.2018.03.019

Benson, M., 2011. The movement beyond (lifestyle) migration: Mobile practices and the constitution of a better way of life. Mobilities 6, 221–235. https://doi.org/10.1080/17450101.2011.552901

Bury, M., 1982. Chronic illness as biographical disruption. Sociol. Health Illn. 4, 167–182.

Campbell, I., Boese, M., Tham, J.-C., 2016. Inhospitable workplaces? International students and paid work in food services. Aust. J. Soc. Issues 51, 279–298. https://doi.org/10.1002/j.1839-4655.2016.tb01232.x

Cheregi, B.F., 2015. The media construction of anti-immigration positions: The discourse on the Romanian immigrants in the British press. Revista Romana de sociologie. 26(3/4), 279–298.

Conradson, D., Mckay, D., 2007. Translocal subjectivities: Mobility, connection, emotion. Mobilities 2, 167–174. https://doi.org/10.1080/17450100701381524

Ezzy, D., 1993. Unemployment and mental health: A critical review. Soc. Sci. Med. 37, 41–52. https://doi.org/10.1016/0277-9536(93)90316-v

Ezzy, D., 2000. Fate and agency in job loss narratives. Qual. Sociol. 23, 121–134. https://doi.org/10.1023/A:1005459701480

Fanon, F., 2008. Black Skin, White Masks. Pluto Press, London.

Favell, A., 2008. The new face of east–west migration in Europe. J. Ethn. Migr. Stud. 34, 701–716. https://doi.org/10.1080/13691830802105947

Findlay, A., Prazeres, L., McCollum, D., Packwood, H., 2017. 'It was always the plan': International study as 'learning to migrate.' Area 49, 192–199. https://doi.org/10.1111/area.12315

Fox, J.E., Moroşanu, L., Szilassy, E., 2015. Denying discrimination: Status, 'race,' and the whitening of Britain's new Europeans. J. Ethn. Migr. Stud. 41, 21. https://doi.org/10.1080/1369183X.2014.962491

Genova, E., 2016. To have both roots and wings: Nested identities in the case of Bulgarian students in the UK. Identities 23, 392–406. https://doi.org/10.1080/1070289X.2015.1024125

Gilmartin, M., Coppari, P.R., Phelan, D., 2020. Promising precarity: The lives of Dublin's international students. J. Ethn. Migr. Stud. 1–18. https://doi.org/10.1080/1369183X.2020.1732617

Goffman, E., 1956. The Presentation of Self in Everyday Life, University of Edinburgh Social Sciences Research Centre monographs; 2. University of Edinburgh Social Sciences Research Centre, Edinburgh.

Goffman, E., 1963. Stigma: Notes on the Management of Spoiled Identity. Prentice-Hall, Englewood Cliffs, NJ.

Goffman, E., 1990. The Presentation of Self in Everyday Life. Penguin, London.

Gomes, C., 2015. Footloose transients: International students in Australia and their aspirations for transnational mobility after graduation. Crossings J. Migr. Cult. 6, 41–57. https://doi.org/10.1386/cjmc.6.1.41_1

Greenberg, J., 2011. On the road to normal: Negotiating agency and state sovereignty in postsocialist Serbia. Am. Anthropol. 113, 88–100. https://doi.org/10.1111/j.1548-1433.2010.01308.x

Huot, S., Rudman, D.L., 2010. The performances and places of identity: Conceptualizing intersections of occupation, identity and place in the process of migration. J. Occup. Sci. 17, 68–77. https://doi.org/10.1080/14427591.2010.9686677

Kovačević, N., 2008. Narrating Post/Communism: Colonial Discourse and Europe's Borderline Civilization, BASEES/Routledge Series on Russian and East European Studies; 47. Routledge, London.

Lamont, M., 1992. Money, Morals, and Manners: The Culture of the French and American Upper-middle Class, Morality and Society. University of Chicago Press, Chicago.

Lamont, M., 2000. The Dignity of Working Men: Morality and the Boundaries of Race, Class, and Immigration. Russell Sage Foundation, New York.

Lamont, M., Aksartova, S., 2002. Ordinary cosmopolitanisms – strategies for bridging racial boundaries among working-class men. Theory Cult. Soc. 19, 1–25. https://doi.org/10.1177/0263276402019004001

Lehmann, W., 2009. Becoming middle class: How working-class university students draw and transgress moral class boundaries. Sociology 43, 631–647.

Lopez Rodriguez, M., 2010. Migration and a quest for 'normalcy.' Polish migrant mothers and the capitalization of meritocratic opportunities in the UK. Soc. Identities 16, 339–358. https://doi.org/10.1080/13504630.2010.482422

Manolova, P., 2017. On the Way to the Imaginary West: Bulgarian Migrations, Imaginations, and Disillusionments. (Unpublished thesis). Birmingham University, Birmingham: Department of Political Science and International Studies.

Manolova, P., 2018. 'Going to the west is my last chance to get a normal life': Bulgarian would-be migrants' imaginings of life in the UK. Cent. East. Eur. Migr. Rev. 1–23. https://doi.org/10.17467/ceemr.2018.01

Manolova, P., 2020. Aspiring, ambivalent, assertive: Bulgarian middle-class subjectivities and boundary work through migration. East Eur. Polit. Soc. Cult. 34, 505–528. https://doi.org/10.1177/0888325419837349

Marc, L., 2009. What's So Eastern about Eastern Europe? Oldcastle Books, Harpenden.

Marcu, S., 2015. Uneven mobility experiences: Life-strategy expectations among Eastern European undergraduate students in the UK and Spain. Geoforum 58, 68–75. https://doi.org/10.1016/j.geoforum.2014.10.017

Maury, O., 2017. Student-migrant-workers. Nord. J. Migr. Res. 7, 224–232. https://doi.org/10.1515/njmr-2017-0023

Maury, O., 2020. Between a promise and a salary: Student-migrant-workers' experiences of precarious labour markets. Work Employ. Soc. 34, 809–825. https://doi.org/10.1177/0950017019887097

Mishhova, D., Kostadinova, T., 2018. Reconceptualising space, borders and identity in Bulgaria: The Kosovo crisis and EU accession, in: Scott, J.W. (Ed.), Post-cold War Borders – Reframing Political Space in Eastern Europe. Routledge, London.

Misztal, B.A., 2001. Normality and trust in Goffman's theory of interaction order. Sociol. Theory 19, 312–324. https://doi.org/DOI: 10.1111/0735-2751.00143

Murphy-Lejeune, E., 2002. Student Mobility and Narrative in Europe: The New Strangers, Routledge Studies in Anthropology. Routledge, London.

Olwig, K.F., 2018. Migration as adventure: Narrative self-representation among Caribbean migrants in Denmark. Ethnos 83, 156–171. https://doi.org/10.1080/00141844.2016.1209538

Pan, D., 2011. Student visas, undocumented labour, and the boundaries of legality: Chinese migration and English as a foreign language education in the Republic of Ireland. Soc. Anthropol. 19, 268–287. https://doi.org/10.1111/j.1469-8676.2011.00159.x

Parutis, V., 2014. 'Economic migrants' or 'Middling transnationals'? East European migrants' experiences of work in the UK. Int. Migr. 52, 36–55. https://doi.org/10.1111/j.1468-2435.2010.00677.x

Raghuram, P., 2013. Theorising the spaces of student migration. Popul. Space Place 19, 138–154. https://doi.org/10.1002/psp.1747

Robertson, S., 2013. Transnational Student-migrants and the State: The Education-migration Nexus. Palgrave Macmillan, Basingstoke.

Robertson, S., 2018. Friendship networks and encounters in student-migrants' negotiations of translocal subjectivity. Urban Stud. 55, 538–553. https://doi.org/10.1177/0042098016659617

Ryan, L., 2011. Migrants' social networks and weak ties: Accessing resources and constructing relationships post-migration. Sociol. Rev. 59, 707–724. https://doi.org/10.1111/j.1467-954X.2011.02030.x

Ryan, L., Mulholland, J., 2014. 'Wives are the route to social life': An analysis of family life and networking amongst highly skilled migrants in London. Sociology 48, 251–267. https://doi.org/10.1177/0038038512475109

Samaluk, B., 2016. Migration, consumption and work: A postcolonial perspective on post-socialist migration to the UK. Ephemera 16, 95.

Sandu, D., Toth, G., Tudor, E., 2018. The nexus of motivation-experience in the migration process of young Romanians. Popul. Space Place 24, e2114. https://doi.org/10.1002/psp.2114

Sardar, Z. 2008. Foreword to the 2008 edition, in: Fanon, F. (Ed.), Black Skin, White Masks. Pluto Press, London.

Sawir, E., Marginson, S., Nyland, C., Ramia, G., Rawlings-Sanaei, F., 2009. The social and economic security of international students: A New Zealand study. High. Educ. Policy 22, 461–482. https://doi.org/10.1057/hep.2009.4

Sayer, A., 2005. Class, moral worth and recognition. Sociology 39, 947–963. https://doi.org/10.1177/0038038505058376

Scheuer, S., 2017. Misbrug af østeuropæiske studerende på det danske arbjedsmarked. LO – Landsorganisationen i Danmark. https://lo.dk/wp-content/uploads/2017/11/2221- ny-su-rapport-oesteuro-stud-2017.pdf

Simola, A., 2018. Lost in administration: (Re)producing precarious citizenship for young university-educated intra-EU migrants in Brussels. Work Employ. Soc. 32, 458–474. https://doi.org/10.1177/0950017018755653

Snel, E., Faber, M., Engbersen, G., 2015. To stay or return? Explaining return intentions of Central and Eastern European labour migrants. Cent. East. Eur. Migr. Rev. 4, 5–24.

Somers, M.R., 1992. Narrativity, narrative identity, and social action: Rethinking English working-class formation. Soc. Sci. Hist. 16, 591. https://doi.org/10.2307/1171314

Somers, M.R., 1994. The narrative constitution of identity: A relational and network approach. Theory Soc. 23, 605–649. https://doi-org.ezproxy.its.uu.se/10.1007/BF00992905

Thomas, S., 2017. The precarious path of student migrants: Education, debt, and transnational migration among Indian youth. J. Ethn. Migr. Stud. 43, 1873–1889. https://doi.org/10.1080/1369183X.2017.1286970

Valentin, K., 2012. Caught between internationalisation and immigration: The case of Nepalese students in Denmark. Learn. Teach. 5: 56–74. https://doi.org/10.3167/latiss.2012.050304

Valentin, K., 2015. Transnational education and the remaking of social identity: Nepalese student migration to Denmark. Identities 22, 318–332. https://doi.org/10.1080/1070289X.2014.939186

van Riemsdijk, M., 2010. Variegated privileges of whiteness: Lived experiences of Polish nurses in Norway. Soc. Cult. Geogr. 11, 117–137. https://doi.org/10.1080/14649360903514376

Veličković, V., 2019. Eastern Europeans in Contemporary Literature and Culture: Imagining New Europe. Palgrave, London.

Vertovec, S., 2007. Super-diversity and its implications. Ethn. Racial Stud. 30, 1024–1054. https://doi.org/10.1080/01419870701599465

Volet, S.E., Ang, G., 1998. Culturally mixed groups on international campuses: An opportunity for inter-cultural learning. High. Educ. Res. Dev. 17, 5–23. https://doi.org/10.1080/0729436980170101

Wacquant, L.J.D., 2008. Urban Outcasts: A Comparative Sociology of Advanced Marginality. Polity, Cambridge.

Wilken, L., Dahlberg, M.G., 2017. Between international student mobility and work migration: Experiences of students from EU's newer member states in Denmark. J. Ethn. Migr. Stud. 43, 1347–1361. https://doi.org/10.1080/1369183X.2017.1300330

5 Should I stay or should I go?

The social and geographical trajectories of Eastern European graduates

Introduction

While the previous chapters have dealt with aspirations prior to departure and experiences of studying in Denmark, this chapter turns towards my interlocutors' lives upon their graduation.[1] According to Allan Findlay et al. (2017), scholarship focused on international students tends to reduce the phenomenon to a geographical binary between staying or returning, while marginalising other potential outcomes such as onward migration to a third country. This presumption may be related to the fact that the phenomenon has been typically interpreted in isolation from other mobilities (Findlay et al., 2017), as 'the only group who migrate primarily in order to enhance their human capital, and ostensibly for fixed time periods' (Baláž and Williams, 2004, p. 218). In response to this prevailing understanding, researchers have stressed the importance of examining the way that students' lives unfold upon graduation (Bryła, 2018; Geddie, 2010; Mosneaga and Winther, 2013) in combination with return rates, labour market outcomes, and other long-term effects of student mobility (Wiers-Jenssen, 2013). The latter seems particularly important since national governments across the world and supranational regions, such as the EU, have entered into a 'race for talent' (Geddie, 2015), turning student migrants into a sought-after good. Indeed, since the first decade of the 21st century, they have increasingly been viewed as prospective highly skilled workers and a means for boosting knowledge-intense labour markets and countering ageing populations (Hawthorne, 2009). On the other side of the coin – that is, from the perspective of sending countries – mobile students may contribute to knowledge and capacity building in their home countries (presuming that they return with improved skills), yet they may also represent lost talent to foreign labour markets (Chankseliani, 2016; OECD, 2017).

In this chapter, I seek to move beyond the conventional 'stay and return construct' when unravelling the Eastern European student migrants' multi-faceted social and geographical trajectories as they evolve following their graduation from a Danish university. I am particularly interested in the ways they narrate their present lives with respect to the goals they had set for themselves when they initially arrived in Denmark, how a Danish degree positions them upon graduation, and the ways they imagine the future social and geographical trajectories from their current positions. Furthermore, I address the tensions between the national interests of the Danish state to recruit and retain highly skilled labour and the challenges that the international graduates in this study experience in establishing themselves in the Danish labour market.

I begin this chapter by outlining the current policy framework shaping especially non-EU graduates' employment and residence options in Denmark. From then on, the analysis is divided into three overriding parts. The first part focuses on the narratives and strategies of the student migrants keen on staying in Denmark, while the second part explores the narratives of 'the homecomers' and their different connotations attached to homecoming. Finally, the third part deals with the student migrants who engage in onward journeys to third countries.

An evolving policy framework

Before exploring my interlocutors' narratives of their post-graduation trajectories, I provide a brief discussion of the current policy framework shaping their options for employment and residence in Denmark following their graduation (see also Ginnerskov-Dahlberg and Valentin, forthcoming). In continuation with the findings discussed in previous chapters, an important distinction exists between graduates from inside and outside the EU in terms of premises for staying in Denmark. I have previously emphasised that the most potent cornerstone of EU citizenship is that it provides access to a common space of equal rights and free movement (Ahrens et al., 2016). Hence, upon graduation, EU/EEA and Swiss students can stay and work in Denmark under the EU regulations on freedom of movement and do not need a residence or work permit. EU/EEA and Swiss students are further entitled to unemployment benefits ('dagpenge') if they have been a member of a recognised unemployment insurance fund for at least one year and have a registered address in Denmark. In contrast, policies facilitating transition of students from non-EU countries into the Danish labour market are less straightforward and even characterised by frequent policy changes and adjustments.

In the following, I discuss the most important immigration policies shaping the experiences of non-EU students in Denmark upon their graduation based on information presented by the Danish Agency for International Recruitment and Integration.[2] Throughout my first wave of fieldwork in Denmark (2013–2015), I encountered non-EU students talking about their upcoming Green Card application. Between 2007 and 2016, non-EU graduates could apply for a Green Card following their graduation. The Green Card Scheme provided non-EU graduates with the possibility to obtain a three-year residence permit under a points system (with possibilities for further extension of a maximum of five years). However, the scheme was discontinued in 2016 due to a claimed mismatch between the academic qualifications of the Green Card holders and the low-skilled work that they often end up performing (Niraula and Valentin, 2019).

Today non-EU/EEA students get a job-seeking permit following their graduation, which allows them to stay up to six months in Denmark after completion of study to search for a job. In this period, students may only work up to 20 hours per week and they do not have the right to unemployment benefits from the unemployment insurance fund, commonly referred to as 'a-kasse.'[3] In addition to the job-seeking permit, master's and PhD graduates have since 2015 been able to apply for a so-called Establishment Card with the aim of allowing international graduates to 'establish themselves' in Denmark. From 1 July 2020, a foreign national with a Danish bachelor's or professional bachelor's degree can also be granted an Establishment Card. It is the only scheme directly intended for international graduates, who should apply within one year of graduating (until 1 July 2020 this period was only six months).

The Establishment Card, however, comes with certain conditions: Graduates cannot receive unemployment benefits and they must demonstrate that they have sufficient funds to support themselves for the upcoming year, which is over DKK 89,376 a year (approximately 12,000 euros). Moreover, the student needs to declare twice the bank assets if he or she has a non-EU spouse (approximately 24,000 euros). A residence permit under the establishment scheme can be granted for a period of up to two years. From 1 July 2020, the Establishment Card may be extended by an additional year for foreign nationals employed in a job *relevant* to the completed educational programme.

Following the expiration of the Establishment Card, graduates must apply for a new residence permit using one of the other schemes. Other relevant schemes for international non-EU graduates include the Pay Limit Scheme, which allows graduates to enter into the labour market by having a job offer that pays more than DKK 445,000 a year (approximately 60,000 euros).[4] To put this number in perspective, it is interesting to note that the average salary for new graduates (whether local or foreign) in the field of humanities was DKK 408,000 in 2019 (approximately 55,000 euros). Different rules (such as having a lower salary) apply to students who enter into research and, for instance, become PhD students. Students with the 'right' job profile may also apply through The Positive List, which lists professions experiencing a shortage of qualified professionals in Denmark. However, none of the areas or jobs on the list (updated January 2021) would apply to the educational profile of the non-EU graduates in my study.

Graduation: attempts at settling in Denmark

In search of recognition

For Erina, who viewed a Danish master's degree as a ticket out of Bosnia and Herzegovina, finding a job in Denmark constituted a crucial first step for long-term migration. During an interview not long before graduating, she seemed anxious when addressing her upcoming job search, where she was required to find employment within as briefly as six months if she wanted to stay in Denmark

> So yeah, I have like six months to find a job here and there is more at stake for me than people who came here to get an exchange experience – you know, a university-laid-back experience – and after that they go back to their own country. So yes, the level of seriosity is different. I'm frustrated about the different opportunities for non-EU and EU citizens. So many people have so many opportunities in the European Union and they don't even think about that. Some of them are not even using their possibilities or they are just taking it for granted. It's just very frustrating because I have to put so much effort, so much stress, think about papers all the time, think about am I eligible to apply for that with my passport and visa. People here have so much more opportunity than I do and they are not using it.
>
> (Erina, Bosnia and Herzegovina)

Clearly, Erina's uncertain migration status filled her with frustration and anger. In the quote, she uses the mobility freedom of EU citizens as a yardstick for evaluating her own situation. Stef Jansen (2009, p. 824) speaks of 'zones of humiliating entrapment' in his analysis of people's engagement with mobility regulations in Bosnia and Herzegovina and Serbia. Exploring how forms of 'geopolitical affect' emerge from engagement with visa regimes, Jansen (2009, p. 824) argues that regulation, embodied in state-issued documents, informs people's understandings of themselves and their 'collective place in the contemporary world.' Erina's narrations indicate that she experienced the EU visa regimes as 'a blatantly humiliating materialization of the inversion of European geopolitical hierarchies' (Jansen, 2009, p. 828) despite that she – in contrast to Jansen's research subjects – was residing *outside* the borders of her home country. Her narrations thus underline how the sense of entrapment may follow non-EU citizens when living in locations other than their home countries. The stress caused by excessive paperwork and opaque regulation made Erina feel like a second-class citizen in Europe. To counter what she described as a geopolitical stigma, she accentuated her impressive CV and value as an employee for future employers:

> If I do not succeed in Denmark to find a suitable job, I think that some countries will be more than interested in me. For example, because of my diverse education – this will be my second master's degree – I'm really trying my best to invest in myself. When I come to an interview at a job, I want to make sure that I get the best job. I don't mind cleaning but it does not make sense to do that like my fellow students are doing it for two years now. If I'm not accepted here, I will do the same thing as I

did in Bosnia. If I'm not appreciated here, I will just go somewhere else. With that level of education, I will have a good salary I think.

(Erina, Bosnia and Herzegovina)

In the quote, Erina draws symbolic boundaries (Lamont and Molnár, 2002) between herself and her classmates willing to subject themselves to low-skilled and low-paid jobs like cleaning. She presents an ontological narrative of herself as above what she experiences to be a humiliating treatment of non-EU citizens. On several occasions, she made it perfectly clear to me that she would not settle for employment less than her intellectual merits. As indicated, many of the students adhered to a narrative that a meaningful life involved a job in line with one's academic credentials (Galasińska and Galasiński, 2010). I previously showed how this quest functioned as an important impetus for studying abroad in the first place, yet for many, it also became a deal-breaker when deciding where to stay in the world following their graduation. In addition, it is interesting to note that Erina's future 'geographical coordinates' seemed highly uncertain. She had no plans to return to Bosnia and Herzegovina following her graduation yet, at the same time, she remained uncertain if Denmark would evolve into a long-term destination.

While my interlocutors initially imagined Denmark as a guarantor of a 'seamless labour market integration for graduates with local qualifications' (Robertson and Runganaikaloo, 2014, p. 216), they woke up to a very different reality following their graduation. Like Erina, Anastasia from Ukraine was reluctant to subject herself to humiliating work conditions. She did not want to stay in Denmark – or any other Western country for that matter – if staying meant that she would work in a low-skilled job. Anastasia knew of many examples of Eastern European graduates who had ended up in a 'low-skilled treadmill' where they remained years after having graduated from a Danish university. Hence, she feared that she would become one of these individuals if embarking on a similar path. She furthermore distanced herself from the Ukrainian women who, out of desperation to migrate to a Western country, saw marriage as their only feasible strategy. Why, she asked herself, would young, intelligent women want to get ahead in life on the basis of anything other than their own skills and merits? Akin to Erina's descriptions, Anastasia had confidence in her skills prior to her education – particularly a competitive internship she had done at an international organisation in Copenhagen as a part of her university studies. However, she gradually understood that having a local degree and relevant work experience was not necessarily sufficient for getting a job:

I applied for a lot of jobs. I think I was applying there unsuccessfully for jobs and internships for more than six months, but I was refused all the time so I eventually just gave up. I heard that getting jobs is all about your networks.

(Anastasia, Ukraine)

In spite of having completed a prestigious internship in the Danish capital, Anastasia believed that her professional network was insufficient for finding employment. In contrast to her earlier convictions of Denmark being a place that offered opportunities to individuals on the basis of their merits and skills, she now deemed social connections imperative for getting ahead professionally.[5] Another important reason which prompted Anastasia's return to Ukraine was the Ukrainian revolution beginning in 2014, which ignited a plethora of patriotic sentiments in her:

> All Ukrainians who cared about what was going on politically wanted to come back because it was a time of big chances and big challenges. And I felt that I need to go back and that I can do more in Ukraine than I can do in Denmark.
>
> (Anastasia, Ukraine)

Anastasia saw it as her 'patriotic duty' to return to Ukraine (Lulle and Buzinska, 2017, p. 1364). Her strong belief that she was contributing to a positive change in her home country by returning appeared to ease any remaining disappointment of failed attempts to enter the labour market in Denmark. Even though Anastasia was back in Ukraine, she did not rule out the possibility of going somewhere else. At one point, she even applied to a new master's programme in the US, thinking that she would add an additional repertoire of credentials to her educational profile, yet did not receive a scholarship.

Erina and Anastasia's narrations illustrate how student migration is not a static movement from one destination to another. Rather, migration emerges as an ongoing process where the involved are forced to adapt their expectations in line with their surrounding realities, not seldom leading to unfulfilled promises that, in turn, prompt new mobilities. Throughout this chapter, I will discuss how the students' geographical trajectories upon their graduation indicate that the conventional 'stay and return construct, dominant in the literature on student migration, is too simplistic for understanding international students' future movements (Geddie, 2015; Tan and Hugo, 2017; Wu and Wilkes, 2017). Essentially, the non-EU graduates' narrations of life were not characterised by a wish to engage in 'unlimited global mobility' (Gomes, 2015, p. 46), Nor did they dream of a free-moving lifestyle characterised by intentional unpredictability and temporality (Engbersen and Snel, 2013). Rather, they were highly conscious of the various legal barriers connected to international border crossing, and 'that their plans are so closely intertwined with the decisions of the regulatory body is ever present' (Robertson, 2011, p. 107). Akin to the EU migrants in the study of Susanne Bygnes and Marta Erdal (2017, p. 114), many dreamed of settling down longer-term and living 'grounded, secure and stable lives.' As non-EU citizens, aspirations of migration were, however, complicated by their uncertain legal status and future destinations highly conditioned on being granted a visa (see also Mosneaga and Winther, 2013).

In line with earlier discussions of global navigation strategies, the graduates did not want to settle for just *any* other country. Those eager to reside outside the borders of their home countries remained focused on destinations in the West. Affirming the assumption that our integrity and identity are shaped by recognition from others (Honneth, 1996), the students expressed a particular affinity for countries with a history of migration, led by the assumption that they would be recognised as humans of equal worth in these societies. Following Goffman (1963, p. 15), 'we believe the person with a stigma is not quite human' and the students clearly wanted to avoid ending up as stigmatised in their future host society. Indeed, Erina's and Anastasia's narrations exemplify well how graduates were focused on dodging countries where their label as 'Eastern European immigrants' could risk becoming a stigmatising attribute in the labour market and broader society, leading to social and economic marginalisation.

Despite the fact that many policy-makers talk about international students as desired immigrants, studies (Alho, 2020; Lulle and Buzinska, 2017) have shown that they also fall victim to the same discrimination and prejudice that 'regular immigrants' face. Essentially, the feeling of remaining an immigrant – an external component rather than an integrated part of society – eventually made Erina conclude that it was time for her to leave Denmark. Although she was previously hesitant to return to Bosnia and Herzegovina, she saw no other viable options due to mobility limitations brought by her non-EU passport. While back in Bosnia and Herzegovina, she wrote me the following:

> I am much more content when I came back from Denmark. Even tough, everybody told me that I was crazy because I left Denmark, I knew perfectly well it is not a country for me. To be honest, I didn't want to live in a country where the biggest obstacle for having a proper job was my foreign name. It was very frustrating. There are other reasons as well: from social exclusion to bad weather. At the end, Denmark has actually helped me in realizing what I definitely don't want in life. That's why for over a year now, I am working to go in a completely different country, continent. Hopefully, in a couple of months I will be given my impressions from Australia.
>
> (Erina, Bosnia and Herzegovina)

The quote sums up the complex range of emotions which characterised Erina's departure. Staying in Denmark was contingent on finding a 'proper job,' yet when this pursuit failed, it seemed pointless for her to stay. Feelings of being unwanted and stigmatised due to her 'foreignness' stretched from concrete day-to-day situations to an abstract societal level. Thus, she hoped that Australia – what she referred to as a 'vibrant, multicultural country' – would make life as a migrant less complicated. Essentially, this resembles findings from the ethnographic study by Polina Manolova (2017, p. 274) of how failed migration projects for Bulgarian migrants in the UK made them reach the conclusion that the 'real West' – in the shape of 'more advanced,' 'better organised,' and 'more open' countries – was elsewhere. Like the young migrants in Manolova's study, Erina and Anastasia re-projected the West into different countries across the globe, pinpointing the US and Australia as particularly desirable destinations for onward migration and further development of 'Western merits.' In this sense, dreams of 'the West [were] never abandoned but sustained and reproduced as a telos, always deferred into the upcoming future' (Manolova, 2017, p. 285).

Staying against the odds

Scholars have highlighted romantic love as a powerful pull factor for making people move (Mai and King, 2009; Riaño, 2015). For some students, love was also an important motivation for wanting to stay in Denmark (see also Mosneaga and Winther, 2013). Even though a master's degree in Denmark had been a part of Isidora's initial plan of long-term settlement outside North Macedonia, her Danish partner had become *the* overriding reason for wanting to stay in the country. Like many other students, Isidora moved to Copenhagen almost directly after graduating in 2015 to improve her chances of finding employment. For non-EU graduates particularly, prospects of building a life in Denmark are not solely dependent on their level of integration or eagerness for staying in the country but, to a large extent, their labour market success. Despite having relevant work experience from internships and graduating with top marks, Isidora was surprised by local employers' reluctance to hire her. For Isidora 'graduation' marked the beginning of an extremely stressful period in her life. As emphasised, non-EU students are not entitled to welfare benefits while 'establishing themselves' in the Danish job market. To support herself during her search for 'skilled jobs,' Isidora was therefore employed in various 'random,' low-skilled jobs:

> I was in retail – different positions within retail and sails, and customer service and stuff like that because I am not allowed, I can't get a-kasse [unemployment benefits] because I am not a part of the European Union. When you have this establishment visa, you are not entitled to get a-kasse, so for me that was the reason that I had to work. I was not on a-kasse while searching for a job. That made the process of searching for a job longer and more tough than for Danes and people from EU countries.
>
> (Isadora, North Macedonia)

To enhance her possibilities for finding employment, Isidora even did a voluntary internship while working full-time as a waitress in a restaurant. The additional internship was motivated by her fear that future employers would refrain from hiring her due to a potential gap between her graduation date and relevant work experience. By doing an internship in line with her educational qualifications, she could demonstrate a continuation of valuable experiences within her area of expertise. In addition, Isadora also worked hard on improving her Danish skills because she had become increasingly aware that fluency in English was not sufficient for securing a desirable job in Denmark. While studying for their Danish master's degrees, my interlocutors were generally undetermined if they wanted to make the timely investment required to learn a new language – especially when deeming Danish to be a 'niche language' only spoken by a few million people. Yet, every graduate in my study eventually arrived at the realisation that possibilities for employment in Denmark were limited without fluency in Danish.

The non-EU students found themselves in a particularly stressful situation, as their legal right to reside in Denmark depended on finding employment in due time (six months) – that is, unless they managed to get their hands on an Establishment Card, which could grant them up to, at that time, two years to search for employment. The frustrating job search and sense of constant rejection meant that Isidora on various occasions was close to giving up on her ambitions of staying in Denmark on a long-term basis. Worries and stress related to not knowing whether she could stay in the country grew as her visa expiry date came closer. In her study of international students in Australia, Hannah Soong (2014) highlights how the uncertainty of not knowing whether the students would accomplish their overall goal of more permanent migration to Australia or not constituted their greatest challenge. The precariousness meant that they faced 'exceptional levels of anxiety not knowing if they could remain as migrants in Australia after their studies' (Soong, 2014, p. 4).

Since students studying abroad often develop meaningful relationships and may even 'put down roots,' the idea of having to uproot oneself and start again in their country of origin may also trigger anxiety (Robertson and Runganaikaloo, 2014, p. 214). For Isidora, her Danish partner remained the single most important motivation for continuing to struggle. Amidst searching for employment, she even considered moving to another EU country with relatively lenient immigration regulation: 'If I continue struggling for a year more, then it would not be worth for me staying here just not using what I studied.' Isidora was determined to find employment that reflected her intellectual capabilities. It is important to realise that for the non-EU students, it was not only a question of finding a job that they themselves deemed relevant and interesting but it had to be accompanied by a yearly salary of minimum DKK 445,000 a year (level of 2021) as stipulated by Danish immigration regulation and more specifically the Pay Limit Scheme. As mentioned, the average salary for new graduates (whether local or foreign) in the field of humanities was DKK 408,000 in 2019. The fact that the average salary of students within their position and field of studies has been consistently below the salary requirements of the Pay Limit Scheme gives an important clue as to why many of my interlocutors struggled tremendously to find jobs with 'acceptable' salaries.[6]

Eventually it was not the salary that secured Isidora's continued presence in Denmark, but marrying her Danish partner. When she found a 'skilled job' after approximately two years of searching, it still paid DKK 2000 less a month than the minimum salary required by the Pay Limit Scheme. Essentially, Isidora's narrations support the results of studies underlining the importance of marriage for non-EU citizens to fulfil their educational projects and transition into the labour market in EU countries (Neveu Kringelbach, 2015; Seminario and Le Feuvre, 2019). Romina Seminario and Nicky Le Feuvre's (2019) study of Peruvian student migrants in Switzerland shows how obtaining a Swiss university degree is rarely enough to guarantee access to the upper reaches of the Swiss labour market. In most cases, such qualifications needed to be combined with marriage to a Swiss (or EU) citizen before the graduates could settle legally in the host country and start a career that reflects their educational credentials. While Isidora was happily married, she admitted that their marriage (after approximately one and a half years of dating) was fast-tracked by her 'insecure migratory legal status' (Goldring and Landolt, 2011, p. 329). Her explanations indicate how restrictive immigration policies may position international graduates in a difficult situation where they see themselves constrained to contract a marital relationship at a faster pace than they desire (Riaño, 2015). Isidora's story also suggests how, in spite of having educational credentials from a local university, she was deeply dependent on her Danish spouse for staying in Denmark. In addition to being legally married, her husband, for example, had to provide the couple with an apartment of more than 60 square metres and demonstrate a significant amount of savings in his bank account.

In the fall of 2020 – approximately five years after their graduation – Isidora and Christina were the only 2 out of the 11 non-EU graduates still remaining in Denmark. While there are many resemblances between their stories, paths, and strategies for staying in Denmark, their trajectories after graduation also differ on several important points. In contrast to Isidora, Christina did not have a Danish partner and she did not stay in Denmark continuously after graduating even though she too began her post-graduation journey in different low-skilled jobs. She seemed frustrated when reliving the first period as a graduate:

> The last two years I was in Denmark I was working hard labour. I messed up my body, I had to go to therapy for my back. For seven months, I worked as a supervisor for the cleaning staff at a hotel. I started as a cleaner and then worked my way up. It was a gruelling experience. I worked very long hours and you don't stop until the work is done. Some days I would have maybe 300 rooms to clean and I would only have 10 people to do that. [...] I was very stressed, I was losing weight plus it was very difficult to find housing in Denmark, so I was moving a lot. In four years, I moved five times.
>
> (Christina, North Macedonia)

The quote accentuates how the combination of a demanding low-skilled job and unstable housing affected Christina's physical and mental well-being negatively. At one point, she did an internship during the weekdays while cleaning full time on the weekends, starting at 6:00 am. Therefore, Christina worked seven days a week. Notably, there are striking resemblances between her narrations and those of the hardworking EU students discussed in Chapter 4. Without the scholarship, Christina was also completely reliant on her own efforts to support herself abroad. Graduation involved a 'divestment passage' – entailing a negatively experienced separation from accustomed ontological narratives and performances of uncertain duration – and the incorporation of new facets into her ontological narrative. Therefore, she experienced a marked contrast between the roles and performances constituting her life as a master's student and her life as a graduate, the latter involving a deep struggle with 'finding social involvements conducive to the performance of valued identities' (Ezzy, 1993, p. 50). In retrospect, she felt that she had lived a sheltered life while studying, which had failed to prepare her for the harsh realities awaiting her after the completion of her studies.

Christina's narrations suggest that her after graduation realities were tightly linked to her precarious legal status. The notion of 'precarious legal status,' introduced by Luin Goldring and Patricia Landolt (2011, p. 329), captures the multiple and variable forms of 'less than full status,' involving the absence of key rights or entitlements usually associated with the full or nearly full status of citizenship and permanent residence. Individuals with a precarious legal status may include 'documented' but temporary workers, students, and refugee applicants, as well as people with unauthorised forms of status. On the basis of interviews with immigrant workers in Canada, Goldring and Landolt accentuate a strong linkage between having a precarious legal status and precarious employment, that is, work that is 'unstable and insecure, offers limited rights, protections, and benefits, and allows workers limited autonomy, recourse, or control' (2011, p. 326). Their analysis foreground how a shift to more permanent legal status is not necessarily accompanied by a reduction in job precarity. Indeed, Christina's narrations illustrate well how my interlocutors generally found it difficult to escape the 'low-skilled treadmill' in spite of numerous efforts to upgrade their CVs such as doing unpaid internships relevant for their field of studies.

The 'straw that broke the camel's back' occurred when Christina was subjected to exploitation at the housing market: 'Combined with the lifestyle that I had, I just could not do it anymore, so I decided to come back to Macedonia. The only thing worse than leaving was staying.' Returning to Macedonia, then, was not an active decision but the outcome of a lack of viable alternatives abroad. Therefore, 'home, unsurprisingly, became the default destination [when] unable to achieve a sustainable transnational transience' (Gomes, 2015, p. 48). The abrupt departure was also part of the reason why it took several months for Christina to accept (once again) being a resident in North Macedonia's capital, Skopje:

Well, I have gotten used to being back. I had a hard time being here when I first came. But I think I got over it relatively fast, it is mostly because the company where I work now is not representative of what the labour market is here. It's a British company and it has a flat hierarchy and the people are young and vibrant. So, it's like a typical start-up atmosphere. If I had to be employed in a government position, where it's mostly middle-aged men and women working, it would not have been as easy. It's maybe similar to what I experienced in Denmark. It helped a lot that I got this job.

(Christina, North Macedonia)

In the quote, Christina distances herself from the North Macedonian labour market when drawing attention to the similarities between the work environment of her new workplace and the conditions she associates with Denmark such as a flat hierarchy. As I will return to, there was a tendency among those interlocutors returning to their home countries to accentuate continuation between their lives in their home countries and Denmark – even among those who, like Christina, had less pleasant memories of parts of their life in Denmark. Christina's job in North Macedonia was relatively well paid and characterised by acceptable working conditions, yet she was ready to go abroad whenever the opportunity arose due to diverse issues such as the lack of opportunities for saving up and the amount of air pollution in Skopje. During a conversation on Skype, Christina underlined her new realities by showing me a mouthpiece that she had to wear when biking in public.

Nation-states differ in their political status in the international hierarchy, which affects their citizens' mobility rights (Moret, 2020). Christina felt trapped in North Macedonia due to the juridical obstacles of not being an EU citizen. While she was more than ready to go abroad again, the mobility restrictions that accompany a North Macedonian passport hindered her to do so. In North Macedonia, she considered several potential destinations for migration: At one point, she was determined to go to New Zealand but deemed the procedures too complicated and costly. She came very close to getting a position in a Dutch company but was eventually not hired due to visa obstacles. She even attempted to get a Bulgarian citizenship, which, if granted to her, would make it possible to work and reside more or less freely inside the EU. When I asked her if she was considering returning to Denmark during an 'online conversation' in the fall of 2018, she made it clear: 'I could imagine returning under the right circumstances. I would not go there just for the sake of going there.' In late 2019, she nonetheless sent me a text stating that she had returned to Denmark after being offered a job with a salary above the minimum rate required by the Pay Limit Scheme. She was partly able to get the job because of connections she had developed while working in North Macedonia. While Christina was thrilled by the prospects of reuniting with Denmark, she feared losing the job and that she once again would have to return to North Macedonia on short notice. When she found a Danish boyfriend, her concerns about being forced to leave Denmark only increased. In several conversations in 2020, Christina described how she found the possibilities for planning her future somewhat limited in Denmark and the fear of deportation – in case she lost her job again – constituted a constant worry. Hence, residence stability and citizenship considerations remained a paramount concern (Mosneaga and Winther, 2013).

The advantages of having an EU citizenship?

European and national authorities have encouraged young Europeans to make use of their 'freedom of mobility' within the EU for educational and labour movement (Favell, 2008; Simola, 2018). In theory this means that graduates with an EU citizenship should find it easier to settle in Denmark than the non-EU nationals who have been the focus of this chapter so far. In spite of having a more favourable legal status for intra-EU immigration in comparison to non-EU graduates, I was surprised by the resemblances between the two groups' narrations of (failed) attempts to settle in Denmark. Indeed, many of my interlocutors from EU member states similarly realised that an EU citizenship and a local degree was not necessarily sufficient for finding employment abroad (see also Simola, 2018) – at least when it came to finding employment *relevant* to their academic skills (Wiers-Jenssen, 2013). For Ania, the lack of favourable job prospects entailed that she, after more than two years in Denmark, felt compelled to return to Poland. During our meeting on a hot summer day in Krakow – approximately three years following her graduation – she seemed frustrated when recalling her search for highly skilled jobs in Denmark:

> Back then, I hoped I could find a good job in Denmark – it kept me motivated to do all these weird jobs but after two years, I could not see this perspective, yeah … No one wanted to hire me. It would have been very different if there was a company who wanted me and maybe I would have stayed in Denmark if I had gotten a chance to work *a normal job* – not in a supermarket or something like that.
>
> (Ania, Poland)

I have previously described how the incapability of aligning her life with a desired life trajectory in combination with aspirations of 'normality' made Ania long for a life in a Scandinavian welfare society, which she believed could offer her better opportunities for thriving on a personal level. However, as the quote indicates, life in Denmark was characterised by unexpected levels of hardship involving 'weird jobs' that primarily served the purpose of getting by. Convinced that normal jobs were reserved for individuals of Danish origin, she felt at distance from the 'normality' and principles of meritocracy that she previously associated with Denmark. As an EU citizen, Ania's narrations indicate that there were other less formal obstacles for belonging fully in Denmark (Moret, 2020). Moreover, despite the fact that she had worked long hours as a cleaner while studying, her student identification had served to uphold some state of normality and balance in her then challenged ontological narrative. Graduating, however, meant a narrative disruption – *a divestment passage* – where she experienced a complete disconnection from desired role performances fundamental for a positive self-understanding (Ezzy, 1993).

In many ways, Ania's experiences echo the narrations of David who, despite having a solid local network as a master's student in Denmark, felt surprisingly alone upon his graduation. In line with the rationale of many graduates, David reckoned that it would be easier to find a job by moving to Copenhagen. His EU citizenship, in combination with the fact that he had worked throughout his studies, even made him eligible for Danish employment benefits, which provided him with some financial stability. However, he was completely taken off guard by the difficulties of establishing himself in Copenhagen. One of the main obstacles confronting him amidst his job search was the hurdles of finding accommodation. Since David no longer had access to student housing, he had to tackle the housing market in the private rental sector by himself. Initially, he stayed at several places in the outskirts of the city before finally finding a more permanent living arrangement in a shared, overpriced flat. The constant search for residence, in combination with his lack of Danish proficiency, complicated the task of finding a job that reflected his academic qualifications. Researchers have underlined that the residential environment plays an important role in people's everyday lives and that residential satisfaction influences whether people move away from or stay in their current location (Eskelä, 2015). As exemplified by David, many graduates – especially those moving to Copenhagen – found it difficult to gain a foothold in the housing market and often relied on rather unstable, short-term leases. The exhausting process of searching for permanent accommodation complicated goals of settling down in Denmark on a long-term basis. Moreover, since David had worked part-time as a dishwasher during the entire duration of his studies, he was short of relevant experience in his field of study and valuable contacts needed to 'boost' his search for skilled jobs. Eventually he decided 'to settle' for a job at a restaurant that he had gotten via his contacts in the service industry. While one should be careful to label highly skilled workers working in low-skilled jobs as 'failures' (Niraula and Valentin, 2019), David feared that his chances to get a job in line with his academic qualifications diminished every day he was an employee in the restaurant. Approximately two years after graduating from the university, he therefore decided to 'throw in the towel' and return to Hungary. I met up with David for dinner at a restaurant in central Budapest where he reflected on his time in Denmark in the following way:

DAVID: I could have stayed [in Copenhagen] and if not that restaurant then another one. I knew so many people and they could just refer to me to another place. But the problem was that I really did not see the endpoint in that, because let's say that I stay at the restaurant and I do my shifts and I do the work and on the side I still try to find a proper job that matches my education – that was no guarantee that that could happen. I think my biggest enemy in Copenhagen was how much everything and every company was competitive. Like even when students attend the university they immediately get chosen by these companies and they start to work for them – thereby getting training prior to their education. I think that if more time had passed by chances for finding a job would have been lower and lower.

METTE: Why?

DAVID: Because they would just look at my CV and, I don't know, the date of me finishing the university would be far away in the past and I could not really show anything. Another aspect during my time in Copenhagen is that I felt really burned out. This whole job search. I felt mentally drained.

(David, Hungary)

David was convinced that he could have stayed in Copenhagen if he continued working at a restaurant. Yet, despite having an extensive network in the service industry, his contacts were of little value for finding employment that matched his educational profile. David's narrations underline how it is not enough for international graduates to have a network in Denmark. In line with the experience of non-EU graduates discussed earlier, he foresaw himself entering a low-skilled treadmill if he remained in Denmark. Thus, while he previously found the societal conditions in Hungary depressing, his life circumstances in Denmark turned his home country into an increasingly attractive option and, in sharp contrast to earlier, he was no longer convinced that the West offered a superior mode of living. I return to David's post-graduation trajectory and its many 'migration-twists' later in this chapter.

Akin to the descriptions of the non-EU graduates, the stories above illustrate how many EU movers too grew increasingly pessimistic when accessing their possibilities for getting jobs corresponding to their education, training, and experience. Their decision to leave Denmark was prompted by feelings of existential impasse and the sense that Denmark lacked meaningful opportunities for existential advancement (Hage and Papadopoulos, 2004). Somewhat ironically and truly discouraging, their experiences after graduation foregrounded a similar plethora of emotions as those prompting their departure from their home countries in the first place. They believed that their access to the Danish labour market was hindered by their status as foreigners, not speaking Danish, and a deficiency of valuable contacts. Some were convinced that they would have been more favourably positioned with a degree in natural science or a diploma from a business school. Essentially, my interlocutors' narrations support previous studies which suggest that highly skilled migrants from Eastern European countries are more likely to return back home or 'move on' if they work in jobs below their educational level (Pungas et al., 2012; Snel et al., 2015).

During the fall of 2020, Peter, Borge, and Ada were the only 3 remaining in Denmark out of 16 interlocutors originating from EU member states. The presence of Peter and Borge was particularly surprising since they both nearly capitulated and returned to their home countries at different moments during their journeys. Moreover, neither of the two had graduated from the university but dropped out prior to writing their master's theses. Previously, I described how money, which Peter's grandmother had saved for her funeral, secured his continued stay in Denmark. I also discussed how Borge at one point had been increasingly keen on returning to Romania and residing among his 'own people.' Yet, notwithstanding Peter's financial obstacles and Borge's contrasting emotions, both had become increasingly rooted in Denmark. If seeking to provide an answer to what distinguishes the stories of Peter, Borge, and Ada from the 13 EU graduates who left Denmark, an important factor appears to be the fact that they all found employment that they were passionate about, even if Borge and Peter did not have jobs that were directly linked to their field of study. In fact, Peter had become a successful entrepreneur and set up his own business in Denmark, and Borge worked as a minister in a Romanian orthodox church located in a smaller Danish town. Since Borge did not get paid for his work in the church, he was also employed at a factory to support himself and his family. Ada, on the other hand, began her career as an intern and worked her way up within an area related to her field of studies. While the professions of the three graduates were extremely diverse, their description of their paths after graduation fits – in contrast to the examples of EU movers discussed earlier in this section – Ezzy's (1993) notion of an 'integrative passage,' entailing that they engaged in activities that supported and reaffirmed valued identities. Undeniably, their 'migration success' was also assisted by their EU citizenship, since neither of the three graduates earned above the minimum amount stipulated by the Pay Limit Scheme.

I earlier emphasised the importance of a Danish partner – and in some cases legal marriage – for non-EU graduates' possibilities for staying in Denmark. However, without being affected by the demanding immigration regulations, the narrations of the three EU movers also suggest that having a partner, and more broadly a local network, played an important role in their continued presence in Denmark. The study of Erik Snel et al. (2015) on the return intentions of Polish, Bulgarian, and Romanian labour migrants in the Netherlands highlights that inclinations to return are not primarily conditioned by labour market successes in host countries. Rather, the intensity of transnational activities (for instance, frequent contact with social network in home countries) and the migrants' socio-cultural integration (including having non-migrant social networks abroad) in the host countries appear to be pivotal factors for shaping return intentions (see also de Haas et al., 2015). Notably, Peter and Ada were both living in Copenhagen with their Danish partners and they both had extensive social networks. In addition to the, in his words, 'invaluable' stability and emotional support provided by his Danish girlfriend, Peter explained that the dorm he had moved to while studying in Copenhagen – mainly consisting of Danish residents – had become like a second family to him. Over lunch with him and his Danish girlfriend on a warm summer day in Copenhagen, he laughingly told me that he had become one of those 'socially closed Danes' that international students often complained about. In Ada's case, her Danish partner was the main reason she initially came to Denmark to study and she had become an ingrained part of his network in Denmark. In addition, both Peter and Ada were able to communicate fluently in Danish. Borge's trajectory seems different in the sense that he married a native Romanian and had an extensive network of mainly Romanian migrants, many of whom he knew from the environment surrounding the church. While his connection to his home country seemed stronger than in the case of Peter and Ada, he described how his dense network of other Romanians made up for not being in Romania and that he did not have any plans to return. This strengthens Jill Ahrens et al.'s (2016, p. 94) point, that when conditions to 'return are unfavourable or problematic, relocating to a place with vibrant ethnic enclaves that reproduce most elements of the "home culture" can appear like a good substitute or make a return unnecessary.'

Homecoming

A sense of continuity

Ania never considered going anywhere else than Poland after having decided to leave Denmark. For her, the main pull factor was her family and the thought of being around them on an everyday basis after several years apart. Returning to Poland, however, meant coping with the demotivating societal conditions that she previously had been eager to escape. Even though Ania initially found her 'dream job' in Polish academia as a PhD student, she was discouraged by the 'very different' unstructured work conditions in comparison to the transparency and structure which, in her view, characterised the Danish labour market. A 'ridiculously low salary' meant that she eventually quit her job at the university. Instead, she became employed as a Danish translator at an international company, which, although far away from her academic merits, was comparatively well paid in a Polish context. To her own surprise, fluency in Danish had become a valuable merit in her post-graduation path. Essentially, Ania's narrative resonates with findings presented by Vladimír Baláž and Allan Williams (2004) on returning student migrants from Slovakia after having studied abroad in the UK. When examining students' transition to the labour market they concluded that 'there is a need to look at a range of competences, rather than narrower measures of qualifications and formal courses of studies' (Baláž and Williams, 2004,

p. 234). Moreover, Ania was not contemplating any new international adventures but had terminated her international career for the time being. Her main priority, she informed me, was now to create decent financial conditions that would allow her to lead a desirable life in Poland.

While Ania had felt at a distance from the 'normal conditions' that she initially anticipated from Denmark, it is interesting to note that aspirations of 'normalcy' remained a pivotal point of orientation for her upon her return to Poland. Yet, instead of viewing migration as instrumental in achieving a state of normality, she was determined to carve out a 'normal space' for herself in Poland by surrounding herself with 'normal people.' Through her job, she remained in frequent contact with Scandinavians, which, she claimed, served to uphold a sense of normality in her everyday life:

> Like I said, I have some Swedish people at work and I co-work with some Danish people and it gives me the sense that yeah … I'm in a *normal* environment [laughing]. I can say that I have a little Denmark in Poland right now, like I'm trying to have at least.
>
> (Ania, Poland)

It is interesting to note that although Ania in many ways felt like a *stranger* in Denmark and at a distance from the social security enjoyed by locals, she continued to idealise the Scandinavian welfare model and what she called 'Scandinavian behaviour.' Akin to Christina's narrative of the Danish-like start-up atmosphere at her office in Skopje, Ania seemed keen on presenting her life in Poland as being characterised by the values she associated with Denmark. While physically in her home country, she sought to distance herself from certain societal conditions when narrating her return. Thus, in Ania's ontological narrative lingered a sense of being 'different' from most people in her home country and that her choice to return was not synonymous with embracing the Polish society in its entirety.

This sense of being different or indeed *above* certain conditions in one's home country also characterised the narrations of Jacob, who initially worked in Copenhagen following his graduation. While in Denmark, he decided to change his career path and, consequently, moved back to Hungary to pursue a new bachelor's degree in Budapest. After having spent years away from Hungary, he was curious about how a reunion with his natal country would feel. I spoke to Jacob after he had lived in Budapest for a year, where he underlined that he still did not feel fully at home. When observing his immediate surroundings and the Hungarian society more generally, he felt more like a tourist than an insider: 'I have been in Budapest for more than a year now and I still find myself observing things like a tourist from time to time, one who has a kind of Scandinavian view of things.' Although he found life in Budapest 'quite awesome,' he remained critical of Hungarian national politics, which he successfully managed to 'block out mentally' to stay sane. Similar to Ania, Jacob seemed focused on stressing a continuity between his life in Hungary and the values he associated with Scandinavia. Underlining that he had internalised a Scandinavian gaze became a way to present himself as not quite an 'ordinary Hungarian' and to distance himself from the surrounding society. Thus, both Ania's and Jacob's ontological narrative seemed, once again, to nurture from the narrative of the 'Eastern European Westerner' – that is, a self-proclaimed Western-minded and modern individual.

Maybe because many of my interlocutors initially viewed student migration as a mark of distinction, – a way to cement a symbolic boundary between 'the leavers' and 'the stayers' (Krivonos and Näre, 2019) – it seemed to be of great importance for some homecomers to accentuate close alliance between their ontological narratives and 'Scandinavian values' upon their return. At times, it felt as if they were trying to convince me – or potentially to a greater extent themselves – that returning did not entail turning their back on core values that they had sworn allegiance to during previous interviews and conversations. Since both Ania and Jacob previously had been convinced that there was no future for them in their home countries, there might also have been an element of shame connected to their return. It is important to note how 'mobility' and 'immobility' are not neutral terms but denote a hierarchy of power (Forsberg, 2019; Franquesa, 2011). Mobility, Tim Cresswell (2006, p. 15) claims, is 'self-evidently central to Western modernity.' To be mobile thus signifies progression: 'A modern citizen is, among other things, a mobile citizen' (Cresswell, 2006, p. 20). In a similar vein, Jaume Franquesa (2011) writes:

> Society appears then to be asymmetrically divided: on the one hand we find the 'mobile cosmopolitans,' an active force associated with time, progress, capital, universalism, power, and agency; on the other hand we have the 'immobile locals,' relegated to a passive role and associated with place, backwardness, tradition, localism, and powerlessness.
>
> (pp. 1016–1017)

In this sense, 'immobility' may symbolise a potentially stigmatising marker, which further explains why some homecomers felt a need to counter and defend themselves against what they experienced as an 'immobility stigma.'

Family first

Etel's post-graduation trajectory is particularly noteworthy since she worked several years in Denmark in a highly paid, permanent position after having completed her studies. In an e-mail from 2018, she remarked: 'Denmark is treating me nicely and I have no reason to leave at the moment.' Therefore, I was surprised when Etel one year later announced that she had quit her job and was returning to Budapest together with her Hungarian boyfriend. Even if migrating for Etel had been successful – if equating success with a well-paid job – there had been other aspects of her life where she felt disconnected from the Danish society. Despite having lived in Denmark for almost six years, her social life, for instance, remained a disappointment. She had also maintained frequent contact with friends and family back home and longed to be closer to them, even though her parents were '100 per cent against' her going back when deeming Denmark to be a better country than Hungary for leading a 'good life.' Regardless of her parents' wish, Etel and her Hungarian boyfriend were keen on reuniting with their long-lost home country. In line with the cases discussed earlier, Etel's story strengthens the assumption that migrants' decision to return is not only conditioned by their labour market success in the host country (Snel et al., 2015), but also factors such as their social life and, as indicated earlier, their accommodation arrangements. While I was sharing a pizza with Etel and David in Budapest in the late summer of 2019, Etel nonetheless indicated that her decision to resettle in Hungary might have been somewhat hasty and that yearnings for friends and family had blurred her ability to see the Hungarian labour market conditions clearly. She was tired of the long hours and the low salary in comparison to the Danish one. Thus, despite the fact that she had managed to get a good job in an area with relevance for her education, she remained open to going abroad again.

On the basis of qualitative interviews with international students in Australia, Catherine Gomes (2015) seeks to nuance the common assumption that student mobility is linked to a long-term strategy to return to the country of origin. Rather, she argues that the majority of the students in her study foresaw a transnational lifestyle upon their graduation. Aspirations for transnational mobility even took precedence over familial and cultural connections to their home nation. While some of my interlocutors were eager to stay mobile (or at least reside outside the borders of their home countries), others described how the wish to remain close to their family and friends grew increasingly important and became their main leading star upon graduation (see also Fong, 2011). Etel's narrative of 'successfully leaving' Hungary for Denmark and 'successfully returning' to Hungary with the growing wish to leave again accentuates the students' complicated relationship with their home country and transnational mobility.

Akin to Etel's longings to return, Georgi initially regarded an education in Denmark as the first step to long-term migration but became increasingly convinced that he wanted to return to Bulgaria upon his graduation: 'At some point, I felt like I wanted to come back home. I just started to feel like this, missing my family, missing my friends. To be honest, I simply just wanted to be back in Bulgaria.' In contrast to Gomes' (2015) findings among international students and Etel's wish to leave Hungary for the second time, Georgi's narrations suggest a sense of fatigue with leading a life outside the borders of his home country and a strong yearning to be around friends and family. Hence, Bulgaria was never a default destination in the absence of a better alternative or a result of failed migration (Snel et al., 2015), but essentially Georgi's 'first pick.'

Returning to Romania had also been an outspoken aim ever since Clara embarked on her student journey in 2013. Like Georgi, she never applied for any jobs in Denmark following her graduation and she had no ambition to migrate again. Some years into her return to Romania, she had even married her long-term (Romanian) boyfriend. Similar to five years earlier, when I interviewed her about her future plans, she narrated her return to Romania as a question of patriotic aims and aspirations of nation-building (Holloway et al., 2012; Thomas, 2017). She said: 'I am still fond of this country, and I always thought that whatever job I will do here it will make a difference and in Denmark, I will be just one out of many people.'

For some returnees, homecoming meant pausing aspirations of building a career that reflected their (initial) academic interests. As noted, many also eventually realised that migration (at least to Denmark) did not automatically lead to a desirable career trajectory. In addition, some found that a 'Western degree' did not necessarily have the impact in their home countries that they initially imagined. After having stayed some time in Denmark following his graduation, Bogdan decided to return to Romania due to difficulties in finding employment that did not involve newspaper delivery. He partly deemed this failure a result of his lack of professional network, which had been difficult for him to develop simultaneously with working full-time next to his studies. The fact that he had fallen in love with his home country again however eased his disappointment and sparked an urge to return.

While settling in Bucharest brought Bogdan geographically closer to friends and family, he could only find work far away from his field of studies. In fact, he worked as a computer technician, assisting primarily English and Danish customers. Even though Bogdan could utilise his Danish skills, he seemed pessimistic when assessing his possibilities for finding 'relevant jobs' in the immediate future, but found comfort in his life and intellectual pursuits outside working hours. Moreover, while residing in Romania, he decided to further educate himself within the area of IT to make himself more attractive to a greater range of employers. Bogdan's 'change of direction' is indicative of a broader tendency among the graduates. Later in this chapter, I will discuss several examples of how some of my interlocutors engaged in *additional education*, often, like Bogdan, turning to the area of IT, to boost their CVs.

Even though Clara was happy being back in Romania, she had also found employment at odds with her initial expectations:

> It's a very philosophical way of feeling my life actually. Of trying to make a change for the benefit of the country. But in the end, I'm working as a tourist guide. So, I'm actually doing that [laughing]. I'm actually changing the way that tourists think about this country.
>
> (Clara, Romania)

In the quote, we get a sense of how Clara came across as a bit hesitant when telling me the details of her post-graduation path and that she was supporting herself partly as a self-employed tourist guide in Romania and partly – as became evident further into our conversation – by her husband. Maybe because she had not found the type of job that she initially imagined she would get with a Western master's degree, it seemed important for her to insist on continuation between her studies and her current profession. While she argued that the master's degree did not play a role in getting the job, she noted how her studies 'helped [her] understand better how we communicate' as well as the 'correlation between language and emotion.' Moreover, throughout our conversation, she continuously stressed a link between her patriotic ambitions and her work on changing tourists' perception of Romania. Simultaneously with drawing attention to the importance of her work, Clara revealed that she too was considering a 'change of direction' by returning to the university – this time in Bucharest – to study psychology. Interestingly, her plan to change career path was less a question of being dissatisfied with her work as a tourist guide, but rather driven by fear of being judged by her surroundings for her choice of employment and in particular the gaze of her father:

> I have to defend myself. Even my father says, 'Yeah, so you studied abroad and you did this and that and are you happy with your life? Can you support yourself?' […] I think my father, well he is judging me more than he says. Actually, I think that he is just trying to overcome a possible disaster. Like he is pushing me to be independent. To, even now that I'm married, to still have my own income, because he believes that he has given me everything in order for me to become independent. Even though he does not want to admit it, he considered supporting me in Denmark an investment so that I in the future would be so well-paid that I could support him when he retires.
>
> (Clara, Romania)

I earlier described how Clara's father worked ten months a year in Dubai to support his family in Romania as well as Clara's studies in Denmark. The quote above accentuates how her father appeared to have had great faith in a degree from a Western country and that, due to its symbolic worth, it would automatically lead to a highly paid and respectable job. During our conversation, Clara also underlined that her father – like Etel's parents – had initially been against her returning to Romania, thereby making his disappointment in her post-graduation trajectory twofold. Her story underlines how student migration, for some, was deeply entrenched in family expectations, which constituted an additional burden and led to feelings of indebtedness (Thomas, 2017). This resonates with the findings by Allan Findlay et al. (2017, p. 196) of how students originating from less economically advantaged countries experienced that their return to their home countries was seen as 'a sign of failure and disappointment' by their families. Clara's narrations further suggest a strong sense of indebtedness to her father, who sponsored her education, but also feelings of shame for not living up to his *grand* expectations.

Throughout our conversation, however, Clara stood up for her 'right to immobility' (Forsberg, 2019, p. 325). As a part of this quest, she was focused on presenting narratives that countered the dominant narrative of Romania as 'underdeveloped and unsafe,' which, according to her, summed up the way that most (Western) people viewed the country from the outside. For instance, Clara presented me with the example of two Spanish tourists, who had been surprised by how safe Romania felt as a site of tourism. In the following quote, Clara narrates an incident where she accompanied the Spanish tourists on a trip to the Romanian countryside:

> I just parked the car with a lot of things inside because my trunk is a little bit small. I usually have to leave something on the backseat. And they [the Spanish tourists] were totally surprised that I had no panic of being robbed. Because nowadays in Spain you cannot leave anything on the side, because you risk having one of your windows smashed.
>
> (Clara, Romania)

Essentially, the quote accentuates how Clara's 'struggle of narration' takes place at two levels. Firstly, in relation to the tourists, where her actions of leaving valuables at the backseat of her car functioned as a way to cement a positive narrative of Romania as 'safe.' Secondly, her retelling of the 'car incident' can be interpreted as an attempt of impression management during the interview and a way to justify her return. Not only did she construct Romania as 'safe' but she also juxtaposed it to the 'unsafe' conditions in Spain – a Western European country – where a similar action would have resulted in one's car windows getting smashed. She thereby challenged the dominant narrative of Western superiority, while simultaneously questioning the notion that migration to the West necessarily is a logical and better choice than returning to one's home country in Eastern Europe. Later in this chapter, I will discuss examples of how similar narrative patterns were present among graduates engaging in onward migration to other countries in the eastern parts of Europe.

Homecoming in the EU's immediate outside

Approximately one year into her master's degree, Maia knew that she did not want to stay in Denmark following her graduation. It was a combination of various factors – the people, the weather, but above everything, she foresaw great difficulties in terms of getting the career she wanted if staying. For instance, Maia reckoned that a job as a government official would be difficult to get due to her educational profile and lack of Danish proficiency. A life outside the borders of Georgia was seen as a possibility but by no means a necessity. For her to consider long-term migration, the destination had to offer a 'cosmopolitan ambiance' unthinkable in a country like Denmark. At one point, following a six-month internship in a prestigious think tank in

Brussels, she was keen on staying in the 'European epicentre,' yet found the environment in Brussels way too competitive. Moreover, her legal status as a non-EU citizen generally complicated potential destinations inside the EU. Returning to Georgia thus seemed to be the most logical option upon her graduation. Similar to students from EU countries, Maia also described being close to friends and family as an important motivation for returning.

Due to her lack of professional network in her home country, Maia initially deemed her chances of finding employment in the public sector poor. Yet, to her own surprise, she was hired in a high-profile job in the public sector after only three months of job search without the help of any local acquaintances. When I asked her if she regarded her Danish diploma to be an asset in her job search, she quickly replied: 'What I think helped me to get a job was my internship. Well actually, I'm 100 per cent sure.' Even though Maia did not consider her Danish degree as a drawback in any way, she was convinced that the symbolic value of her Brussels-based internship (in combination with a great deal of luck) trumped a Danish master's degree in terms of opening doors in the Georgian labour market. When discussing the roots of her well-being, she emphasised the importance of having found an internationally oriented job. She, for instance, travelled frequently to countries like Sweden and Germany, thereby managing to unite a 'cosmopolitan mode of living' (particularly travels to the West) with her desire to stay close to family and friends.

Like Maia, Anastasia had found meaningful employment in an international NGO where she worked with various issues central to her educational profile. Anastasia believed that two factors were pivotal for her to 'stand out in the pile of CVs.' First, her Danish degree and, secondly, her internship in Copenhagen. Importantly, it was not so much a degree from the specific university or even Denmark which in Anastasia's view appealed to Ukrainian employers, but the symbolic value of having a degree from a Western country. 'Western merits,' she claimed, was not only a question of having specific skills but guaranteed certain desirable personal values:

> Going abroad, having this Western education – like not Ukrainian degree – is a very big advantage. If you talk about the job market, having a Western education is something that is recognized by the employers – especially in the non-governmental sector and the non-service sector. Because we are recognized as people who carry Western work ethics and like Western values, Western approaches, which are of course by the Ukrainian standards, better.

> (Anastasia, Ukraine)

In the quote, Anastasia narrates a Western education as something with great transformative potential and a means of symbolic distinction. By accentuating the value of Western education, Anastasia aligns her ontological narrative with the Western metanarrative of progress and modernity, while simultaneously drawing symbolic boundaries between herself and people with a Ukrainian university degree. She thereby accentuates continuation between her life in Ukraine and the West. I previously noted how Anastasia considered staying in Denmark following her graduation if she found the 'right job.' Nonetheless, she did not regret returning to her home country, and she expressed an overall satisfaction with her life back home. While she remained open to further possibilities for education and professional advancement in the West, she foresaw her future in Ukraine and underlined that further education remained in line with the goals of nation-building. Akin to Maia's ontological narrative, Anastasia did not construct an opposition between future transnational mobility and building a life in her home country.

While Anastasia and Maia mainly narrated their return to the EU's immediate outside in positive terms, I spoke to other non-EU graduates determined to go abroad again whenever the opportunity arose. Esmira from Bosnia and Herzegovina, for instance, stated: 'I definitely do not plan to stay here. I already have some plans to go back to Scandinavia.' Upon her return, she initiated a third master's degree located partly in Italy, partly in Bosnia and Herzegovina, with the hope that it would optimise her opportunities for securing future employment. Neither Mikko nor Gojko described homecoming as an 'active decision.' Upon his return to Moldova, Mikko told me: 'It was not that I did not want to stay in Denmark.' Rather, it was when he suddenly lost his accommodation in Denmark that he saw no other option than moving in to his parents' house to finish his master's thesis 'in peace and quiet.' In a similar manner, Gojko stressed how returning to Serbia was the result of his master's thesis taking a longer time to finish than he initially estimated, leaving no time within the time range of his residence permit to search for jobs in Denmark. Another issue was that he did not have the DKK 89,376 in his bank account required for applying for the Establishment Card. Thus, Gojko saw no other alternative than relocating to Serbia, despite the fact that he had gotten top marks throughout his master's degree and would have liked to continue within research in Denmark:

> It was not a great feeling [leaving Denmark]. When it happened it was just a temporary thing, I will just continue to look for jobs and stuff actively after I come back to Serbia. But nothing came along, and three years after graduation I'm still staying here.
>
> (Gojko, Serbia)

The quote accentuates how returning to Serbia, initially intended to be a temporary stopover, turned out to be a longer-term solution for Gojko. In Serbia, he found employment in a British company somewhat aligned with his master's degree and was paid €700 a month, which, according to Gojko, was above the average salary for Serbian citizens. However, in comparison to his colleagues in the UK, he was paid a lot less – despite the fact that he in several cases was more skilled: 'It's frustrating when you are doing a good job, but you get paid much less just because you are from an Eastern European country.' In many ways, a Western degree had not brought the possibilities and lifestyle Gojko had anticipated and he did not feel esteemed as a person with a Western education. Instead, he felt that his Serbian nationality remained the overriding fix point for foreign employers – a stigmatising attribute overshadowing his work results. This sometimes made him feel that all his efforts had been in vain and he had become less convinced of the symbolic worth of a degree from a Danish university following his graduation. A degree from a university in the UK, he claimed, would have positioned him more favourably.

Returning to Serbia confronted Gojko with a limited sense of agency. Although his current salary was sufficient to lead a decent life in his home country, he explained how travelling to other countries – even neighbouring countries like Croatia – was a 'no go' due to the costs involved. He felt that the friendships and international network that he had developed abroad were decomposing due to his involuntary immobility. In addition, his return involved a 'reunion' with the discouraging societal conditions from which he had remained at a comfortable distance in Denmark, such as a malfunctioning infrastructure, poverty, and corrupted politicians. Thus, Gojko seemed ambivalent in his *presentation of self*. On the one hand, he did not want to present an ontological narrative, where he assigned himself the role of a victim due to his Serbian citizenship and 'bad luck.' On the other hand, it was clear that he felt victimised by the global visa regime and societal conditions in Serbia:

> Coming back here full-time was like a shock. Nothing really works. I'm not an easily depressed kind of person. In that sense, it's ok here. I have friends, I can hang out with people – I can get it out of my mind. However, in a sense being here does get me down occasionally. I'm thinking, 'Shit, what am I doing here?' or 'This was not the way that it was supposed to be.' I feel stuck.
>
> (Gojko, Serbia)

Gojko's narrations clearly indicate a sense of entrapment or what Ghassan Hage (2009) calls 'stuckedness.' When I asked Gojko if he had plans to migrate again, his answer was univocal: 'I definitely don't want to stay long-term, but it's difficult to find options to leave.' His desire to migrate again – preferably to a country in Scandinavia – was a response to existential immobility and a strong wish to move forward in life, physically and socially. Yet, structural constraints – such as his legal status as a non-EU citizen – limited his options for migration, which paved the way for a pronounced sense of powerlessness. Gojko's narrative thereby cements how 'power is not so much located in the pole of mobility, as an intrinsic attribute of it, but rather in the capacity to manage the relation between mobility and immobility' (Franquesa, 2011, p. 1028).

Compared to Gojko, Mikko seemed more ambivalent and indecisive when reflecting on whether to stay in Moldova or migrate to a foreign country in the future. While Mikko had found a 'rather interesting job' in line with his educational profile, he described how returning to Moldova felt peculiar in light of the amount of young people 'fleeing' the country: 'So many of my friends left that I can count the people who stayed on one hand.' The scale of young, highly skilled Moldovan citizens leaving the country meant that the question of whether to leave or stay remained a constant point of orientation throughout Mikko's everyday life:

> I don't want to create the impression that I'm depressed, but there is a lot of uncertainty around my future. Why are thoughts about leaving Moldova always around me? Because it's an everyday conversation, migration is the issue and it's discussed at all kinds of levels – family, friends, mass media, government. Migration is the number one problem for Moldova today. A million out of four million Moldavians have already left the country and 40 per cent of them have higher education. Migration is a part of daily discourse – every day, from morning to evening. My friends who have well-paid jobs and who are respected are also thinking about migration. They are not happy with the political life and they want different cultural things.
>
> (Mikko, Moldova)

The quote sheds light on an important issue – namely the pressure to migrate experienced by some youth in high-spending communities (see also White, 2010). Hence, even though Mikko was rather pleased with his life in Moldova's capital, Chişinău, he felt that there was a societal expectation of him to leave the country. Akin to the young Moldavians in Pamela Abbott et al.'s (2010) study, he was left in a dilemma: Whether to try to develop his life in Moldova or to look for opportunities elsewhere.

Onward journeys

Transnational ties and 'random' destinations

For some graduates, homecoming was not necessarily an easy transition, especially for those moving back into their parents' house after having lived on their own. As Paul sarcastically noted: 'That's another issue you should do research on – coming back is almost as difficult as going away. It's one of the things where there should be a law about: You don't move back to your parents!' Indeed, Paul dreaded a life sentence in a call centre if staying in Romania. For that reason, he was determined to migrate to another European country immediately after finishing his master's thesis.

I previously noted that Paul was hesitant to move to certain destinations, for instance, Spain and Italy, due to fears that his Romanian nationality would overshadow important facets of his 'actual social identity' (Goffman, 1963). Hence, for Paul, onward migration was not guided by de-facto experiences of racism (King and Karamoschou, 2019). Rather, similar to the student accounts discussed earlier, it was a strategy driven by the ambition to avoid countries where being an Eastern European immigrant would constitute a stigmatising attribute. Upon his graduation, Paul decided to move to Ireland. There were several overriding aspects which shaped his choice of destination. One factor was the issue of *transnational ties* (see also Ahrens et al., 2016) and the fact that his sister was already living in Ireland. Knowing that a cherished family member would be a part of his everyday life provided him with emotional comfort – even in a more practical way such as having a place 'to crash' upon his arrival. Moreover, Paul cherished the fact that Ireland had a long history of immigration, which he linked to an inherent appreciation of cultural diversity:

> The Irish have the experience of the Ireland of the 70s and 60s when they were extremely poor. They were sort of a developing country and they were migrating massively to the UK, the US, and Australia. So, they do have an understanding of this type of migration that the Danes don't have.
>
> (Paul, Romania)

Due to Ireland's history, Paul felt that there was a greater acceptance of migrants and that he, consequently, would 'blend in' better than in Denmark. When he was offered a PhD scholarship, the choice of Dublin as a destination for long-term migration seemed even more obvious. Academia further opened the door for other international ventures, such as a one-year visit as a researcher at an Ivy League university in the US. Thus, Paul felt light-years away from what he now described as the 'dark period' in Denmark – that is, the latter part of his stay – where he feared that his financial dependence on newspaper delivery would sabotage his otherwise promising academic career.

Paul was not the only student whose post-graduation trajectory challenges the 'stay and return construct.' In fact, Alma from Montenegro was in Italy; Ivan from Belarus was in the UK; Zurab from Georgia was in Germany; Maria from Estonia was in Austria; Olga from Poland was in the Czech Republic; Adam from Romania was in Poland; and, finally, David had set sail for Bulgaria. As such, this group of students from both EU and non-EU countries was particularly transnational in the sense that their lives stretched across several national borders (Robertson, 2013). Essentially, none of them had planned for future migration to any of these destinations when they initially moved to Denmark to pursue a master's degree. According to Ahrens et al. (2016, p. 85), scholars tend to presuppose 'that migrants leave their place of origin with a clear idea about the ultimate destination of their journey' thereby ignoring 'the possibility that after settling in one place, migrants may later decide to migrate to another place – or even a number of other places – they had not considered at the start of their journey' (see also King and Karamoschou, 2019; Ramos, 2018). In fact, several of the students indicated that they did not necessarily believe that their current destination would be their final destination. Even though Maria was doing a PhD in Vienna, she did not plan to stay in Austria on a long-term basis: 'I think Vienna is a really lovely city, looks really nice with the parks, art deco houses, and coffee houses. But I don't feel at home here somehow, so that's why no longer-term plans.' Instead, she and her boyfriend were considering moving to Berlin after she had handed in her PhD thesis. Similar to Paul's description of Ireland, Maria was attracted to Berlin's 'openness' and long experience with immigration and multiculturalism.

While Paul's choice of onward destination was a product of transnational ties, onward migration seemed to follow an ad hoc logic for most of my interlocutors. Cristina Ramos (2018, p. 1842) notes how onward migration often is as a reaction to 'a variety of reasons, such as disillusion, discrimination or disappointing job opportunities.' Certainly, many of my interlocutors would have liked to stay in Denmark but found it difficult to get jobs. Ivan from Belarus moved directly from Denmark to the UK to pursue a PhD degree, which he finished at the end of 2019. He explained that choosing the UK was the result of 'excellent opportunities for research,' but also the fact that he felt handicapped by not knowing the Danish language since it complicated his possibilities to follow the national media and thereby his abilities to stay in touch with the surrounding society. He explained: 'I found that in smaller European countries it's harder to be a foreign citizen in comparison to bigger countries like the UK or maybe even Germany because you have a better understanding of the context.'

In comparison to Paul and Ivan, David's journey after graduation was characterised by a greater number of what appeared to be somewhat 'random' destinations. I earlier described how David returned from Denmark to his country of origin, Hungary, when being incapable of finding employment with relevance to his academic profile. Akin to other graduates discussed in this chapter, he too was determined to supplement his Danish master's degree with additional education. In Budapest, he paid for a five-week – long language course with the aim of becoming a teacher. After getting the teaching certificate, it only took few months before finding employment as a teacher at an American institution in Ecuador. While he enjoyed his life in Ecuador, he decided to return to Hungary after one year of teaching, because he could not justify to himself how little he was paid. Although he found employment as an English teacher in Kazakhstan, he terminated his work contract after only a couple of months in the country due to 'unacceptable' working conditions. David felt saddened by being unemployed and back in Hungary – the country he previously had been so eager to escape.

After several months of intensive job search, David finally managed to find a job in Budapest. However, he remained determined to go abroad again whenever the moment offered itself. The turning point came when he fell in love with a Bulgarian woman. He explained how he had 'started self-learning web programming' and that he soon would start to apply for jobs in Bulgaria in the IT industry. David's narrations draw attention to several interesting aspects. One, how David neither navigated his post-graduation journey on the basis of a clearly structured plan nor a clear notion of the ultimate end destination of his voyage. Rather, in line with Gomes' (2015) point, his onward ventures were mostly spurred by disappointing job opportunities and a chase for meaningful employment – interpreted as primarily being in line with his academic merits and skills – which he hoped would allow him to live a fulfilling life. His narrative furthermore accentuates how student migrants' routes and motivations can swiftly change during the migration process. Two, his geographical trajectory highlights how his home country, Hungary, remained an important base in-between the various destinations – thereby underlining the continued significance of the nation-state in spite of having an EU citizenship (Favell, 2008). Three, his story provides yet another example of how some graduates engaged in further education – in his case even several times – to supplement their Danish master's degree to make their profile more attractive for a greater range of employers. The following section goes further into how skills acquired outside one's formal education turned out to be pivotal for some graduates.

Flexible skills

In their study of student migrants in Australia, Robertson and Runganaikaloo (2014, p. 220) point out how their research subjects' narratives, 'despite often feeling subject to the whims of the immigration regime,' also foregrounded individual agency and coping strategies 'in their dealings with governmental processes, finding ways around bureaucratic or legal hurdles.' While many graduates from non-EU countries in this present study felt maltreated by Denmark's immigration regulation and unfairly positioned by the global visa regime, I also wish to highlight how their narratives, akin to Robertson and Runganaikaloo's findings, underlined a great portion of agency and creativity in terms of navigating state regulation. This has already been indicated when, for instance, discussing how marriage for one non-EU graduate functioned as a way to stay in Denmark and enter the Danish labour market with a salary below the pay range stipulated by the Pay Limit Scheme. In the following, I will focus on how skills acquired outside the range of the student migrants' formal education proved valuable for the onward migration (inside the EU) of some non-EU citizens. I will particularly zoom in on Zurab's story, a student migrant from Georgia, and his post-graduating journey from Denmark to Germany.

Simultaneously to studying in Denmark, Zurab had managed to build an impressive CV. He, for instance, did an internship in Brussels, but he also engaged in other extracurricular activities related to software development, which had been a hobby of his since a young age. The latter turned out to be pivotal for his possibilities of remaining inside the EU upon his graduation – even more so than his master's degree from Denmark. While Zurab had been interested in staying in Denmark, he did not deem this viable in light of the Danish immigration regulation:

> I did want to stay in Denmark but it was incredibly hard. The visa requirements were impossible to comply with even though I graduated there. I mean, I examined the visa requirements thoroughly and they were crazy.
>
> (Zurab, Georgia)

According to Zurab, Denmark was asking for 'an insane amount of money' for him to fulfil his ambition of starting up his own company and while telling me this, he asked me with a puzzled look on his face: 'Who has that kind of money after graduation?' Thus, in line with the experiences of other interlocutors from non-EU countries, he came to realisation that the combination of having a Danish master's degree and professional experience from internships did not in itself guarantee access to the upper reaches of the labour market upon graduating. Further, Zurab was also reluctant to accept a job unrelated to his professional interest and he too believed that his lack of Danish proficiency constituted a major deficit for finding relevant employment. The difficulties of settling down made him keen on going to other destinations with less strict immigration regulation and where being highly skilled overruled being a migrant. He decided on Germany, and more specifically Berlin, because he considered the atmosphere 'much more chill' in terms of giving newcomers a fair chance of establishing themselves:

> We have a lot of young people coming here and big part of them don't even know what they want to do, but they are highly skilled and trying to do things and the city is really encouraging such immigration. Here it's very affordable and very vibrant, lots of opportunities to do whatever you want to do, as a researcher, startup person, artist or working for a big company. And most people here are young immigrants, so very easy for most of them to integrate.
>
> (Zurab, Georgia)

The quote accentuates how Berlin, in Zurab's view, offered a more welcoming climate for integration both socially and professionally. In addition, Zurab could (in contrast to Denmark) get by without speaking the local language. Thus, he was confronted by a markedly different openness than what he had encountered in the Danish society, where coming from a non-EU country had proven to be a huge deficit. As such, his experiences of living in Berlin shaped the narrative he presented of Denmark as a closed and insulated country, making 'the vectors of difference between "here" and "there" become the causative factors for migration' (Raghuram, 2013, p. 143). It was also not his Danish university degree that secured his continued stay or even employment in Berlin. In fact, when I asked him if his formal education had been of any usage, he laughingly replied, 'No, not much. I mean, I am still very interested in those topics though and I read about it all the time.' As indicated, his self-taught software skills instead became decisive for his career and onward migration. He explained how, in Berlin, they were keen on attracting people in certain fields: 'I needed a visa here, so it's important that I had a job that's in demand and is something that is good for German economy.' To his luck, this included software developers and since no formal proof of his software skills was required – except for some contract offers, which he quickly established – he found the transition into the German labour market surprisingly smooth. When I last spoke to him in 2020, he had resided in Berlin for more than four years.

Abroad but not a foreigner – onward mobility to Eastern Europe

I previously discussed how Olga grew tired of always feeling like a foreigner in Denmark. While studying abroad, she also experienced a stronger identification with her 'Eastern European roots' and ultimately decided to return to Poland. Disappointed with her job opportunities in Poland, she nonetheless decided to move on to a third country. However, in contrast to previous aspirations, she did not want to settle in a Western European country. Instead, she moved to the Czech Republic. One of the reasons for her choice of destination was that she – despite living in a foreign country – would not feel stigmatised for her Eastern European roots. I encountered a similar reasoning when speaking to Adam, who had relocated to Poland after having spent some years in his home country, Romania. Adam thoroughly expanded on his current living conditions in relation to the past in a particularly generous, direct, and lively manner. Thus, Adam's ontological narrative makes a fitting case for an in-depth exploration of how stigma management was not only intertwined with an overarching metanarrative of the West but also weaved into my interlocutors' encounters with various public narratives of different European countries.

Despite the fact that Adam had not lived in Denmark for several years, we were not far into our Skype conversation before I sensed a strong resentment towards the country. The numerous unsuccessful attempts of finding a job next to his university studies in Denmark – a direct result, he claimed, of his inability to speak the Danish language as well as of his foreign nationality – still infuriated him:

> I was always thinking:' Why? You speak English! It's your second language, why?' Even for washing some stupid dishes, you're still asking for Danish. It's so stupid. It's almost like you are trying to make up excuses to not hire me because I'm not Danish. In Denmark, I felt a closure towards any type of foreigner. What pissed me off about Denmark was the expectations that I got from reading advertisements online that Denmark *wants* people from other countries. They want you. They want you to go there, because they are so open-minded. But they are not. The government wants diversity but the population doesn't.
>
> (Adam, Romania)

Adam felt that Denmark had not given him a fair chance, and, as described earlier, he had terminated his 'migrant career' in a depressed state of mind after only six months in the country. He further confided in me about an 'immature fantasy' playing in his mind from time to time. One day a company from Denmark would offer him a job – an offer to which he would nonchalantly respond:

> Well, I tried to get a job in your country and I really tried to prove that I'm intelligent and that I wanted to contribute and you did not do shit, so now Poland will make money out of me.
>
> (Adam, Romania)

Throughout our conversation, Adam seemed eager to underline the fundamental difference between the treatment he had received in Poland and in Denmark. He emphasised how he had met Polish citizens taking Romanian language classes to get jobs *in* Poland – thereby accentuating Poland's openness towards foreigners and how, in Poland, being from Romania in many ways functioned as symbolic capital rather than as a shortcoming (Bourdieu, 1986). Adam's narrations also highlight the fundamental importance of being treated and viewed as an equal by the host society rather than stigmatised on the basis of one's 'foreignness.' Indeed, he felt accepted by the Polish society and people:

> I once asked a local, 'Do you have any issues with me because I am from Romania?,' and the Polish person said, 'Well, you are white, and you're a Christian,' and I was like, 'Well, that's extremely racist, honestly, but from a pragmatic point of view, I guess I'm alright in Poland.'
>
> (Adam, Romania)

Adam seemingly experienced a strong sense of belonging to his new country. To fortify their level of dedication to Poland, he and his Romanian girlfriend were even considering applying for Polish citizenship. While Adam's narrations at first glance appear to be different from the examples provided earlier, they too constitute an example of stigma management. Due to the rejection Adam experienced in the West, he evidently felt a need to redeem himself and rise above the humiliating treatment. While Clara defended her 'right to immobility' upon her return to Romania, Adam was focused on legitimising Poland as a worthy destination for onward migration. We can observe Adam's impression management in several ways. First, at a more personal level, where he seemed keen on presenting a (counter)ontological narrative as successful in nearly all aspects of his life: He had found a loving partner and a well-paid job (in a Polish context), which even allowed him to save up for an apartment in the future and lead a cosmopolitan lifestyle. The take-home-message intended for his audience (me) was clear: Denmark had not managed to bring him down but rather ignited his thirst for success. Secondly, Adam was focused on countering the stigma attached to Poland by subtracting the country – and thereby himself – from the metanarrative of Eastern Europe as backwards and undeveloped. As emphasised consistently throughout this book, struggles over narrations are ultimately struggles over identity (Somers, 1994). Adam's story illustrates how the different narrative levels are entwined, drawing heavily on the public narrative of Romania he experienced in Denmark and Poland, respectively, to tailor his ontological narrative in line with his current life situation. Interestingly enough, on several occasions he continued to draw on the metanarrative of the West by stressing that Poland was located in Central Europe, thereby insinuating a marked difference between Poland and countries 'further East' – including his home country, Romania:

> Many of my friends left for other countries – mostly to popular destinations for Romanians like Germany, France, England, and Spain. I was highly criticised by my friends when I said I'm going to Poland. They were saying: 'Oh, you are going to a communist country, it's a shitty place.' Like Romanians have a lot of misconceptions about Poland. And I came here and I realised, 'No, Poland is basically Romania but better, because it's exactly like Romania here but better!' People are more developed and have a more civic spirit. I enjoy the fact that there are not a lot of Romanians here and I do not particularly like to be around Romanians honestly. I love my country, but I hate Romanians. I hate the mentality. I hate their wannabe attitude, like they want to be like people in Germany, or people in Denmark, they want to be like America, but they don't want to be like themselves.
>
> (Adam, Romania)

As we sense in the quote, Adam was determined to distance himself from his home country, Romania, while portraying Poland as an unambiguous 'upgrade' on the 'East–West civilizational slope' (Melegh, 2006, p. 2). He especially emphasised Poland's economic success when stating that: 'Poland is officially part of the first world economically. I think it's the most well-developed country out of all ex-communist countries.' Simultaneously, he drew attention to the *sameness* between Poland and countries in Western Europe: 'And in terms of infrastructure and the vibe you get in [Krakow] compared to Aarhus or Copenhagen, it's the same. Poland is like Denmark. They both have infrastructure, highways, buildings, which are well-kept.' Adam even underlined how he saw Poland *ahead* of Denmark and Western European countries in many ways: 'Honestly I feel so safe here. I did not feel safe in the Netherlands or Denmark.' While he regarded Poland as a 'racist country,' he argued that Denmark was in fact 'more racist,' only in a less blatant manner. Thereby, he made it perfectly clear that Poland was not a downgrade from previous migration destinations in the West, which, as indicated in the above quote, went against the perception of many of his friends. Thus, Adam had no intention to return to Romania: 'No, definitely no [shaking his head]. Not even in my wildest dreams.'

Conclusions

This chapter shed light on my interlocutors' narrations of their social and geographical trajectories following their graduation. For analytical clarity, the chapter was divided into three overriding parts: The first part focuses on a group of graduates who were keen on and managed to stay in Denmark; the second part scrutinises the narratives presented by the students who, in one way or another, returned to their home countries after graduation; and, finally, the third part explores the assorted paths of some interlocutors who engaged in onward journeys to a third country, or even a few different countries.

In Chapter 4, I showed how the non-EU students, when compared to students from EU countries, narrated their experiences of student life in Denmark in more positive terms. I linked this tendency to the financial security provided by their scholarships since the regular income facilitated the possibility to participate in voluntary extracurricular activities (potentially beneficial for their career trajectory) and more generally the freedom to prioritise their time and studies as they pleased. In contrast, the EU movers often relied on low-skilled employment to cover their living expenses and had to cut down expenses not directly related to their subsistence. One of the main strengths of longitudinal research is that it allows us to distinguish developments or changes in the characteristics of the target population at both the group and the individual levels. In this chapter, I discussed how graduation introduced a new dimension of uncertainty for the non-EU graduates keen on staying in Denmark when being without any legal guarantee that they could stay (Tan and Hugo, 2017). Consequently, many of them experienced a 'staggered' journey after graduation (Robertson and Runganaikaloo, 2014, p. 211). They first arrived on a student visa, followed by temporary work visas for varying periods after their graduation, while simultaneously trying to fulfil a number of criteria for getting a more permanent work visa. The non-EU students generally experienced their encounters with the Danish immigration regime as highly stressful. Their best option for staying in the country involved getting a job with a yearly salary above the level stipulated by the Pay Limit Scheme (roughly 60,000 euros) – a significantly higher amount than the average salary of university graduates in the field of humanities. Thus, despite the fact that many had completed relevant internships as a part of their studies or engaged in extracurricular activities, getting a job with a salary within this pay range was generally challenging and many graduates choose to leave Denmark. Indeed, their narrations revealed an alarming gap between the Danish state's ambitions to recruit and retain high-skilled labour and the conditions under which non-EU graduates are expected to establish themselves in the Danish labour market. For some, marriage to a Danish citizen turned out to be the only possible way of staying in the country.

While students with EU citizenships are privileged in the sense that they can move and settle in other EU countries without legal constraints, their journeys illustrate how young EU 'free movers' also face challenges in their aspirations of settling down in a fellow EU country (see also Favell, 2008). Akin to the descriptions of the non-EU graduates, their stories accentuate how many grew increasingly pessimistic when assessing their possibilities for getting jobs commensurate with their education, training, and experience in Denmark and how they too felt disadvantaged by their lack of valuable professional contacts. Their stories exemplify how obstacles for making a life abroad go beyond legal boundaries conditioned by one's citizenship and how, if the focus solely remains on legal barriers for migration, we overlook important aspects of the migration process. While legal marriage may function as a potential way for non-EU students to bypass restrictive immigration policy in Denmark, I also highlighted how having a partner even appeared to be fundamental for retaining students from EU countries in Denmark. In addition to having the stability and emotional support from a long-term partner, a central factor uniting the three remaining EU graduates in Denmark was that they had found meaningful employment. While the professions of the three graduates were extremely diverse, their paths after graduation fit Ezzy's (1993) notion of an 'integrative passage,' entailing that they all were engaging in performances that served to uphold (for them) valued ontological narratives.

It is interesting to note that both graduates from non-EU and EU countries highlighted the fundamental importance of Danish language proficiency for entering the labour market in Denmark. This pinpoints specific language challenges that international graduates may face in non-Anglophone destinations. Another factor which may have impaired their study-to-work transition in Denmark is that they graduated from interdisciplinary programmes in social sciences and humanities. This hypothesis is strengthened by Rolle Alho in his study of international graduates in Finland. Despite the fact that international students generally experienced difficulties with finding relevant jobs in the country, Alho underlines that 'interviewees who had studied humanities and social sciences seemed to have experienced somewhat more challenging paths to employment than those who had studied disciplines that prepared more directly to specific professions' (Alho, 2020, p. 17).

It was not only a discouraging labour market in Denmark which made some graduates return to their home countries. A considerable number of my interlocutors described how the wish to stay physically close to their family and friends grew increasingly important while residing abroad. Their experiences of return varied from case to case. While some managed to find interesting and fulfilling jobs relevant to their educational profile, others had to pause aspirations of building a career that reflected their (initial) academic interests upon their return. Their estimation of the value of a 'Western degree,' however, was less univocal than during our earlier conversations in Denmark. In contrast to what many believed when they initially journeyed to Denmark, a Western degree did not always guarantee labour market success in itself. Often, it appeared to be a combination of various factors such as the right academic profile, previous work experience, valuable contacts, and a bit of luck. Obviously, it is difficult to tell if this would have been different if they had graduated from another university in another 'Western country.' While I spoke to students for whom a mismatch between their level of education and career opportunities sparked a wish to go abroad again, others chose to pursue further education – sometimes a second or even a third master's degree – to upgrade their profile and/or explore alternative career paths. Indeed, I gave several examples of student migrants who embarked on new educational journeys after having completed their studies – often within the area of IT – to give their profile a competitive edge in the labour market. I also showed how skills acquired outside their formal education in Denmark – such as learning the Danish language – turned out for some to be an advantage for finding employment.

Maybe because my interlocutors initially viewed student mobility as a mark of distinction – a way to cement a symbolic boundary between 'the leavers' and 'the stayers' – they often felt a strong need to accentuate (continued) close alliance between their ontological narratives and 'Scandinavian values' upon their return. In addition, there was a tendency for them to defend themselves against what they experienced as an 'immobility stigma' after having cancelled their migrant career and thus expressed a need to justify their return. In the chapter, I also discussed how homecoming for those returning to countries outside the European Union had an extra 'juridical layer' due to restrictions imposed by the global visa regime. This made those less satisfied with their employment situation feel confined to their home countries. As such, I highlighted how the students' post-graduation trajectories also reflect differentiated access to mobility.

Finally, I examined the paths and narratives of the graduates, whose paths challenged the dominant 'stay and return construct' by moving on to other countries. I showed how their onward journeys often followed what appeared to be an 'ad hoc' logic and that most of them did not have a clear vision about the ultimate destination of their journey. Onward migration is an ongoing process where routes and motivations can suddenly and swiftly change. Moreover, several of these graduates did not have any plans to remain in their current destinations on a long-term basis but were open to explore new localities. This did not mean that they necessarily had a wish to engage in 'unlimited global mobility' (Gomes, 2015, p. 46). In fact, most of my interlocutors dreamed of 'grounded, secure and stable lives' (Bygnes and Erdal, 2017, p. 114), yet this wish was often difficult to realise due to obstacles that kept on emerging within their social surroundings. While the graduates' onwards paths did not follow a neat plot, I shed light on various factors that steered graduates towards certain destinations. One factor was that of transnational ties and the attraction to family members or romantic partners. In addition, the graduates wanted to avoid locations where one's foreignness would constitute a stigmatising attribute in the labour market and broader society. Therefore, many found countries appealing with a long tradition of migration, and some even chose to migrate to other Eastern European destinations for this reason. I highlighted how the latter choice seemingly entailed the need both to defend their 'non-Western' choice of destination by accentuating its 'Western qualities' in comparison to their home countries and, at the same time, to challenge the narrative of Western superiority by stressing the inferiority of Denmark.

On a more theoretical level, the analyses illustrate how the student migrants' ontological narratives were repeatedly modified in relation to their local surrounding social societies and reflections of experiences in the past. Yet, regardless of whether the students stayed in Denmark, returned to their home countries, or travelled to third countries, their presentations of self were, in one way or another, engaging with metanarratives of Eastern and Western Europe when elaborating on their migration choices.

Notes

1 I use the words 'graduating' and 'graduates' knowing that some of my interlocutors did not formally graduate from the university in Denmark.
2 The majority of this information is taken from the website 'New to Denmark,' created by the Danish Agency for International Recruitment and Integration (SIRI): www.nyidanmark.dk/en-GB (accessed 16 January 2021).
3 The Danish word 'a-kasse' is an abbreviation for 'arbejdsløshedskasse' and means unemployment insurance fund. When you become a member of the a-kasse, you are guaranteed an amount of regular income if you become unemployed. The a-kasse thereby gives you time to look for the right job and pay your bills.
4 This amount has been rising over the years since the Pay Limit Scheme was introduced in 2015, which means that when my interlocutors graduated the

required yearly salary might have been a little bit lower. In 2020, for instance, the yearly salary required was DKK 436,000.

5 Such beliefs echo the experiences of international graduates in Finland who in a similar manner became surprised by the importance of connections in their job searches (Alho, 2020).

6 This information was found at the webpage of Danish Association of Masters and PhDs: https://dm.dk/din-loen/nyuddannet (accessed 16 January 2021).

References

Abbott, P., Wallace, C., Mascauteanu, M., Sapsford, R., 2010. Concepts of citizenship, social and system integration among young people in post-Soviet Moldova. J. Youth Stud. 13, 581–596. https://doi.org/10.1080/13676261.2010.489605

Ahrens, J., Kelly, M., Liempt, I.V., 2016. Free movement? The onward migration of EU citizens born in Somalia, Iran, and Nigeria. Popul. Space Place 22, 84–98. https://doi.org/10.1002/psp.1869

Alho, R., 2020. 'You need to know someone who knows someone': International students' job search experiences. Nord. J. Work. Life Stud. 10, 3–22. https://doi.org/10.18291/njwls.v10i2.120817

Baláž, V., Williams, A.M., 2004. 'Been there, done that': International student migration and human capital transfers from the UK to Slovakia. Popul. Space Place 10, 217–237. https://doi.org/10.1002/psp.316

Bourdieu, P., 1986. The forms of capital, in: Richardson, J. (Ed.), Handbook of Theory and Research for the Sociology of Education. Greenwood, Westport, CT, pp. 241–258.

Bryła, P., 2018. International student mobility and subsequent migration: The case of Poland. Stud. High. Educ. 44, 1–14. https://doi.org/10.1080/03075079.2018.1440383

Bygnes, S., Erdal, M.B., 2017. Liquid migration, grounded lives: Considerations about future mobility and settlement among Polish and Spanish migrants in Norway. J. Ethn. Migr. Stud. 43, 102–118. https://doi.org/10.1080/1369183X.2016.1211004

Chankseliani, M., 2016. Escaping homelands with limited employment and tertiary education opportunities: Outbound student mobility from post-Soviet countries. Popul. Space Place 22, 301–316. https://doi.org/10.1002/psp.1932

Cresswell, T., 2006. On the Move: Mobility in the Modern Western World. Routledge, London.

de Haas, H., Fokkema, T., Fihri, M.F., 2015. Return migration as failure or success? The determinants of return migration intentions among Moroccan migrants in Europe. Int Migr. Integr. 16, 415–429.

Engbersen, G., Snel, E., 2013. Liquid migration: Dynamic and fluid pat-terns of post-accession migration, in: Glorius, B., Grabowska-Lusinska, I., Kuvik, A. (Eds.), Mobility in Transition: Migration Patterns after EU Enlargement, IMISCOE Research. Amsterdam University Press, Amsterdam, pp. 21–40.

Eskelä, E., 2015. Housing Talent Residential Satisfaction among Skilled Migrants in the Helsinki Metropolitan Area. The Faculty of Science of the University of Helsinki, Finland.

Ezzy, D., 1993. Unemployment and mental health: A critical review. Soc. Sci. Med. 37, 41–52. https://doi.org/10.1016/0277-9536(93)90316-v

Favell, A., 2008. Eurostars and Eurocities: Free Movement and Mobility in an Integrating Europe, Studies in Urban and Social Change. Wiley-Blackwell, Malden, MA.

Findlay, A., Prazeres, L., McCollum, D., Packwood, H., 2017. 'It was always the plan': International study as 'learning to migrate.' Area 49, 192–199. https://doi.org/10.1111/area.12315

Fong, V.L., 2011. Paradise Redefined. Stanford University Press, Stanford, CA.

Forsberg, S., 2019. 'The right to immobility' and the uneven distribution of spatial capital: Negotiating youth transitions in northern Sweden. Soc. Cult. Geogr. 20, 323–343. https://doi.org/10.1080/14649365.2017.1358392

Franquesa, J., 2011. 'We've lost our bearings': Place, tourism, and the limits of the 'mobility turn.' Antipode 43, 1012–1033. https://doi.org/10.1111/j.1467-8330.2010.00789.x

Galasińska, A., Galasiński, D., 2010. The Post-communist Condition: Public and Private Discourses of Transformation. John Benjamins, Amsterdam.

Geddie, K., 2015. Policy mobilities in the race for talent: Competitive state strategies in international student mobility. Trans. Inst. Br. Geogr. 40, 235–248. https://doi.org/10.1111/tran.12072

Geddie, K.P., 2010. Transnational Landscapes of Opportunity? Postgraduation Settlement and Employment Strategies of International Students in Toronto, University of Toronto, Toronto.

Ginnerskov-Dahlberg, M., Valentin, K., forthcoming. Unpredictable mobilities: Post-graduation trajectories of international students in Denmark.

Goffman, E., 1963. Stigma: Notes on the Management of Spoiled Identity. Prentice-Hall, Englewood Cliffs, NJ.

Goldring, L., Landolt, P., 2011. Caught in the work-citizenship matrix: The lasting effects of precarious legal status on work for Toronto immigrants. Globalizations 8, 325–341.

Gomes, C., 2015. Footloose transients: International students in Australia and their aspirations for transnational mobility after graduation. Crossings J. Migr. Cult. 6, 41–57. https://doi.org/10.1386/cjmc.6.1.41_1

Hage, G., 2009. Waiting out the crisis: On stuckedness and governmentality. Anthropolo Theory. 5, 463–475.

Hage, G., Papadopoulos, D., 2004. Ghassan Hage in conversation with Dimitris Papadopoulos: Migration, hope and the making of subjectivity in transnational capitalism. Int. J. Crit. Psychol. 12, 95–117.

Hawthorne, L., 2009. The growing global demand for international students as skilled migrants, in: The Migration Policy Institute Talent (Ed.), Competitiveness and Migration: The Transatlantic Council on Migration. Verlag Bertelsmann Stiftung, Brussels.

Holloway, S.L., O'Hara, S.L., Pimlott-Wilson, H., 2012. Educational mobility and the gendered geography of cultural capital: The case of international student flows between Central Asia and the UK. Environ. Plan. Econ. Space 44, 2278–2294. https://doi.org/10.1068/a44655

Honneth, A., 1996. The Struggle for Recognition: The Moral Grammar of Social Conflicts. MIT Press, Cambridge, MA.

Jansen, S., 2009. After the red passport: Towards an anthropology of the everyday geopolitics of entrapment in the EU's 'immediate outside.' J. R. Anthropol. Inst. 15, 815–832. https://doi.org/10.1111/j.1467-9655.2009.01586.x

King, R., Karamoschou, C., 2019. Fragmented and fluid mobilities: The role of onward migration in the new map of Europe and the Balkans. Migr. Etn. Teme 35, 141–169.

Krivonos, D., Näre, L., 2019. Imagining the 'west' in the context of global coloniality: The case of post-Soviet youth migration to Finland. Sociology 53, 1177–1193. https://doi.org/10.1177/0038038519853111

Lamont, M., Molnár, V., 2002. The study of boundaries in the social sciences. Annu. Rev. Sociol. 28, 167–195. https://doi.org/10.1146/annurev.soc.28.110601.141107

Lulle, A., Buzinska, L., 2017. Between a 'student abroad' and 'being from Latvia': Inequalities of access, prestige, and foreign-earned cultural capital. J. Ethn. Migr. Stud. 43, 1362–1378. https://doi.org/10.1080/1369183X.2017.1300336

Mai, N., King, R., 2009. Love, sexuality and migration: Mapping the issue(s). Mobilities 4, 295–307. https://doi.org/10.1080/17450100903195318

Manolova, P., 2017. On the Way to the Imaginary West: Bulgarian Migrations, Imaginations, and Disillusionments. (Unpublished thesis). Birmingham University, Birmingham: Department of Political Science and International Studies.

Melegh, A., 2006. On the East-West Slope: Globalization, Nationalism, Racism and Discourses on Central and Eastern Europe. Central European University Press, New York.

Moret, J., 2020. Mobility capital: Somali migrants' trajectories of (im)mobilities and the negotiation of social inequalities across borders. Geoforum 116, 235–242. https://doi.org/10.1016/j.geoforum.2017.12.002

Mosneaga, A., Winther, L., 2013. Emerging talents? International students before and after their career start in Denmark: International students in Denmark. Popul. Space Place 19, 181–195. https://doi.org/10.1002/psp.1750

Neveu Kringelbach, H., 2015. Gendered educational trajectories and transnational marriage among West African students in France. Identities 22, 288–302. https://doi.org/10.1080/1070289X.2014.939190

Niraula, A., Valentin, K., 2019. Mobile brains and the question of 'deskilling': High-skilled South Asian migrants in Denmark. Nord. J. Migr. Res. 9, 19–35. https://doi.org/10.2478/njmr-2019-0008

OECD, 2017. Education at a Glance 2017: OECD Indicators, OECD Publishing, Paris, https://doi.org/10.1787/eag-2017-en.

Pungas, E., Toomet, O., Tammaru, T., Anniste, K., 2012. Are Better Educated Migrants Returning? Evidence from Multidimensional Education Data. Norface Migration Discussion Paper. 1–33.

Raghuram, P., 2013. Theorising the spaces of student migration. Popul. Space Place 19, 138–154. https://doi.org/10.1002/psp.1747

Ramos, C., 2018. Onward migration from Spain to London in times of crisis: The importance of life-course junctures in secondary migrations. J. Ethn. Migr. Stud. 44, 1841–1857. https://doi.org/10.1080/1369183X.2017.1368372

Riaño, Y., 2015. Latin American women who migrate for love: Imagining European men as ideal partners, in: Enguix, B., Roca, J. (Eds.), Rethinking Romantic Love: Discussions, Imaginaries and Practices. Cambridge Scholars Publishing, Cambridge, pp. 45–60.

Robertson, S., 2011. Cash cows, backdoor migrants, or activist citizens? International students, citizenship, and rights in Australia. Ethn. Racial Stud. 34, 2192–2211. https://doi.org/10.1080/01419870.2011.558590

Robertson, S., 2013. Transnational Student-Migrants and the State: The Education-Migration Nexus. Palgrave Macmillan, Basingstoke.

Robertson, S., Runganaikaloo, A., 2014. Lives in limbo: Migration experiences in Australia's education–migration nexus. Ethnicities 14, 208–226. https://doi.org/10.1177/1468796813504552

Seminario, R., Le Feuvre, N., 2019. The combined effect of qualifications and marriage on the employment trajectories of Peruvian graduates in Switzerland. J. Int. Migr. Integr. 22, 205–226. https://doi.org/10.1007/s12134-019-00730-8

Simola, A., 2018. Lost in administration: (Re)producing precarious citizenship for young university-educated intra-EU migrants in Brussels. Work Employ. Soc. 32, 458–474. https://doi.org/10.1177/0950017018755653

Snel, E., Faber, M., Engbersen, G., 2015. To stay or return? Explaining return intentions of Central and Eastern European labour migrants. Cent. East. Eur. Migr. Rev. 4, 5–24.

Somers, M.R., 1994. The narrative constitution of identity: A relational and network approach. Theory Soc. 23, 605–649. https://doi-org.ezproxy.its.uu.se/10.1007/BF00992905

Soong, H., 2014. Transnational Students and Mobility: Lived Experiences of Migration. Routledge, London.

Tan, G., Hugo, G., 2017. The transnational migration strategies of Chinese and Indian students in Australia. Popul. Space Place 23, e2038. https://doi.org/10.1002/psp.2038

Thomas, S., 2017. The precarious path of student migrants: Education, debt, and transnational migration among Indian youth. J. Ethn. Migr. Stud. 43, 1873–1889. https://doi.org/10.1080/1369183X.2017.1286970

White, A., 2010. Young people and migration from contemporary Poland. J. Youth Stud. 13, 565–580. https://doi.org/10.1080/13676261.2010.487520

Wiers-Jenssen, J., 2013. Degree mobility from the Nordic countries: Background and employability. J. Stud. Int. Educ. 17, 471–491.

Wu, C., Wilkes, R., 2017. International students' post-graduation migration plans and the search for home. Geoforum 80, 123–132. https://doi.org/10.1016/j.geoforum.2017.01.015

6 Conclusion

This book originates in the increasing number of students travelling from Eastern to Western Europe via the channel of higher education (Genova, 2016; Lulle and Buzinska, 2017; Marcu, 2015). Instead of targeting one of the most popular countries and largest receivers of international students, I have focused on the case of Denmark – an 'off-beat study destination,' characterised by lesser-known universities in a country where the main language is not a major world language (Eskelä, 2013, p. 145). The number of students coming to study in Denmark from Eastern European EU member states has more than doubled in recent years, particularly concentrated in English-medium, master's level study programmes. This increase of incoming Eastern European students has led to a public outcry on the rising costs these students presumably bring to the Danish taxpayers financing the state-driven education. Denmark is not the only country where students from Eastern European countries have been increasingly debated in a negative manner. Elena Genova (2016, p. 392), for instance, notes how 'Bulgarian migrants and university students in particular have recently fallen into the spotlight of British media, firmly positioned within fervent immigration debates.' Accounts like this underline how all international students no longer are unconditionally 'welcome' in Western European countries (Luthra and Platt, 2016).

Drawing on insights developed through a longitudinal, ethnographic study (2013–2020), I have sought to shed light on the evolving narratives of 27 full-degree, master's students from different post-socialist countries and thereby provided a window into the lives of this relatively understudied group of individuals. To bring my interlocutors' experiences to the forefront, I drew on conceptual tools found in the literature on narrativity and dramaturgy. The findings presented in this book are divided into three analytical chapters, each focusing on one of three overarching dimensions: (1) the student migrants' motivations for going to Denmark, (2) the student migrants' narratives connected to living and studying in Denmark, and (3) the student migrants' social and geographical trajectories after graduation. In this concluding chapter, the main themes and contributions presented in the three analytical chapters are summarised and discussed in relation to the existing literature on student migration/mobility.

The complex paths to Denmark – beyond economic logic

A central claim of this book is that we cannot understand the Eastern European students' paths to Denmark without paying sufficient attention to the meanings they attach to their pre-mobility position and 'the broader economic, cultural and social environments wherein these decisions are formed' (Van Mol, 2014, p. 40). The narratives presented by my interlocutors suggest that the international 'immobility' of previous generations – due to travel restrictions imposed by communist regimes – constituted a significant factor for their aspirations of pursuing an education outside the national borders (see also Ginnerskov-Dahlberg, 2021). The fact that the students established a causal link between their parents' resentment about the travel restrictions prior to 1989 and their own desire to cross borders accentuates how narratives circulate between generations and carry the momentum of the past into the present and the future (Liechty, 2003). The students particularly foregrounded how their parents had 'handed over' a narrative of travelling as an intrinsic value while simultaneously encouraging them to explore the world from a very young age. By attaching symbolic value to cross-border movement, the students regarded themselves as fortunate to have come of age in an era where people are less confined to the nation-state. In this light, study abroad – and in particular to destinations in the West – equals taking advantage of opportunities the previous generations were denied.

The students' motivations for going abroad were not solely based on their parents' experiences of restricted mobility, but the result of a combination of individual, subjective circumstances and broader (current) social structures in their home countries. When delving further into their narratives we find an intricate interplay between a sense of existential fatigue, stemming from the societal conditions and opportunities available to them in their home countries, and a powerful metanarrative of the West, informing their dreams of a different mode of existence that could grant them the possibility to lead a 'normal life.' Metanarratives are master stories with a global currency in which social actors are entangled and that often have become naturalised to the extent that people seldom question their supposed 'truths' (Somers, 1994, 1992). I accentuated how the students narrated Eastern and Western Europe hierarchically in spatial and temporal ways (see also Brooks et al., 2012; Brooks and Waters, 2011; Fong, 2011; Soong, 2014). Accordingly, none of my interlocutors seemed to question the narrative of the West as 'superior' or Eastern Europe as 'backward.'

Their explanations for why Eastern European countries occupied unfavourable positions on the East/West civilisational slope (Melegh, 2006) had a strong historical focus, accentuating negative socio-economic effects

caused by the communist regime. Although the Iron Curtain lost its physical representation with the destruction of the Berlin Wall, communism, the
students claimed, left a dark mark on their home countries and paved the
way for current disturbing societal conditions, such as corruption and nepotism. When feeling hindered from getting jobs reflecting their educational
level, they attributed their lack of 'the right' social connections in their home
countries as one of the main reasons for being incapable of imagining a
future there. The students' 'migration narratives' were marked by a sense of
existential stagnation (Hage and Papadopoulos, 2004; Jansen, 2009) and
aspirations of transforming themselves into the people 'they ought to be'
outside what they saw as the restraining context of their home countries
(Kennedy, 1994, p. 4). Following Goffman's (1963, 1959) dramaturgical
model, this entailed the possibility to live their lives in a Western context
where they hoped to gain a better podium to *perform* in accordance with
desired roles. They furthermore aligned their ontological narratives with the
metanarrative of the West to accentuate certain personal qualities – one of
the most important being a progressive mindset fit and ready for a life outside the national borders. In this sense, most students did not present themselves as average citizens in their home countries but rather as part of an
ambitious and forward-thinking clique diverging from the mass (Buchowski,
2006) – a group of 'Eastern European Westerners.'

According to Sarah Lipura and Francis Collins (2020, p. 54), the literature on student migration is characterised by 'an overemphasis on narrow
conceptualisations of choice, reinforcing a neoliberal narrative that frames
students and their families as strategic calculating actors, removing scope
to consider the more-than-rational and more-than-economic drivers of student mobilities.' As noted, Eastern European students have become the focal
point in an at-times heated political debate in Denmark. Politicians have
raised concerns that students enrol in Danish universities to take advantage of the fee-free tertiary education and the possibility of obtaining study
grants – only to leave the country shortly after their graduation. In contrast to
this at-times one-sided portrayal of Eastern European students, the findings
presented in this book accentuate the complexity surrounding their motivations for pursuing an education in Denmark and their entanglement with
wider historical and socio-economic factors. Indeed, the findings discussed
above illustrate the complexity that underpinned the students' choice of
study destination and how it cannot be reduced to a question of rational
economic calculation (see also Krivonos and Näre, 2019; Manolova, 2017;
Sliwa and Taylor, 2011). This is not to say that financial considerations play
no role at all. Factors such as the availability of English-medium master's
programmes and the cost of education are indeed fundamental in turning
Denmark into an accessible destination. For all my interlocutors, free education – either in the shape of a scholarship or free tuition (and sometimes even
the Danish study stipend) – constituted a precondition for studying abroad in

the first place. Free education, they hoped, could also pave the way for financial independence from their parents. Importantly, this does not mean that the students were without any academic ambitions or that education (for non-EU students) merely functioned as a means to get a residence permit in Denmark. In fact, short-term goals of improving one's skills and obtaining an academic degree coexist with long-term aspirations of settling down and were all considered integral to a desirable life (Ginnerskov-Dahlberg and Valentin, forthcoming).

Towards a broader conceptualisation of youth mobility

Following Somers (1994, p. 120), researchers should remain critical towards dominant conceptual narratives, that is, the stories and explanations that scholars elaborate for themselves and others about their object of investigation. On a broader level, the empirical findings presented in this book indicate that the dominant narrative of 'youth migration' deserves more attention. There has been a tendency to treat student migration as something inherently different from other forms of cross-border movement such as labour migration. According to Olwig and Valentin (2015, p. 249), study abroad has long been viewed 'as the privilege of a small, select group of young people who were able to travel for educational purposes because they either had wealthy parents or were the fortunate recipients of scholarships.' The perceived privileged nature of international student mobility has made some researchers suggest that the phenomenon shares characteristics with tourism (Amit, 2010; Bento, 2014; Kenway and Fahey, 2007; King, 2002; Murphy-Lejeune, 2002; Trower and Lehmann, 2017; Waters et al., 2011). One of the main attractions of taking an education abroad (in addition to knowledge acquisition) is the possibility to explore a new cultural environment – preferably in a country with a pleasant climate (Rodríguez González et al., 2011). For some students, enthusiasm related to a new cultural setting may even trump the accumulation of knowledge (Trower and Lehmann, 2017) – a view that also has been prevalent in studies dealing with students participating in Erasmus exchange. In an analysis of Erasmus students' motivations for going abroad, Miha Lesjak et al. (2015, p. 861) found that students engaged in Erasmus mobility programmes primarily for 'having fun activities,' although the students may still benefit academically from participating in the exchange programme. Elizabeth Murphy-Lejeune (2002) foregrounded the hypothesis that young mobile Europeans may be particularly prone to embrace European integration:

> One of the main differences between expatriates and students is the greater flexibility which youth confers. Without family responsibilities or other ties, students are in a state of family and economic 'lightness' and their affective and mental horizon should be more unobstructed.

As a result, their integration into a different environment might prove easier, faster and more comprehensive.

(p. 6)

Murphy-Lejeune's statement is indicative of a dominant understanding of youth mobility that is still widespread among researchers today – namely as a life phase linked to a narrative of lightness, fun, and flexibility (see also Lipura and Collins, 2020). While Europe arguably has changed a lot since Murphy-Lejeune's oft-cited book saw the light of day, the findings from the present study support the importance of refraining from speaking of youth mobility in the singular. Instead, as Russell King (2018, p. 7) accentuates, the overarching notion of 'youth' is not only socially and culturally constructed but also a contextual, a situational, and, indeed, a relational property. King's way of approaching the notion of youth is thus in straight line with the study design which underpins this book – both methodologically and theoretically – where the social world is approached and understood relationally.

The empirical findings presented in this book serve to pinpoint the difficulties of deducing dominant understandings of youth migration prior to one's empirical analysis. While mobility, for the Canadian middle-class travellers in Vered Amit's (2010, p. 67) study, represented a 'time out' from adult commitments, my interlocutors' narrations paint up a markedly different scenario. Certainly, for the students from Eastern European countries, mobility was deeply entangled in adult commitments and long-term aspirations. Whether they departed from countries inside or outside the EU, cross-border mobility carried an outspoken wish of creating a brighter future for themselves and sometimes even hopes to support their immediate networks. As established, Denmark was intertwined with aspirations of long-term migration to the West and yearnings of symbolic movement free from the weight of a communist shadow. This strengthens studies claiming that global student flow should be examined within broader practices of migration (King and Raghuram, 2013; Luthra and Platt, 2016; Olwig and Valentin, 2015).

Indeed, my interlocutors' narratives accentuate the seductive power of 'the West,' which bear a strong resemblance to the students from East Asia, in Rachel Brooks and Johanna Water's (2011, p. 48) study, who shared a similar belief 'that it is impossible to fail in the "West".' Hence, my interlocutors had given much consideration to the future value and usage of a Danish master's degree prior to their departure. Even those who returned to their home countries upon graduation were convinced that a 'Western degree' would function as a means of distinction in the labour market. As such, this differs markedly from other accounts of student mobility within Europe. Interviewing UK students who took their entire degree abroad, Brooks et al. (2012) for instance found that the students in their sample only had vague career plans and generally thought little about the weight of their decision to study abroad on their future career. The authors underline how this contrasts with previous findings among students in Asia. Comparing Brooks et al.'s findings to this study also serves to accentuate important spatial disparities *within* mainland Europe and that the symbolic (and practical) value of educational mobility may differ considerably for Eastern European students and Western European students. Consequently, this strengthens and further expands the reach of Brooks et al.'s (2012, p. 294) claim 'that more attention needs to be paid to these significantly different geographies of student migration.'

An additional insight, which relates to the dominant view of youth mobility illustrated by the quote by Murphy-Lejeune, concerns the question of European integration. Even though this book did not focus on European integration *per se* nor did it address whether European student mobility fosters a European mindset, my findings indicate that students' sense of Europeanness may depend on their point of departure in Europe. Indeed, the vast majority of my interlocutors experienced their Eastern European heritage as a discrediting attribute in Denmark and felt that they were treated as second-class European citizens in the West. This misfortunate narrative of Eastern Europe, they claimed, functioned as a yardstick for evaluating them as persons – a stigma that often overshadowed the complexity of their full personality (Goffman, 1963). In fact, life in Denmark appeared to make some students more aware of regional and national borders and, consequently, more detached from an overarching European narrative. Essentially, this stood in marked contrast to their earlier ontological narrations as progressive, Western-oriented, and 'EU-loving.' In a sense, this follows Christof Van Mol's (2013) assumption that the development of a European identity through student mobility is not self-evident for all European nations but, instead, subject to a range of different personal, economic, and political factors.

My interlocutors' narratives of student life in Denmark also underline how youth may signify a precarious and uncertain life phase, affirming the assertion that all student lives are not characterised by privilege and 'spatial emancipation' (Kenway and Fahey, 2007, p. 168), but that some are subjected to labour market exploitation and migration intermediation (Lipura and Collins, 2020; Robertson, 2018, 2013; Valentin, 2015). In contrast to the students from non-EU countries sponsored by scholarships, most EU movers were completely reliant on paid work in Denmark to get by abroad. The large salary differences between their home countries and Denmark further complicated their possibilities for receiving substantial parental support. Due to a general lack of relevant study jobs, the work available was often very time-demanding, low-skilled, and several were subjected to exploitation at their workplace. I accentuated how the lives of student migrants from EU countries were characterised by a 'divestment passage' (Ezzy, 1993), entailing a separation from one's accustomed status of uncertain duration. Indeed, 'student' was just one of many identities (King and Raghuram, 2013). For those who struggled the most with the lack of money, student migration was less about 'having fun activities' (Lesjak et al., 2015) and more about an everyday struggle for survival. In sharp contrast to their lives in their home countries, Denmark became synonymous with 'dirty, dull and dangerous jobs' (Favell, 2008, p. 704), living in the ghetto, difficulties of dedicating themselves to their university studies, and feeling forced to cut back on expenses not directly related to their subsistence. Hence, they described a marked tension between their ontological narratives – their self-understanding of who they 'are' based on who they 'used' to be – and their actual practices in Denmark. Their physical labour and, even more so, a constant worry for the uncertain future appeared to have a negative impact on the students' overall well-being, many referring to depression-like symptoms. Throughout this book, I have thus highlighted the fluidity of narratives (Somers, 1994, 1992) and how students' ontological narratives are challenged and become redefined by changing practices and overarching narratives of space, place, and people.

Similar to the argument regarding the dominant narrative of youth migration, the empirical findings highlight how one should be cautious to treat the notion of 'privilege' as a fixed category (Valentin, 2015). Despite the fact that the majority of the EU movers estimated that they came from 'middle-class' families in their local context, the precarious mode of existence characterising their lives in Denmark underlines the importance of paying close attention to the situational and relational nature of privilege. Essentially, this echoes Shanthi Robertson's (2013, p. 160) findings from Australia, which show that student migrants occupy 'a spectrum of experiences in between those of the unskilled and highly vulnerable labour migrant and the elite and resourced global knowledge worker.'

The results presented in this book also elucidate the variation existing within the broad group of Eastern European students. The explanations from the non-EU students sponsored by scholarships suggest that they – when compared to the EU movers – were privileged in the sense that they were not driven by the same acute need for 'cool cash' to finance their studies abroad. Because of their relative financial security, they enjoyed a different degree of freedom to engage in valued activities and focus on their studies. Thus, they could mould their CVs in desirable directions through extra-curricular activities and socialise with like-minded peers. Indeed, the ontological narratives of the students sponsored by scholarships were not challenged by student migration in the same ways as the EU movers' who struggled to perform their accustomed roles and narratives within the frame of their new practices and demanding life conditions in Denmark. All of the scholarship students also managed to graduate from their respective master's programmes on time, in sharp contrast to several of the EU movers, some of whom returned to their parents' house in order to breathe and write up their master's theses, while six students dropped out of their programmes completely.

Evolving stories

A main contribution of the study presented in this book lies in its methodological framework, particularly the longitudinal approach to fieldwork, where I have followed and studied the same group of individuals over a period of seven years. In contrast to most qualitative studies on student migration, where interviews are conducted at one point in time only, this study design brings the ability to shed light on the student migrants' stories as they evolve in different, often unpredictable, directions (Robertson, 2018). Lipura and Collins (2020, p. 352) argue that there has been a tendency for researchers on student migration to treat the life course of students as 'biologically determined, linear and progressive rather than also considering the social constructedness, unpredictability and mutability of life course.' This inclination, the authors claim, links to the dominant presumption of internationally mobile students being a privileged group. Certainly, this study of Eastern European students on the move cements how their initial hopes, dreams, ambitions, and life conditions were far from stable but often changed significantly over time. On a broader level, this processual take on student migration indicates that future aspirations should not be mistaken for actual practices or events – thereby strengthening Colin Jerolmack and Shamus Khan's (2014, p. 178) argument that 'what people say is often a poor predictor of what they do.'

For instance, while the majority of my interlocutors initially perceived a Danish university degree as an important step towards more permanent migration to Denmark, and more broadly the West, many began to revaluate their original migration plans during the course of residing abroad. Often, they were discouraged by the specific combination of being approached as 'Eastern European foreigners' rather than an integrated part of Danish society, and non-native speakers in a non-Anglophone country. By following the students *after* their graduation, I showed how the Danish labour market, in contrast to what many had expected, proved to be extremely difficult to enter if unwilling to settle for a job at distance from their academic competences. Some felt disadvantaged by graduating from interdisciplinary university programmes in social sciences and humanities and being without a professional network (see also Alho, 2020). Since my interlocutors had envisioned Denmark as a 'meritocratic paradise,' which stood in contrast to the nepotism many experienced in their home countries, they were surprised by the importance of social networks for the progression of one's professional career. Consequently, many of those who returned to their home countries expressed that their return was prompted by the lack of attractive options in the West.

The conditions for returning differed for students coming from countries inside and outside the EU. For the graduates from non-EU countries, their best shot at staying in Denmark was getting a job with a yearly salary above the level stipulated by the so-called Pay Limit Scheme (approximately 60,000 euros), which often proved difficult without years of relevant work experience. While students with EU citizenships were privileged in the sense that they could move and settle in other EU countries without legal constraints, their narratives of life after graduation illustrated how even young EU 'free movers' faced challenges in their attempts at settling down in another EU country. Upon graduation, many found themselves in a similar position as when they left their home countries around 2013, namely residing in a place that lacked meaningful opportunities for existential advancement. In 2020, only 5 out of the 27 interlocutors who arrived in Denmark as students remained in the country.

In several cases, students who used to be very critical of the social conditions in post-communist countries began to see their home countries in a different and often less negative light. Some became keen on returning home and increasingly expressed a somewhat patriotic ardour, a tendency, which for the majority represented a considerable deviation from their plans when they initially came to Denmark. The lived experience of migration thus nuanced the narrative of the West as a guarantor of the good life. The students' valuation of a 'Western degree' also seemed less univocally positive compared to earlier and many gradually realised that a Danish diploma was not necessarily a guarantee in itself for a prestigious and highly paid job. Instead, successful employment appeared to be contingent on a combination of various factors such as the right academic profile, previous work experience, valuable contacts, as well as a bit of luck. There were returnees for whom a mismatch between their level of education and career opportunities sparked a wish to go abroad again. Others chose to pursue further education – sometimes even a new master's degree – to upgrade their professional profile and explore alternative career paths.

Following the student migrants' multifaceted social and geographical trajectories as they evolved after their graduation from Denmark allowed me to move beyond the conventional 'stay and return construct' (Geddie, 2010) – thereby accentuating how many engaged in onward migration, sometimes to several new destinations. Indeed, in 2020, seven students resided in third countries, spread out over different countries in both the Eastern and Western parts of Europe. I showed how the graduates' onward journeys often followed an 'ad hoc' logic and that most of them did not have a clear vision about the ultimate destination of their journey (Ahrens et al., 2016; King and Karamoschou, 2019; Ramos, 2018). Common for the students, however, was the dream of settling down long-term and living 'grounded, secure and stable lives' (Bygnes and Erdal, 2017, p. 114). For non-EU citizens, aspirations of migration were complicated by their uncertain legal status and destinations highly conditioned on being granted a visa. The graduates migrating to another Eastern European country narrated it as a 'safe haven' from the stigmatisation they experienced in Denmark and expressed a regained sense of dignity. Against a similar backdrop of an 'Eastern European stigma,' the students moving to new destinations in

Western Europe often draw on favourable public narratives to motivate their choice, such as the country's increased tolerance to foreigners due to its history of previous migration.

In addition to numerous surprising twists in my interlocutors' narratives and migration patterns, certain things remained constant. While the lived experiences of migration served to nuance metanarratives of Europe and the West for my interlocutors, their narrations following their graduation simultaneously indicated that the 'East–West civilizational slope' (Melegh, 2006, p. 2) remained an important point of orientation in their ontological narratives. Regardless of whether they stayed in Denmark, returned to their home countries, or travelled to third countries, their presentations of self were often narrated in relation to metanarratives of Eastern and Western Europe. Those returning home, for instance, emphasised continued alliance between their ontological narratives and the West, typically accentuating the 'Western character' of their professional lives. Further, in their narrations they defended their choice to return to Eastern Europe, which extended beyond conversations with me to everyday talks with friends and families who remained convinced that life was better in the West.

References

Ahrens, J., Kelly, M., Liempt, I.V., 2016. Free movement? The onward migration of EU citizens born in Somalia, Iran, and Nigeria. Popul. Space Place 22, 84–98. https://doi.org/10.1002/psp.1869

Alho, R., 2020. 'You need to know someone who knows someone': International students' job search experiences. Nord. J. Work. Life Stud, 10, 3–22. https://doi.org/10.18291/njwls.v10i2.120817

Amit, V., 2010. The limits of liminality: Capacities for change and transition among student travellers, in: Rapport, N. (Eds.), Human Nature as Capacity. Berghahn Books, New York.

Bento, J.P.C., 2014. The determinants of international academic tourism demand in Europe. Tour. Econ. 20, 611–628. https://doi.org/10.5367/te.2013.0293

Brooks, R., Waters, J., 2011. Student Mobilities, Migration and the Internationalization of Higher Education. Palgrave Macmillan, New York.

Brooks, R., Waters, J., Pimlott-Wilson, H., 2012. International education and the employability of UK students. Br. Educ. Res. J. 38, 281–298. https://doi.org/10.1080/01411926.2010.544710

Buchowski, M., 2006. Social thought & commentary: The specter of orientalism in Europe: From exotic other to stigmatized brother. Anthropol. Q. 79, 463–482.

Bygnes, S., Erdal, M.B., 2017. Liquid migration, grounded lives: Considerations about future mobility and settlement among Polish and Spanish migrants in Norway. J. Ethn. Migr. Stud. 43, 102–118. https://doi.org/10.1080/1369183X.2016.1211004

Eskelä, E., 2013. Migration decisions of skilled migrants. Nord. J. Migr. Res. 3. https://doi.org/10.2478/njmr-2013-0004

Ezzy, D., 1993. Unemployment and mental health: A critical review. Soc. Sci. Med. 37, 41–52.

Favell, A., 2008. The new face of east–west migration in Europe. J. Ethn. Migr. Stud. 34, 701–716. https://doi.org/10.1080/13691830802105947

Fong, V.L., 2011. Paradise Redefined. Stanford University Press, Stanford, CA.

Geddie, K.P., 2010. Transnational Landscapes of Opportunity? Postgraduation Settlement and Employment Strategies of International Students in Toronto, University of Toronto, Canada and London, UK.

Genova, E., 2016. To have both roots and wings: Nested identities in the case of Bulgarian students in the UK. Identities 23, 392–406. https://doi.org/10.1080/1070289X.2015.1024125

Ginnerskov-Dahlberg, M., 2021. Inherited dreams of 'the West'. Eastern European students' paths to Denmark, in: Cairns, D. (Ed.), The Palgrave Handbook of Youth Mobility and Educational Migration. Palgrave Macmillan, Basingstoke.

Ginnerskov-Dahlberg, M., Valentin, K., forthcoming. Unpredictable mobilities: Post-graduation trajectories of international students in Denmark.

Goffman, E., 1959. The Presentation of Self in Everyday Life. Volume 174. Doubleday, New York.

Goffman, E., 1963. Stigma: Notes on the Management of Spoiled Identity. Prentice-Hall, Englewood Cliffs, NJ.

Hage, G., Papadopoulos, D., 2004. Ghassan Hage in conversation with Dimitris Papadopoulos: Migration, hope and the making of subjectivity in transnational capitalism. Int. J. Crit. Psychol. 12, 95–117.

Jansen, S., 2009. After the red passport: Towards an anthropology of the everyday geopolitics of entrapment in the EU's 'immediate outside.' J. R. Anthropol. Inst. 15, 815–832. https://doi.org/10.1111/j.1467-9655.2009.01586.x

Jerolmack, C., Khan, S., 2014. Talk is cheap: Ethnography and the attitudinal fallacy. Sociol. Methods Res. 43, 178–209. https://doi.org/10.1177/0049124114523396

Kennedy, M.D., 1994. An introduction to East European ideology and iden-tity in transformation, in: Kennedy M.D. (Ed.), Envisioning Eastern Europe. Postcommunist Cultural Studies. The University of Michigan Press, Michigan.

Kenway, J., Fahey, J., 2007. Policy incitements to mobility: Some speculations and provocations, in: Epstein, D., Boden, D., Deem, F., Rizvi, F., Wright, S. (Eds.), World Year Book of Education 2008: Geographies of Knowledge, Geometries of Power – Framing the Future of Higher Education. Routledge, New York.

King, R., 2002. Towards a new map of European migration. Int. J. Popul. Geogr. 8, 89–106. https://doi.org/10.1002/ijpg.246

King, R., 2018. Theorising new European youth mobilities. Popul. Space Place 24, e2117. https://doi.org/10.1002/psp.2117

King, R., Karamoschou, C., 2019. Fragmented and fluid mobilities: The role of onward migration in the new map of Europe and the Balkans. Migr. Etn. Teme 35, 141–169.

King, R., Raghuram, P., 2013. International student migration: Mapping the field and new research agendas: Mapping the field and new research agenda in ISM. Popul. Space Place 19, 127–137. https://doi.org/10.1002/psp.1746

Krivonos, D., Näre, L., 2019. Imagining the 'West' in the context of global coloniality: The case of post-Soviet youth migration to Finland. Sociology 53, 1177–1193. https://doi.org/10.1177/0038038519853111

Lesjak, M., Juvan, E., Ineson, E.M., Yap, M.H.T., Axelsson, E.P., 2015. Erasmus stu-dent motivation: Why and where to go? High. Educ. 70, 845–865. https://doi.org/10.1007/s10734-015-9871-0

Liechty, M., 2003. Suitably Modern: Making Middle-class Culture in a New Consumer Society. Princeton University Press, Princeton, NJ.

Lipura, S.J., Collins, F.L., 2020. Towards an integrative understanding of contemporary educational mobilities: A critical agenda for international student mobilities research. Glob. Soc. Educ. 18, 343–359. https://doi.org/10.1080/14767724.2020.1711710

Lulle, A., Buzinska, L., 2017. Between a 'student abroad' and 'being from Latvia': Inequalities of access, prestige, and foreign-earned cultural capital. J. Ethn. Migr. Stud. 43, 1362–1378. https://doi.org/10.1080/1369183X.2017.1300336

Luthra, R., Platt, L., 2016. Elite or middling? International students and migrant diversification. Ethnicities 16, 316–344. https://doi.org/10.1177/1468796815616155

Manolova, P., 2017. On the Way to the Imaginary West: Bulgarian Migrations, Imaginations, and Disillusionments. (Unpublished thesis). Birmingham University, Birmingham: Department of Political Science and International Studies.

Marcu, S., 2015. Uneven mobility experiences: Life-strategy expectations among Eastern European undergraduate students in the UK and Spain. Geoforum 58, 68–75. https://doi.org/10.1016/j.geoforum.2014.10.017

Melegh, A., 2006. On the East-West Slope: Globalization, Nationalism, Racism and Discourses on Central and Eastern Europe. Central European University Press, New York.

Murphy-Lejeune, E., 2002. Student Mobility and Narrative in Europe: The New Strangers, Routledge Studies in Anthropology. Routledge, London.

Olwig, K.F., Valentin, K., 2015. Mobility, education and life trajectories: New and old migratory pathways. Identities 22, 247–257. https://doi.org/10.1080/1070289X.2014.939191

Ramos, C., 2018. Onward migration from Spain to London in times of crisis: The importance of life-course junctures in secondary migrations. J. Ethn. Migr. Stud. 44, 1841–1857. https://doi.org/10.1080/1369183X.2017.1368372

Robertson, S., 2013. Transnational Student-Migrants and the State: The Education-Migration Nexus. Palgrave Macmillan, Basingstoke.

Robertson, S., 2018. Friendship networks and encounters in student-migrants' negotiations of translocal subjectivity. Urban Stud. 55, 538–553. https://doi.org/10.1177/0042098016659617

Rodríguez González, C., Bustillo Mesanza, R., Mariel, P., 2011. The determinants of international student mobility flows: An empirical study on the Erasmus programme. High. Educ. 62, 413–430. https://doi.org/10.1007/s10734-010-9396-5

Sliwa, M., Taylor, B., 2011. 'Everything comes down to money'?: Migration and working life trajectories in a (post-)socialist context. Manag. Organ. Hist. 6, 347–366.

Somers, M.R., 1992. Narrativity, narrative identity, and social action: Rethinking English working-class formation. Soc. Sci. Hist. 16, 591. https://doi.org/10.2307/1171314

Somers, M.R., 1994. The narrative constitution of identity: A relational and network approach. Theory Soc. 23, 605–649.

Soong, H., 2014. Transnational Students and Mobility: Lived Experiences of Migration. Routledge, London.

Trower, H., Lehmann, W., 2017. Strategic escapes: Negotiating motivations of personal growth and instrumental benefits in the decision to study abroad. Br. Educ. Res. J. 43, 275–289. https://doi.org/10.1002/berj.3258

Valentin, K., 2015. Transnational education and the remaking of social identity: Nepalese student migration to Denmark. Identities 22, 318–332. https://doi.org/10.1080/1070289X.2014.939186

Van Mol, C., 2013. Intra-European student mobility and European identity: A successful marriage? Popul. Space Place 19, 209–222. https://doi.org/10.1002/psp.1752

Van Mol, C., 2014. Post-industrial society and European integration, in: Van Mol, C. (Ed.), Intra-European Student Mobility in International Higher Education Circuits: Europe on the Move, Palgrave Studies in Global Higher Education. Palgrave Macmillan UK, London, pp. 23–39. https://doi.org/10.1057/9781137355447_2

Waters, J., Brooks, R., Pimlott-Wilson, H., 2011. Youthful escapes? British students, overseas education and the pursuit of happiness. Soc. Cult. Geogr. 12, 455–469. https://doi.org/10.1080/14649365.2011.588802

Index

abnormality (see: normality)
accommodation (see: housing and students)
alienation 40, 61, 98, 103, 109–110, 112–113, 116, 120, 122, 130, 132–133
Arabic countries 79, 92
audience 36, 43–45, 99, 171

backwardness 7, 65, 129, 156, 171, 181
Balkans 17, 65–66, 124–126, 178
Belarus 7, 30, 78, 165–166
belonging 61, 103, 107, 109–112, 120–121, 126, 130, 151, 170
better lives, aspirations 58, 69, 74, 106, 150
biographical disruption 96, 100, 105, 133
Bologna Process 14
borders, national 3–4, 6, 9, 11, 28–29, 52–54, 66, 68, 70, 76, 78–79, 97, 108, 111, 120, 141, 144, 157, 160, 165, 181–182, 185
Bosnia and Herzegovina 30, 56, 59, 68–70, 75, 78, 107, 140–142, 144, 162
Bulgaria 9, 12–15, 30–31, 55, 58–59, 66, 69, 98, 108–109, 126, 145, 149, 153, 157, 165, 167, 180

citizenship 104, 139, 148–151, 153, 163, 167, 171, 173, 188
civilisation 7, 56, 64–65, 81, 122–124, 181
class 2, 27, 30–31, 34, 40, 44, 63, 93, 95, 117, 141
communism 6–10, 42, 53–57, 60–64, 74–75, 80–82, 171, 181–182, 184
conceptual narratives 27, 42, 183

corruption 70–71, 75, 81, 182, 187
cosmopolitan 2, 108
Czech Republic 30, 55, 165, 169

Danish students 104–105, 112, 114–116, 119
democracy 6, 8–9, 62–63, 80
development 8, 11, 32, 46, 57–58, 67, 74, 79–82, 145, 168, 185
discrediting attributes 47–48, 66, 104, 121–124, 126, 128, 133, 185
discrepancy between past and present 47, 94–95, 107–108
divestment passages 45–47, 99, 117, 132, 148, 151, 185
dramaturgy 5, 18, 27, 36, 43–45, 67, 180, 182

Eastern European Westerners 81, 103, 112, 156, 182
Erasmus 11–12, 54, 76, 90, 98, 183
Establishment Card 140, 145–146, 162
Estonia 30, 89, 98, 102, 165
EU member states 4–5, 9, 11, 15–17, 28, 77, 94, 132, 150, 153, 180
EU movers 19, 78, 90, 98, 102, 106–107, 132–133, 152–153, 172, 185–186
Europeanness 12, 19, 123–124, 126, 133, 185
European Union 2–6, 9–12, 15–19, 28–31, 72, 77–78, 88–91, 93–94, 98, 102–107, 111, 115, 131–133, 138–141, 143, 145–153, 161, 163, 165, 167–168, 172–173, 180, 184–188
existential stagnation 18, 67–69, 163, 182

exploitation 5, 17, 101–102, 132, 148, 185
Ezzy, Douglas 27, 37, 45–46, 100, 117, 148, 151, 153, 173, 185

France 11, 58, 67, 113, 128, 171
front 44–45, 67, 119, 128

gender 22, 24, 30–31, 40, 77, 120
generation 8–10, 53–54, 72, 81, 123, 181
Georgia 7, 30, 53, 160–161, 165, 168
Germany 11, 13, 15–16, 56, 161, 165–166, 168–169, 171
ghetto 119–120, 186
Goffman, Erving 27, 36, 43–45, 47–49, 66–67, 75, 77, 99–100, 103, 105, 121, 123, 125–126, 144, 165, 182, 185

heritage, Eastern European 49, 103, 126, 129, 185
homecoming 19, 139, 154, 156, 158, 160, 162, 164, 174
hope 8, 54, 58, 67–69, 73, 77, 124, 162
housing and students 72, 117–120, 133, 147–148, 151, 157, 162
Hungary 15–16, 19, 28, 30, 54, 59, 62–66, 68–69, 72, 77–78, 89, 92, 102–105, 110–112, 117, 120, 122–123, 151–152, 155–157, 166–167

identity 7, 12, 14, 19, 27, 31–32, 38–49, 64–66, 99–101, 104, 107, 120, 122–123, 125–128, 133, 144, 148, 153, 165, 171, 185
immigration regulation 3, 5, 15–16, 139, 146–147, 153, 167–168, 173
immobility 18, 53, 55, 67, 81, 160, 163–164, 171, 174, 181
internationalisation 2, 14, 30, 113, 124
internships 17, 105–106, 142–143, 145–146, 148, 160–161, 168, 173

King, Russell 2–4, 11–12, 76, 145, 165–166, 183–185, 188

labour exploitation 47, 101, 103, 186
labour market 3, 11, 13–16, 59, 69, 75–76, 82, 101, 105, 131–132, 138–140, 142–145, 147, 149, 152–154, 157, 161, 167–169, 173–175, 184–185, 187
Lamont, Michèle 116, 128, 142

language acquisition 54, 89, 93, 146, 159, 166, 169–170, 173–174, 180
legal status 18, 31, 143, 147–148, 150, 161, 163, 188
lifestyle 10, 31, 55, 62, 74, 80, 91, 95, 97–98, 111, 143, 148, 157, 163, 171
longitudinal, study design 4–5, 18–19, 27, 29, 39, 172, 180, 187
low-skilled work 1, 3, 17–18, 99, 108, 122, 132, 145, 148, 185

media 30, 58, 77, 82, 97, 118, 164, 166, 180
mental health 46, 101
mentality, Eastern European 65–66, 111, 171
meritocracy 77, 82, 122, 150, 187
merits 77, 96, 142–143, 145, 154, 161, 167
metanarratives 42, 52, 56, 61, 65, 80–82, 88, 122, 161, 169, 171, 175, 181–182, 189
methodology 3, 18–19, 27–28, 36, 184, 187
modernity 7, 56–57, 60, 62, 65–66, 74, 82, 119, 133, 156, 161
Moldova 7, 9, 11, 30, 53, 59, 61, 162, 164
money, lack of 28, 31, 35, 55, 57, 68, 71–72, 75–76, 78–79, 81, 88–90, 92–95, 97, 100–102, 105, 109–114, 117, 119–120, 130–132, 153, 168, 170, 186
Montenegro 30, 105, 165

narrative identity 27, 38–39, 42, 45, 49, 99
national citizens 62, 64–66, 77, 111
nationality 4, 19, 27, 31, 34–35, 111, 122–126, 163, 165, 170
nepotism (see: corruption)
nesting orientalisms 64–65
normality 6, 18, 71, 73–74, 76–77, 82, 88, 100, 105, 114, 132, 150–151, 155
North Macedonia 30, 54–56, 59, 71–72, 78, 104–105, 145, 147–149

ontological narratives 42, 44–45, 52, 54, 64–65, 81, 98–100, 103, 107–109, 111–112, 129, 132–133, 142, 148, 151, 155–156, 161–163, 169, 171, 173–175, 182, 186, 189 onward migration 19, 138–139, 145, 160, 164–167, 169, 171–172, 175, 178, 188

patriotism 14, 62, 67, 82, 109, 143, 158–159, 188
Pay Limit Scheme 140, 146–147, 149, 153, 167, 173, 175, 187
performativity 36, 43–46, 100–101, 123, 125, 128, 132–133, 148, 151, 173
Poland 11, 13, 15–16, 28, 30, 53, 75–77, 83–84, 90, 114–115, 121, 128, 130–131, 135, 150, 153–155, 165, 169–172
post-socialism 4, 7–11, 30, 52, 54, 64–65, 82, 103, 129, 132, 188
powerlessness 8, 40, 122, 156, 163
precariousness 2, 18, 29, 75, 88, 90–91, 94, 96, 101, 115, 129, 132, 146, 148, 185–186
presentation of self 27, 43, 76, 175, 189

race 40, 48, 77, 103, 120, 123, 127–128
ranking 15, 59–60, 63, 79, 81
relationality 18–19, 27, 31, 34, 36, 39–41, 44–47, 58, 63, 67, 82, 88, 93, 120, 133, 160, 164, 169, 175, 181, 184, 186, 189
Robertson, Shanti 29, 107, 111, 142–143, 146, 165, 167, 172, 185, 187
Romania 1–2, 4, 10, 12, 15–16, 28, 30–31, 34–35, 55–58, 61–62, 66–67, 69, 78–81, 91–101, 103, 108–110, 114–116, 119, 122–123, 125–127, 129, 153–154, 158–160, 164–165, 169–172
romantic love 13, 58, 76, 145, 175
roots 6–7, 52, 56, 66, 109, 121, 125, 128, 130–131, 146, 153, 169
Russia 7, 9, 53, 58, 80, 121–122

salary 13, 17, 72, 78, 97–98, 102–103, 140, 142, 146–147, 149, 154, 157, 162–163, 167, 173, 185, 187
Scandinavia 13, 15–16, 63, 76, 78–80, 91, 115, 150, 155–156, 162–163, 174
Serbia 30, 54–55, 75, 80, 106, 112, 124–125, 141, 162–163
settlement, long-term 3, 12–13, 58, 64, 72, 79, 82, 92, 129, 131, 134, 140,

143, 145, 151, 158, 166, 168, 173, 183, 188
social identity 41, 47–48, 64, 122, 128, 165
Somers, Margaret 27, 36, 38–43, 45, 49, 54, 65, 99, 103, 107, 120, 133, 171, 181, 183, 186
spoiled identity 47, 125–126
stereotypes 14, 34, 47–48, 66, 121–125, 130
stigma, Eastern European 47–48, 64, 77, 120, 123, 125, 144, 156, 163, 165, 169–170, 175, 188
stigma management 34, 48–49, 67, 120–121, 123, 125, 127–128, 130, 133, 144, 156, 163, 165, 169, 171, 175
SU, the Danish study stipend 5, 16–17, 94, 102, 104, 115
symbolic boundaries 18, 64–66, 88, 111, 142, 156, 162, 174
symbolic interactionism 45, 47

theory 18, 35–36, 38, 43, 45–46
transformation, existential 29, 32, 45, 190
transnational ties 130, 165–166, 175
travelling narratives 53
tuition fee 5, 17, 69, 78–81

UK 11–14, 20, 31, 66, 69, 76, 78–81, 108–109, 117, 123, 126, 145, 154, 163, 165–166, 184
Ukraine 7, 30, 55, 60, 109, 142–143, 161–162
USA 1, 36, 39–40, 42–43, 48, 54, 80–81, 117, 143, 145, 165

visa 6, 141, 143, 145–146, 149, 163, 167–169, 172–174, 188

welfare state 3, 5, 10–11, 35, 63, 77, 82, 91, 115–116, 131, 145, 150, 155
Western education 59–60, 81, 158, 161, 163, 174, 184, 188
Westerners 67, 112, 119, 125, 129, 156
Western gaze 125, 129, 133
Western-oriented 8, 57, 59, 66, 185

Yugoslavia 7, 19

Taylor & Francis eBooks

www.taylorfrancis.com

A single destination for eBooks from Taylor & Francis
with increased functionality and an improved user
experience to meet the needs of our customers.

90,000+ eBooks of award-winning academic content in
Humanities, Social Science, Science, Technology, Engineering,
and Medical written by a global network of editors and authors.

TAYLOR & FRANCIS EBOOKS OFFERS:

A streamlined
experience for
our library
customers

A single point
of discovery
for all of our
eBook content

Improved
search and
discovery of
content at both
book and
chapter level

REQUEST A FREE TRIAL
support@taylorfrancis.com

Printed in the United States
by Baker & Taylor Publisher Services